BANK FINANCIAL DECISION ANALYSIS

FOR LOTUS® 1-2-3®

DAVID R. DURST, DBA
Professor of Finance
The University of Akron

DONALD G. CONNER, CBA, CIA
Vice President, Comptroller,
and Chief Financial Officer
Industrial Trust and Savings Bank

MACMILLAN PUBLISHING COMPANY
New York
COLLIER MACMILLAN PUBLISHERS
London

Lotus ® and 1-2-3 ® are registered trademarks of
The Lotus Development Corporation.

Macmillan Publishing Company
866 Third Avenue, New York, New York 10022

Collier Macmillan Canada, Inc.

ISBN 0-02-331000-6

Printing: 1 2 3 4 5 6 7 8   Year: 9 0 1 2 3 4 5 6 7

QUICK REFERENCE GUIDE TO OPERATIONS

The computer operations are controlled by programmed instructions. Do not attempt to operate these programs like a normal manual cursor movement spreadsheet. Attempts to operate the program in this manner will cause the program to not perform as designed. Observe the instructions on the screen and do not attempt to rush through the program operations until you are familiar with the flow of the program. Remember, computers permit type ahead procedures and this may cause questions to be answered before displayed on screen thereby causing the computer to loop through operations not desired by the operator.

1) Back-up copies should be made prior to the first usage. Use the back-up copies in normal operations. Place the original disks in a safe place and retain for later support in case a disk is accidentally damaged.

2) If using a LOTUS 1-2-3 spreadsheet version other than 2.01 or another spreadsheet program, consult Chapter Two, Changing Spreadsheet Versions, *before proceeding.*

3) Start-up procedures:

Make sure the spreadsheet program is "installed" or is compatible with your computer equipment.

A. Dual disk drive system — If system is on and A> is displayed, place Lotus system disk in drive (A) and BFDA program disk "B" in drive (B). Type 123 to load program. If system is not on, DOS must first be loaded either with the DOS disk or Lotus system disk with DOS installed. The date should be entered if prompted. The BFDA introduction screen will be loaded automatically. Remove the Lotus system disk and replace with the BFDA program disk "A" in drive (A). Select disk drive option 2 and the program will advance to drive (A) for operational instructions.

B. Single disk drive system — If the system is on and A> is displayed, place the Lotus system disk in disk drive and type 123 to load the Lotus system. When the system instructs the program disk to be entered, place BFDA program disk "B" in the disk drive. Select disk drive option 1. Before full usage of all files, the disk drive option must be changed at the main disk menu and at each individual file menu on disk "B" with menu option "X". Set the disk drive option to a single disk drive system. This may be changed to either single or dual at the user's option if systems are later changed. See above if system is off for instructions about DOS.

C. Hard disk drive system — When a hard disk system is used, a special directory should be established (i.e.\BFDA) and the Lotus system and BFDA program copied to this directory. The directory then may be located by entering C>CD\ BFDA and depressing the "ENTER" key. The system may be started by typing

123. This directory will have an AUTO123 file in BFDA so no other AUTO123 files should be included in this directory. See Chapter Two for installation procedures.

    D.   A 3.5 Inch Disk Drive — Disk A and B may be copied to one 3.5 inch disk. See Chapter Two "Problem Solving with BFDA" for directions.

4)   Special Key Operations:

A limited number of special key instructions are used by the program. The program may be removed from the macro-commands at any location by depressing and holding down the "CTRL" key while depressing the "BREAK" key. The program may then be restarted at the individual file menu by depressing and holding down the "ALT" key while depressing the "M" key. Should the user desire to return to the main disk menu rather than the individual file menu, one should use the "ALT" and "Z" keys rather than the "ALT" and "M" keys. A limited number of other similar key uses may be used in some files and are illustrated on the respective screens. Normally these special keys are used very little since the menus provide the ability to exit files. Use the "ALT" and "M" combination if the program sequence is broken through an operational error and must be restarted. Any data entered prior to the error will be retained.

Operational Problems:

A problem/solution list is included in Chapter 2 "How to Use BFDA". One should review this list prior to using the program for the first time.

Preface

The approach to teaching commercial bank management in collegiate business schools has changed rapidly in the last few years. From a very descriptive "here's what banks do" approach, texts and courses have evolved into analytical, decision-oriented courses in which students are able to familiarize themselves with a rapidly changing industry, as well as practice their analytical and decision-making skills learned in other courses. These changes have been an extension of the increased emphasis on financial decision making in the basic financial management course. The presence of microcomputers on campus has created a whole new learning methodology and has increased the analytical capability of the student. With the aid of very user friendly software, students are able to (1) learn complicated concepts by changing one variable and observing its impact upon others (sensitivity analysis); (2) prepare more detailed analyses and reports; and (3) spend their time and talents on their summary analyses and less on crunching numbers.

Bank Financial Decision Analysis (BFDA) for LOTUS 1-2-3 provides another classroom tool for decision-oriented courses related to depository institutions. The BFDA package includes two diskettes of LOTUS 1-2-3 driven models for the personal computer supported by this text. The software is extremely easy to use and requires very little computer and LOTUS 1-2-3 familiarity. For the many undergraduate and graduate business schools that have computer and LOTUS 1-2-3 capability, the package offers many ways to use LOTUS 1-2-3. The value and usefulness of the package are as follows:

A. BFDA provides the instructor with a relatively easy way to (1) offer computer applications for students; (2) provide additional instruction and tutoring in important financial concepts outside the classroom, thus offering alternative ways of learning; and (3) provide common software for class problem assignments, case preparation and pre-input analysis for bank simulation games.

B. BFDA offers students a powerful package enabling them (1) to experience the value of a PC as a number cruncher, using their valuable time for preparing analyses and summaries; and (2) to learn finance concepts and variable relationships another way, by easily altering independent variables and seeing, in an instant, the change in the dependent variables. All BFDA programs have a tutorial program, data input, print and save capabilities; (3) to develop their planning, financial analysis and decision-making skills. Text problems, cases, simulation bank, data, or real bank data may be inputted, and ratios, variance analysis, and projections are provided rapidly. With the MACRO print capability of LOTUS 1-2-3 , their assignments are prepared for classes or reports in a few seconds with the touch of a single key; (4) to enable the student user to see the versatility and scope of the PC, and LOTUS 1-2-3, and to develop skills which may be transferred to the workplace. PCs and LOTUS 1-2-3 software will be present in almost all of the financial firms where students will interview or work; (5) to enable the user to quickly review financial concepts and perform assignments without lengthy preparation time. With this text, instructions on almost all screens, and the use of the LOTUS 1-2-3 MACRO commands in the programming, the student is in "finance" and out of computer jargon in a few minutes. These programs only use LOTUS 1-2-3 to drive the software; there is absolutely no LOTUS 1-2-3 programming or editing required.

Bank or depository institutions management courses, texts, cases and simulation games have traditionally been presented from the perspective of senior management and have emphasized decision-making issues at that level, such as bank strategy, funds management, capital adequacy, etc. While the "big picture" is important, it is more the perspective of the instructor than of the students who must wait twenty years to make important decisions. Meanwhile, in the next twenty years, hundreds of specific, basic decisions will be required, and many will have to be correct if the person is to reach top management. At the same time, deregulation and competition are forcing more number crunching related to pricing and costing at all levels of management. Financial planning of decision alternatives has become more important, and up to recently, financial planning has involved more talk in the classroom than practice.

The BFDA package offers an opportunity to develop decision-making skills for students in areas they will work in within the next three years, not twenty. It provides a chance to practice and do financial planning, not just discuss it. BFDA has been developed by a banker/professor team, and it has a good educational/practical balance for students.

The BFDA package was designed to supplement most commercial bank management texts, especially Commercial Bank Financial

<u>Management</u>, 3rd edition, by Joseph Sinkey. Below are a few highlights of the package, the details of which follow in the text.

1. BFDA includes two diskettes covering seventeen specific areas and many more specific models.

2. The software is supported by this detailed text, which covers concepts, directions, definitions and assignments.

3. All models are MACRO-driven.

4. All models have tutorial programs.

5. All models have input capability.

6. All models have print and save options and provide a summary report.

7. Many models have graphs, thus utilizing the graphic capability of the computer.

8. BFDA screens and reports provide excellent transparency masters to aid instructors and students with their presentations.

9. MACRO commands are used for most cursor movements, enhancing input efficiency.

10. All MACROS and formulas have been written using cell locations rather than range names to help the student analyze the models.

In conclusion, we would like to thank the editors of the Macmillan Publishing Company for their support of this project and for providing us the means to share it with our colleagues and students. We would also like to thank Denise Deemer for her word processing assistance. We invite your comments and suggestions in our attempt to make this package more effective. Please send them to Dr. David R. Durst, The University of Akron, Department of Finance, Akron, Ohio 44325. Please direct any program operational questions in writing to Donald G. Conner, R.R. 2, Box 570B, Yorktown, Indiana 47396.

Contents

CHAPTER 1

Introduction to BFDA

INTRODUCTION

BFDA for LOTUS 1-2-3 provides the opportunity to use the power of the personal computer (PC) to learn financial concepts and improve decision-making skills. The BFDA package includes this manual and two diskettes containing seventeen models or programs to be used with LOTUS 1-2-3. The purpose of this chapter is to provide an overview of the BFDA package; the next chapter explains how to use BFDA.

ELECTRONIC SPREADSHEETS AND LOTUS 1-2-3

Most of us have worked with large multi-column accounting worksheets. Do you remember the feeling you had when a number at the beginning of your worksheet had to be changed and everything that followed had to be erased, recalculated and written down? With the PC and an excellent electronic spreadsheet program like LOTUS 1-2-3, we now have a worksheet with rows and columns and places or cells. We can define the cell with a name or formula (the value of the cell in terms of other cells) so that when a number at the beginning of the worksheet is changed, changes are made instantly in all related places or cells.

Why not use this electronic spreadsheet to assist in the learning of financial concepts? Why not provide the spreadsheet forms, headings and layout, provide for automatic and sequential cursor movement, and let the computer do the work while we study a variety of bank financial decision-making topics? This idea sounded good to the authors, and here it is! With BFDA, the LOTUS 1-2-3 program, and the macro models (automatic cursor movement) on the diskettes, you have a powerful learning and number-crunching tool.

THE OBJECTIVE OF BFDA

For the Student

The BFDA diskettes and manual are designed to support bank management texts, cases and bank simulation games. These dynamic

1

planning and decision models assist in learning financial concepts and applying them to realistic decision-making situations like loan and deposit pricing, bank financial analysis, etc. The models were developed with learning as the focal point. Computer programs are essentially relationships between variables. The relationships (formulas) can be disguised or hidden, or, in the case of BFDA, can be easily displayed to enhance the learning process.

Another purpose of BFDA is to enhance the decision-making skills of the students who may later work for depository institutions. Competition has and will continue to intensify in the industry, and future managers must (1) practice more financial planning, (2) make more decisions based on analytical number crunching rather than generalizing and (3) use the PC or its equivalent more and more in the decision-making process rather than just as a huge file drawer. With BFDA, one can do financial planning, focus on the numbers associated with a decision and use the PC as a decision-making tool.

While BFDA, in this form, is primarily a learning tool, and not operational models, the student is exposed to many real and practical areas of commercial bank decision making. Further, even though the knowledge of LOTUS 1-2-3 required for this package is minimal, the student is working with LOTUS 1-2-3, a spreadsheet program found in just about every financial institution. The BFDA models can easily be adapted later to the workplace, and many students may use their BFDA macro and analytical tools for other classroom applications.

BFDA was developed for students with minimal computer skills. The models use the LOTUS 1-2-3 automatic, programmed, cursor movement (Macros), which requires a single pointed finger and knowledge of the alphabet. At the same time, the computer or LOTUS expert can dissect, analyze and change (prepare a backup) the models. And, for the novice, LOTUS 1-2-3 is useful because every time the cursor is moved to a new cell, the formula calculation is displayed at the top of the screen. BFDA offers something for everyone's stage of PC and LOTUS 1-2-3 development.

For the Instructor

BFDA was developed as a learning/teaching aid for college bank or depository institution courses. It is intended to supplement banking texts, casebooks, and bank simulation models. The BFDA models cover most areas covered in a course and most case areas, and many models are very useful pre-input and output analysis tools for simulation games. The report printing capability of each program provides appendices supporting case solutions, simulation inputs and text problem assignments. Some instructors may prefer to use a more descriptive textbook, but may want to use the dynamic capabilities of BFDA (1) to reinforce concepts discussed in the text and (2) to provide the computer/spreadsheet usage required by the college. All a student needs for BFDA is a pointed finger and knowledge of the alphabet. All the instructor has to do is say, "Read the BFDA text and do the assignment."

THE BFDA MENU

The BFDA models and their identifying letters are listed below, along with a brief description of the model.

Model A -- Bond Analysis and Accounting. Input bond variables and study accounting entries associated with bond purchase and income accrual. Compare straightline with level yield accrual of premium and discount.

Model B -- Money Market Yields, Duration, Rate Theory, and Forward Interest Rates. A series of programs related to financial market concepts. Calculate varied yields on money market securities. Use the duration calculator. Analyze nominal interest rate components such as the real rate, price level expectations and risk. Input two actual interest rates and receive an estimated, implied forward rate.

Model C -- Capital Budgeting Analysis. Analyze a fixed asset expenditure using payback, net present value and internal rate of return.

Model D -- Deposit Pricing Model. Create and price/cost a deposit account that will achieve a return on assets goal.

Model E -- Depreciation/Tax Accounting. Analyze varied methods of depreciating fixed assets. Compare financial (book) and tax timing differences, deferred taxes and associated accounting entries.

Model F -- Loan Pricing Concepts. Price a loan with a specific return on equity goal. Select from among prime plus, prime times or market-based rates. Establish a rate structure for varied risks assumed.

Model G -- Marginal Cost of Funds. Analyze the bank marginal cost of funds using varied methods and assumptions.

Model H -- Customer Profitability Analysis. Review and analyze the profitability of a loan and/or deposit customer.

Model I -- Bank Financial Statement Analysis. Analyze twenty financial ratios for five years or five banks. Analyze and decompose return on assets, return on equity, and the internal capital generation rate in the Profitability/Capital Growth Analysis model.

Model J -- Income Statement as a Percent of Average Assets. Analyze the changes in the bank ROA by detailing the income statement ledger accounts per average assets.

Model K -- Bank Performance Analysis. Analyze and establish a regulatory rating for the bank, using the Uniform Bank Performance Report available from regulatory agencies.

Model L -- Loan Loss Reserve Analysis. Evaluate the sufficiency of the bank loan loss reserve.

Model M -- GAP and Net Interest Margin Analysis. Review the basic concepts of GAP management. Study the variables affecting changes in the net interest margin and net interest income. Set up different GAP and NIM situations, and study the effect upon net interest margins and income.

Model N -- Rate Sensitivity Analysis. Analyze the balance and rate impact of interest-sensitive assets and liabilities by reviewing a rate sensitivity model. Review and analyze the report to the bank asset/liability committee.

Model O -- Pro Forma Financial Statements Model. Project the next five periods of the bank income statement and balance sheet. Study the percentage changes, projected net income, and funds (surplus/deficit) under varying assumptions.

Model P -- Capital Planning Model. Input the bank asset growth rate, return on assets, dividend payout, target capital/asset ratio and study the equity capital required over fifteen periods. Input sale of new equity.

Model Q -- Bank Financial Statement Review. Identify bank ledger accounts as revenue, expense, asset, contra-asset, liabilities or capital. The model scores your test and the answers, and displays the accounts in financial statements.

TEXT CHAPTER ORGANIZATION

Each chapter of this book is associated with the models on the diskettes. Each chapter is organized in the following way:

A.   Introduction and Concepts -- Introduces and/or reviews the financial management concepts involved in the program, the interrelationship of variables, and learning objectives (capability) of the program.

B.   Applications -- Illustrates the value of the program for planning and/or decision making for cases, simulation games, etc.

C.   Menu and Screens -- The menu and major screens displayed in the program are presented with definitions and user guidelines. Terms and words on the screen are defined, and instructions are provided where necessary.

D.   Sample Problems -- Several problems are provided to allow the student to input data and quickly see the solution. Later, students may use their own problems with the software.

HOW TO USE THIS BOOK

This book is intended to get you started and to keep you going with BFDA. First, read this and the next chapter, which describes the equipment and a few procedures needed to "boot up" BFDA. Then go on to the later chapters. Each chapter provides instructions and detailed references to various program menus and screens in BFDA. This book does not provide instruction in LOTUS 1-2-3. You are not required to know LOTUS 1-2-3, except for loading the software in the computer. BFDA uses LOTUS 1-2-3 as a tool to emphasize bank financial decision concepts. For the experienced LOTUS 1-2-3 user, a review of the programming, macro commands and setup may be of interest.

When a model is assigned for study, try the following approach, varying it to your needs and capabilities later.

1.   Read the chapter associated with the model assigned to gain an overview of the program objectives, menu and screens.

2.   Load and boot up the LOTUS 1-2-3 and BFDA - B diskette and proceed to Menu A (see the next chapter).

3.   Select the appropriate model and read through the tutorial screens. No data may be entered in the tutorial.

4.   Return to the model menu and review the rest of the menu areas. Program default data, loaded by the authors, will be present on all data input screens. Vary the inputs and note the changes in solutions. As long as you do not save a report at the conclusion of your input experiment, the diskette will not store (save) your input and the default data will appear next time you boot up the program. The default data in most models are used in the end-of-chapter problems, so be sure to keep an original copy for reference.

5.   Develop and organize your program data, perhaps using the Data Input Sheets at the end of most chapters.

6.   Enter your data and then cycle through again to prove your entries.

7. Finally, review and analyze the results of your input. Remember, BFDA models provide a way to learn concepts and analyze economic and business decisions. Completing items 1-6 above without this last step is easy. Data entry and number crunching followed by complete and thorough analysis (what happened and why?) is a task completed.

EXPLORING PROGRAM MACROS AND FORMULAS

Program operations in BFDA models are controlled by LOTUS macro commands, including cursor movements, file retrieve and save, print instructions, and, in several files, the calculate command. The LOTUS 1-2-3 novice should not attempt to alter the spreadsheet layouts or formulas unless so directed by the program. Any changes made may affect program operations. The LOTUS 1-2-3 expert should tinker with a working copy, with the original tucked safely in the disk filebox. The macros for each model may be located by using the F-5 function key and typing macros. Review the formula for any calculated variable by moving the cursor to the cell location desired. The formula or equation will be listed at the top of the screen. If the formula is longer than one line, depress the F2 edit key and use the arrow keys. Be careful not to change the equations when in the edit mode. Return to the macro by depressing the escape key, followed by the return to menu routine.

CHAPTER 2

How to Use BFDA

This chapter reviews the computer equipment and software needed to run BFDA and details the procedures for booting and problem solving. Read this chapter carefully the first time, and use it as a reference to minimize computer time and maximize financial analysis time. It is important to note that BFDA utilizes the LOTUS 1-2-3 software to drive the self-contained MACRO programs. All cursor movement is controlled by the MACRO. You will not be required to do any spreadsheet programming, editing or arrow key cursor movement to run BFDA. This comprehensive MACRO feature distinguishes BFDA from other educational spreadsheet-driven software.

EQUIPMENT AND SOFTWARE REQUIREMENTS

The following equipment and software are required to operate BFDA:

1. An IBM-PC, XT, AT or compatible model capable of supporting LOTUS 1-2-3 version 1-A or later versions or the Student Edition of LOTUS 1-2-3. DOS 2.0 version formatted for system only or installed on LOTUS System Disk should enable user to use a computer with a memory capacity of 256K. Higher levels of DOS or a full DOS disk and/or a higher version of LOTUS 1-2-3 may require memory requirements beyond 256K. The size of some files may cause a "memory full" indicator to be received on 256K machines unless the DOS system only is used.

2. A computer graphics (preferably color) capability is optional; some models have graphics.

3. The diskettes supplied with BFDA have printer settings preset for Epson or compatible narrow-carriage printers. If your printer is not compatible, the print commands may be located for reviewing and changing by depressing the F5 (or GO TO) key, followed by range name P. This will move the cursor to the Print macro location. Refer to your printer manual for the required printer setup string routines (\nnn format) if changes are required.

7

4.   A DOS 2.0 version or higher. Higher DOS versions, if loaded fully, may limit the use of a 256K memory.

5.   LOTUS 1-2-3, Version 1-A Systems Disk or later versions capable of supporting Version 1-A. If version 1-A is used, or if another spreadsheet program is used other than LOTUS version 2.01, the BFDA files with file extension letters WK1, must be converted or renamed to match the file extension letters of the spreadsheet in use before one is able to save new data to the files. Review the instructions presented later in this chapter. This must be completed before proceeding.

6.   Blank, formatted, high-quality, double-sided, double-density diskettes for creating BFDA working copies.

MAKING A WORKING COPY OF BFDA DISKETTES

BFDA programs are designed to store the user data on the BFDA diskettes. Remember, when new data are inputted and saved, they replace the original disk data. Make several working copies for specific assignments. Be sure to write the identical information appearing on your original BFDA diskettes on the working copies with a felt-tip pen. Use the DOS DISKCOPY or other copy programs to make your working copies. Keep your original BFDA diskette in a cool, dry place in a disk case or file.

COMPUTER START-UP FOR BFDA

The following steps should be taken to load the BFDA program:

1.   If the computer is off, place the DOS diskette (or spreadsheet diskette with DOS) in the A disk drive (left or top) and turn on the computer, monitor and printer. After a brief warmup period and disk drive check, the computer will load the DOS and stop at the date prompt. Enter the date in the format indicated in the computer manual (i.e., 10-1-1987) and press the enter key. The program will then advance to the time prompt. Enter the time if desired (not required). Do so using military time (e.g., 2:30 p.m. is 14:30 hours). Press the enter key after entering the time or press the enter key to advance if the time is not entered. If the A> prompt is showing, load the LOTUS 1-2-3 system diskette and proceed to step 3.

2.   If the computer is on and the A> prompt is not showing, exit from the current program to the A> prompt position. An alternative procedure is to load the DOS diskette in the A disk drive and depress the CTRL, ALT, and DEL keys simultaneously. This simultaneous Control, Alternate,

Delete command will reboot the computer. Load the LOTUS 1-2-3 system disk and proceed to Step 3.

3.   Disk drive option and LOTUS 1-2-3, Version 2.01.   BFDA is delivered with a dual disk drive option installed on both diskettes using LOTUS Version 2.01. If your computer has a single disk drive, hard disk drive, or if a spreadsheet version other than 2.01 is to be used, follow the instructions in (A) and/or (B) below before using the program for the first time.

    A.   Procedures are installed on both disks which permit the selection of a single disk drive option, dual disk drive option, or a hard disk drive option. Refer at this time to step 4 below.

    B.   If the spreadsheet version to be used is not LOTUS Version 2.01, refer to "Changing Spreadsheet Versions," later in this chapter. Note that there are other ways to perform a conversion from 2.01. Review your manuals or software if desired.

4.   Disk drive selection

    A.   Dual disk drive: When using the dual disk drive option, disk B should be placed in drive B before loading the spreadsheet software. This will permit the BFDA program to load the first file without an additional operation. If the spreadsheet software is already loaded, use the normal file retrieve instructions (/FR) and retrieve the "Auto123" file on disk B. The program will then ask the user to remove the spreadsheet program from drive A and replace it with BFDA disk A. Note that the dual disk drive option will not work as provided if used with spreadsheet software which requires that the spreadsheet software remain in one disk drive during operation. See item 2 in the following sample screen.

    B.   Single disk drive: When using the single disk drive option after installation, load the spreadsheet software, and when the spreadsheet format appears, remove the spreadsheet software disk. Place BFDA disk A in the disk drive and use the normal file retrieve procedure to retrieve the "Auto123" file. If disk B is placed in the disk drive, it also contains an "Auto123" file. Proceed through the screens to the main disk menu. For single disk drive installation, depress the "X" menu item. The screen below will then be displayed. The program will then request the user to select a disk drive option, which, with a single disk drive, is number 1. If an error is made in the selection, proceed to the main menu. Then make your correction in the disk drive option screen below, by depressing the X key. (Note: If using a spreadsheet other than LOTUS 1-2-3, 2.01, one must convert or rename the file extensions of the BFDA files to match that of the spreadsheet prior to converting to a single disk drive option. Changing options executes a save command. See Changing Spreadsheet Versions in a later section.)

C. Hard Disk Drive: Prepare a backup copy of both BFDA diskettes and use the copies for the installation. The file extensions on the user's software should be reviewed before installation. The BFDA files are configured to LOTUS version 2.01 with WK1 file extensions. File extensions may be changed if you are using another LOTUS version by using the utility disk provided with the LOTUS 1-2-3 software or the DOS Rename (REN) program with REN *.EXT *.EXT with the last EXT associated with new extension letters. Use the Rename program before the BFDA files have been loaded in the hard drive. Review the directory listing of all files. File extensions must be changed if using a LOTUS 1-2-3 version than 2.01, or if using another compatible spreadsheet program. File names other than the "AUTO123" file (introduction file) start with "BFDA" (i.e. BFDAMENU, BFDAA, BFDAB, BFDAC, etc.).

A special directory should be established on the hard disk for the BFDA files. These disks as delivered contain one "AUTO123" file on each disk, which automatically boots BFDA when LOTUS 1-2-3 is loaded. Since only one "AUTO123" file may be included in a directory, it is very important that one installs the BFDA programs on the hard disk in the proper sequence.

The authors suggest a directory titled "BFDA." Once the directory has been established, LOTUS, followed by the BFDA disks (DISK B FIRST, THEN DISK A) should be copied to the directory. Note that LOTUS must be on the same directory as the BFDA files.

The directory is established by starting at the root directory. The following directions considers disk drive A as the primary floppy drive and disk drive C as the hard disk drive.

1. After the system has been booted a C> prompt should appear on the screen. This should be the root directory, but may be tested by typing and entering CD\.

2.   The new directory may then be established by typing and entering MD\BFDA.

3.   Transfer to the new directory by typing and entering CD\BFDA.

4.   The LOTUS spreadsheet should now be installed in this directory.   Refer to the installation instructions provided with the spreadsheet software. After the software has been installed, test the installation by typing and entering, at the C>, the numbers 123.   The spreadsheet should then load. Select the exit command and return to the C> prompt before loading the BFDA files.

5.   (NOTE: DISK B IS COPIED FIRST).   At the C> prompt, place BFDA disk B in disk drive A and type Copy A:*.* and enter. This instructs your computer to copy all the files from the drive A diskette to the hard drive C. When the copy operation is complete and the C> prompt appears, place the BFDA A diskette in drive A and repeat the copy installation with Copy A:*.* and enter. Failure to copy the BFDA B diskette first, followed by BFDA A will place improper files on the hard disk.

6.   Now restart LOTUS by typing 123 at the C> prompt.   The BFDA introduction file will appear. Review the introductory screens and proceed to the menu.

7.   The final steps of the hard disk installation require a few menu controlled operations. Select "X" from the main menu. A special menu for selecting the drive option will then appear. Depress the "3" for the hard disk option. This same operation must also be completed on each of the BFDA files K, L, M, N, O, P, and Q. From the main menu select the file K, followed by menu item "X" from the file K menu. Depress "3" for the hard drive option, then exit the file to the main menu. Repeat for each file L through Q. When these steps have been completed, the BFDA program has been installed for hard disk operation.

The BFDA program then may be located, when starting each time, by typing and entering CD\BFDA to reach the proper directory. Then type and enter 123. The program should then load without any additional operations.

* * *

SPECIAL INSTALLATION PROCEDURES

PROGRAM IS DELIVERED USING A DUAL DISK DRIVE SYSTEM WHICH REQUIRES REMOVING THE LOTUS SYSTEM DISK FROM DRIVE A AND PLACING BFDA DISK A IN DRIVE A AFTER THE LOTUS SYSTEM IS LOADED. THIS DEFAULT SYSTEM MAY BE CHANGED BY FOLLOWING THE PROCEDURES BELOW. ADDITIONAL SIMILAR PROCEDURES MUST ALSO BE FOLLOWED ON MODELS K, L, M, N, O, P AND Q.

NOTE: BE SURE BACKUP COPIES OF BOTH ORIGINAL DISKS HAVE BEEN MADE AND THE ORIGINALS STORED BEFORE COMPLETING THESE PROCEDURES.

1 - SINGLE DISK DRIVE OPTION: SETS SYSTEM FOR DISK A AND DISK B TO BE USED IN SAME DISK DRIVE.

2 - DUAL DISK DRIVE OPTION: SETS SYSTEM FOR DISK A TO REMAIN IN DRIVE A WHILE IN USE AND DISK B TO REMAIN IN DRIVE B. LOTUS SYSTEM DISK MUST BE REMOVED AFTER LOADING AND REPLACED BY DISK A.

3 - HARD DISK DRIVE OPTION

4 - CANCEL INSTALLATION PROCEDURES WITHOUT MAKING ANY CHANGES.

* * *

5. Using the BFDA diskettes (with the BFDA main program menu on the screen): A special menu approach has been used to enable you to see the menu file on the screen. Type the letter of the model desired. If the menu selection cursor is not blinking (under column F), restore the macro by depressing the control and break keys simultaneously, followed by Alt M. Models A through J are on BFDA diskette A, while Models K through Q are on diskette B. You may change the disk drive option from the main menu by selecting X on the main menu. This procedure may be useful if an error or omission was made earlier.

Keyboard macro commands control the cursor movements in all data entry files (except Model N). Macros are collections or storehouses of keystrokes or programs that control the movement of the cursor or other sequences of activities. The alternative entails moving the cursor with the arrow keys for every input. LET THE MACROS RUN THE BFDA PROGRAMS! If the macro sequence and cursor have been interrupted or an error is made, follow the control/break, Alt M (menu) or an Alt letter, per instructions on the screen, which will return you to the top of the screen.

Macro commands and formulas have been written using cell locations rather than range names to aid the user in following calculations and commands. Learning and instruction have been the primary concerns of the authors. LOTUS 1-2-3 has many efficient capabilities that have not been used in order to focus on concepts and instruction.

6.   Special BFDA keys and procedures

a.   Depressing the control (CTRL) key followed by the break key removes the macro command or is the first step to take if you want to restart the cursor movement or the menu item.

b.   After control/break, depress the Alternate (ALT) and Z keys if the main menu is desired or (ALT) and M if you want to return to the specific program menu.

c.   Watch the cursor instructions on the screen, usually at the bottom.

CHANGING SPREADSHEET VERSIONS

If you are using a LOTUS 1-2-3 version other than 2.01, use the following procedure or others in your operational manual to convert the 2.01 spreadsheet screens to other versions.

1.   Prepare a working copy of both original disks before proceeding.

2.   When changing from LOTUS Version 2.01 to the 1-A version, a disk manager procedure is available for changing the file names. Load the 1-A version with LOTUS 1-2-3, and select "File Manager" from the access menu. Then note the disk drive where the BFDA diskette is located. Then select "Rename" and change each file listed, including the file extension, i.e., .WKS. Use the extension associated with the 1-A, all file extensions on both disk A and disk B must be renamed to the version used.

3.   If you are using The Student Edition of LOTUS 1-2-3, the file extension names must be changed. A disk manager file is not available in the student version. The student version stores files with an extension of .WKE, while the 2.01 version uses .WK1. Below are four procedures, any one of which can be used to convert BFDA for use with the student version.

A.   If you have access to the utility disk from a regular LOTUS program, step 2 above may be used.

B. Use the DOS Rename (REN) program. Load DOS and insert your BFDA A or B diskette in a disk drive. Type REN *.EXT *.EXT with the last EXT associated with the <u>new</u> file extension letters. Type Directory (DIR) to view the changes in the file extensions.

C. If the utility disk is not available, you may elect to retrieve each file using the student version and save it to another disk. This will require two new formatted disks. Retrieve each file, one at a time, and save it to the new disk. Write "Student Version" on the new diskettes. Use care when completing this conversion to avoid damaging one of the original disks or convert from a BFDA backup copy. The student version will support the dual disk/single disk option installation procedures.

D. Another method begins by making a backup copy of each disk. Using the student version, retrieve each file, one at a time. After retrieving, use "file erase" to remove the old file name from the disk; then return or save the file to the same disk. This procedure will rename the file extensions (.WKE) used by the student edition. Do not erase a file until it has been retrieved into RAM memory.

4. If using a "clone" spreadsheet program, review the file storage names. LOTUS 1-2-3, Version 2.01, stores files with an extension of .WK1. If a different version is used, follow the steps provided by the software or in the above #3 paragraph to rename all the files. This procedure is required because the files will be saved to unused sectors on the BFDA disk, and space does not permit additional files.

PROBLEM SOLVING WITH BFDA

If problems arise in operating BFDA, refer to the following problem solution aids. Note that problems are underlined, followed by solutions.

<u>Want to return to model menu.</u> Depress and hold the CTRL key while striking the Break key, followed by depressing the ALT key while striking the M key.

<u>Wish to terminate use of a model (without saving) and return to main menu from location other than file menu.</u> Depress and hold the CTRL key while striking the Break key, followed by depressing and holding the ALT key while striking the Z key.

Automatic cursor movement is lost.   The screen indicator shows
that the program is in ready mode and not CMD mode.   Depress and
hold the ALT key while striking the M key to restart at the model
menu.

The screen reflects a split of assorted data after an attempt to
perform an operation. Depress the /WTC keys and then depress and
hold the ALT key while striking the M key to restart at the model
menu.

An attempt to enter data or perform an operation results in an
indicator labeled "Protected Cell." Depress the escape (ESC) key
and restart at the program menu (ALT M). If the same results are
again obtained at the same location, check to see if cell
protection has been entered or recopy the file from the original
disk to the work copy disk.

The BFDA program will not load, and a "memory full" indication is
received.   Review computer RAM memory size. If using LOTUS 1-2-
3, boot only using the 123 command rather than LOTUS.   While the
program is designed for computers with 256K RAM, it is possible
that more RAM may be required if DOS or the spreadsheet software
used takes substantially more memory than DOS 2.0 (system only)
and the LOTUS Version 1-A. DOS should be installed on the LOTUS
system disk when possible to reduce additional RAM requirements
used to support DOS files not required to run LOTUS and BFDA.

Wish to stop the automatic cursor movement when entering a long
list of data and desire to use arrow keys to move the cursor.
Depress and hold the CTRL key while striking the Break key. Some
spreadsheets will then require striking the ESC key to continue.

"Disk full" indication is received or the save command does not
work.   Recheck the installation requirements for the spreadsheet
software being used, if not LOTUS 1-2-3, Version 2.01.

Message received is "too many nesting levels in MACRO calls".
The continued use of a MACRO without a break has reached the
limits.   Depress ESC key followed by ALT M to clear and begin
again at the program menu.

Graphic selection on the program menu will not function. Recheck
the computer to be sure graphic capability is present. Macro
commands are set only for LOTUS 1-2-3 or fully compatible
spreadsheet software.   Some clones are not compatible in graphic
commands.   Review installation procedure of the spreadsheet
software.

Nothing seems to happen when the ENTER key is depressed (WAIT
indicator may be flashing or automatic (MACRO) cursor movement
has been lost through error). Many of the models are large and
take longer to calculate; check for the WAIT indicator. If the
READY indication is present, restart at the model menu. Striking

the Enter key or other keys while the WAIT is flashing can cause an operational error due to the type-ahead feature in micro-computers.

Spreadsheet version used is other than LOTUS 2.01 version. See "Changing Spreadsheet Versions" earlier in this chapter.

Cursor returns to data entry location when being advanced after data entry. PC's permit "type ahead" ability. If keyboard operations are rushed, or depressed several times rapidly, the cursor may advance past an entry point or a question. Slow down and follow the cursor.

When using BFDA installed on hard disk the introduction file or main menu cannot be obtained. Review installation steps. Disk B must be copied to hard disk first, followed by disk A.

User desires to convert files to 3.5 inch disk. Files may be copied to 3.5 inch disk using procedures similar to installing BFDA on a hard disk. One must be able to copy a 5.25 inch floppy to a 3.5 inch disk. Copy disk B first and then disk A. After copy operations are completed, manually retrieve (File Retrieve) the AUTO123, K, L, M, N, O, P and Q files. Select X on each menu and Hard Drive Option (number 3).

Will BFDA run on spreadsheet software other than LOTUS? BFDA was developed to run on LOTUS Version 2.01 and may be converted to other versions, including the student version. Other spreadsheet clones of LOTUS 1-2-3 may support BFDA, such as V-P Planner, TWIN and Joe Spreadsheet. However, the authors do not assume responsibility for accuracy when they are used with software other than LOTUS software. The internal rate of return (IRR) calculation in some models may not calculate without rate changes in some clones. A provision is made to adjust the internal rate of return (IRR) if errors are indicated when calculating. Some require the spreadsheet software to remain in the computer while in use, thereby eliminating the dual disk drive option provided in the program. The graphic commands are set for LOTUS 1-2-3 only and will not perform with some clones which do not use the same commands.

May BFDA be used on single disk drive computers as well as dual disk drive computers? BFDA as delivered is set for dual disk drive computers but may be converted to single disk drive computers (see "Computer Start-Up with BFDA" earlier in this chapter.)

CHAPTER 3

Model A
Bond Analysis and Accounting

INTRODUCTION AND CONCEPTS

One of the most important financial concepts is the inverse relationship between interest rates and security prices. The Bond Analysis and Accounting Model A enables one to enter specific bond information such as face value, coupon rate, price, maturity, and transaction fees. The model calculates the yield to maturity (semiannual), and the effective interest rate (monthly), and displays the monthly accounting entries related to the bond. As one varies the price of the fixed rate bond, the bond yield varies inversely. Falling bond prices are associated with higher yields, whereas increased bond prices indicate a flow of funds into the bond market and a simultaneous decline in interest rates. Both coupon and zero coupon bonds may be analyzed. Note: This is an educational model which covers most concepts related to bond analysis and accounting. It is not an operational model for the work place. Due to memory constraints the maximum maturity, transaction fees, etc. have been limited.

When the financial institution purchases a bond, the bond is entered in the accounting system (original entry) and a planned income accrual is established. Under generally accepted accounting principles (GAAP), if the bond is purchased for the investment account, it is assumed that it will be held to maturity. Thus, the monthly (or daily) accretion of the discount or the amortization of the premium is established for the term of the bond. If the bond was purchased at a discount (premium), the periodic discount accretion (premium amortization) is added (subtracted or expensed) to (from) the income to make the periodic accounting income and the actual economic income (effective yield) the same. Two common methods of accounting for the premium or discount are presented. The straightline method provides an equal allocation of discount or premium per accounting period. The effective interest, constant yield or actuarial method varies the periodic discount or premium so that the net amount of income per period relative to the book value of the bond is a constant yield. The latter method is the recommended method to use for monthly yield analyses, but the straightline method is simple to set up and make monthly entries. This topic is expanded in the section Menu and Screens.

Bond Prices and Interest Rates

This program illustrates several concepts. It provides a means of illustrating and enhancing the understanding of the inverse relationship between security prices and interest rates. One can vary the price of the bond and note the corresponding impact on interest rates. As long as the coupon rate remains fixed, the yield varies inversely with the price. The bond value is the present value of the expected interest and principal discounted at the market yield:

$$\text{Bond Price} = \sum_{t=1}^{N} \frac{\text{Interest per period}}{(1+i)^t} + \frac{\text{Principal}}{(1+i)^N}$$

In the above expression the bond value (price) is the sum of the discounted coupon interest returns for "t" periods, followed by the return of the principal (face amount) at the end of the nth period or at maturity. The bond contract fixes the interest, principal, interest per payment and maturity. As one changes the price, the "i" or yield varies inversely.

Yield and Price Changes with Varying Maturity

Long-term bond prices tend to vary more significantly than short-term bond prices, especially zero coupon bonds. This is often explained in terms of the smaller volume of trading in long-term issues, which results in larger bid/ask differentials. This can also be explained on a present value basis. For any given yield change, the price of a longer-term bond will vary more than that of a short-term bond. The change in the discount rate has a major impact on the present value of the interest and the face value received in the later periods. Remember, any change in the discount rate in the twentieth period is compounded twenty times! On the other hand, short-term interest rates vary more than long-term rates. Changing the price of a long- and a short-term bond by a specific amount will produce a greater change in the yield of the short-term bond. On a present value basis, any given change in price has a greater impact on the bond or security yield with the shorter maturity. These concepts are illustrated in a problem assignment later in this section or may be proven with the money market yield calculations program in the next chapter.

APPLICATIONS

This model is useful in several ways:

1. It illustrates the price/yield effects of coupon bonds.
2. It provides a visual display of the accounting for bonds in depository financial institutions.

Menu and Screens

Model A has the following menus:

A   -   TUTORIAL
B   -   BOND DATA ENTRY
C   -   COMPARATIVE SCHEDULES
D   -   SAMPLE ACCOUNTING ENTRIES FOR BOND PURCHASE
E   -   SAMPLE MONTHLY ACCOUNTING ENTRIES
P   -   PRINT REPORTS
S   -   SAVE TO DISKETTE (REPLACES CURRENT FILE CONTENTS)
Q   -   QUIT PROGRAM

A   -   TUTORIAL

A brief introduction of the model. Note the assumption that the bonds are booked (recorded) at face value with associated premium or discount contra accounts, rather than recorded at cost. Scroll through the tutorial before inputting data in Menu B.

B   -   BOND DATA ENTRY

The user is able to input five bond variables needed to establish accounting entries. They include:

1.   Transaction Fees -- the brokerage cost of purchasing the bond, if applicable. In this model, transaction fees are added to the cost of the bond and reduce (increase) the amount of the discount (premium) which will be accreted (amortized) over the remaining life of the bond.

2.   Face Value -- enter the maturity value of the bond.

3.   Coupon Rate -- enter the coupon or contract rate of the bond. Input in decimal form. For a zero coupon bond, enter a zero.

4.   Price -- enter the market price of the bond as a percent of the face value. Corporate bonds are quoted in fractions of eighths and must be converted to decimal form before entry. A corporate bond price of 87-3/8 would be entered as 87.375. U.S. Treasury bonds are usually quoted in 32nds and must also be converted to decimal form. A Treasury quote of 97.04 is 97-4/32nds or 97.125.

5.   Number of Months to Maturity -- enter the number of months to maturity up to a maximum of 72. The purpose of the model is to analyze and display the monthly accounting for investment securities, so the maximum maturity in this model is constrained by memory and print space. Monthly accrual of income/expense is common in financial institutions, so maturity is a

function of the number of accounting periods to maturity.

Following the five input variables on the screen, seven other variables are given or calculated. They include:

1. Basis (Month/Year) -- for simplicity, the method of accrual in this program assumes a 360-day year and a 30-day month. Other methods may include a 365-day year and the actual number of days in the month.

2. Total Cost -- the purchase price (price times face value) plus transaction fees is the total cost or outlay.

3. Discount -- the face value less the total cost. Transaction fees lower the amount of the discount (increase the cost) to be accreted (income accrual) over the period to maturity and reduce the yield.

4. Premium -- the total cost less the face value of the bond. A transaction fee increases the cost and the amount of premium amortized (expensed) in the period to maturity and lowers the yield.

5. Coupon Income Accrual -- the total interest income to be accrued over the life of the security. It is the product of the coupon rate times the face value times the time (years) to maturity. The total coupon income accrual divided by the number of months to maturity (or call date, sometimes, in the case of a premium bond) is the monthly coupon accrual -- see Menu C.

6. Yield to maturity -- the discount rate or internal rate of return which equates the total cost of the security and the future cash flows discounted at the yield to maturity. This traditional yield calculation is a semiannual rate, annualized (times 2). The semiannual rate compounded annually would be $(1+\text{semiannual rate})^2 - 1$.

7. Effective Interest Rate -- the discount rate or internal rate of return, which equates the total cost of the security and the future cash flows discounted at the effective interest rate. This yield calculation is a monthly rate (annualized, times 12), and is used to establish the level yield computation of the premium/discount in the effective interest accrual method which follows.

Please note the cursor movements on this screen and the option to return to the top of the screen for new data entry. After inputting the five variables, there is a thirty-second pause (see the wait indicator in the upper right corner of the screen) as the yield to maturity and effective interest rate are calculated.

C - COMPARATIVE SCHEDULES

The monthly accounting schedules comparing straightline and effective interest premium/discount accrual are displayed in a table. One may select either (1) a short form, which displays a four-month schedule of both accounting methods on the same screen or (2) a long form, which permits a review of the monthly accounting of both schedules for the entire maturity of the security. Either the short or long form is available in the printed report. See the discussion of Menu P later in this chapter.

If a bond is purchased at a discount or premium, the discount or premium is allocated to the future earning periods in an attempt to match accounting income with economic income (the actual yield). The straightline method is the traditional allocation method. It is easy to calculate, but as the book value changes in each accounting period (month), the accounting yield (monthly income to book value) also changes. This accounting yield should match the actual effective yield, and the variance tends to bias management's monthly yield analyses. The effective interest or constant yield method is more complicated, but provides a better match of accounting and actual economic income.

The Comparative Schedule lists the first four months of data from the bond subsidiary journal. See Table 1. The book value figure reflects the original purchase price (cost) and the adjustments to book value each month. The discounted bond is slowly written up (Accumulated Discount Accretion) to face or maturity value, while the premium bond is written down (Accumulated Premium Amortization) to face at maturity (see Menu E).

The coupon accrual is the monthly coupon income allocated to the period and is found by multiplying the face amount of the bond times the coupon rate divided by twelve. This would be blank for a zero coupon bond.

The monthly discount accretion or premium amortization is found by dividing the total premium or discount by the number of months to maturity. The monthly income amount for the straightline method is found by adding (subtracting) the coupon interest accrual to (from) the monthly discount accretion (premium amortization). Remember, one is accreting discount (adding to coupon income) to raise the accounting yield to the effective economic yield and amortizing premium (reducing expense or income) to lower the accounting yield to the approximate economic yield.

Under the effective interest method, the monthly income accrual is calculated <u>first</u> by multiplying the effective monthly rate (rate/12) by the month-end book value. The amount of monthly premium is determined by subtracting the monthly income accrual from the monthly coupon interest accrual. It is subtracted with the premium bond because the effective yield is less than the coupon rate and the income accrual should approximate the effective yield. The amount of monthly discount is determined by subtracting the coupon interest accrual from the monthly income accrual. It is a residual amount after starting with the effective yield desired, compared to the straightline method, where the yield is the residual and the premium/discount is fixed. The discount is thus added to the coupon income accrual because the effective rate on a discounted bond exceeds the coupon rate.

To illustrate the above discussion, a premium and a discount bond example has been constructed. Enter the data first for the premium bond, then for the discount bond. After Data Entry

Table 1

Comparative Schedule - Premium Bond (Menu C)

BASED ON STRAIGHTLINE ACCRETION AND AMORTIZATION

NET BOOK VALUE	COUPON ACCRUAL	DISCOUNT ACCRETION	PREMIUM AMORT	MONTHLY INCOME	YIELD
1,050,000.00	8,333.33	0.00	694.44	7,638.89	8.7302%
1,049,305.56	8,333.33	0.00	694.44	7,638.89	8.7359%
1,048,611.12	8,333.33	0.00	694.44	7,638.89	8.7417%
1,047,916.68	8,333.33	0.00	694.44	7,638.89	8.7475%

BASED ON EFFECTIVE INTEREST (CONSTANT YIELD)

NET BOOK VALUE	COUPON ACCRUAL	DISCOUNT ACCRE-TION	PREMIUM AMORT	MONTHLY INCOME	YIELD
1,050,000.00	8,333.33	0.00	527.61	7,805.72	8.9208%
1,049,472.93	8,333.33	0.00	531.53	7,801.80	8.9208%
1,048,940.86	8,333.33	0.00	535.48	7,797.85	8.9208%
1,048,405.38	8,333.33	0.00	539.46	7,793.87	8.9208%

Comparative Schedule -- Discount Bond (Menu C)

BASED ON STRAIGHTLINE ACCRETION AND AMORTIZATION

NET BOOK VALUE	COUPON ACCRUAL	DISCOUNT ACCRE-TION	PREMIUM AMORT	MONTHLY INCOME	YIELD
950,000.00	8,333.33	694.44	0.00	9,027.77	11.4035%
950,694.44	8,333.33	694.44	0.00	9,027.77	11.3952%
951,388.88	8,333.33	694.44	0.00	9,027.77	11.3869%
952,083.32	8,333.33	694.44	0.00	9,027.77	11.3785%

BASED ON EFFECTIVE INTEREST (CONSTANT YIELD)

NET BOOK VALUE	COUPON ACCRUAL	DISCOUNT ACCRE-TION	PREMIUM AMORT	MONTHLY INCOME	YIELD
950,000.00	8,333.33	491.02	0.00	8,824.35	11.1465%
950,491.02	8,333.33	495.59	0.00	8,828.92	11.1466%
950,986.61	8,333.33	500.19	0.00	8,833.52	11.1466%
951,486.80	8,333.33	504.84	0.00	8,838.17	11.1466%

(Menu A) has been completed, review the comparative schedule (Menu B), using the short form (1). Return to the paragraphs above for instructions and prove the numbers on the screen with your calculator.

Data Entry (Menu A)

	Premium Bond ----->	Discount Bond
Transaction Fee	0	0
Face Value	$1,000,000	$1,000,000
Coupon Rate	10%	10%
Price	105	95
Maturity (Months)	72	72

D   -   SAMPLE ACCOUNTING ENTRIES FOR BOND PURCHASE

Menu D presents the original purchase journal entries for the bond data entered in Menu B. In this example the bonds are recorded at face value, with associated contra accounts for premium or discount. See the Bond Accounting Entries (Table 2) which follows this section.

E   -   SAMPLE ACCOUNTING ENTRIES FOR MONTHLY INCOME

The monthly journal entries for income-related accounts are presented for both straightline and constant yield methods. The coupon interest accrual is recorded first, followed by the discount/premium entries. Discount accretion (write up) is an income account, while premium amortization is a contra-income or expense account.

The second screen in Menu E, presented below, is designed to analyze the accounting entries for two other coupon bond-related variables: purchased interest and coupon payments.

* * *

GENERAL LEDGER ENTRIES TO RECORD PURCHASED INTEREST AND INTEREST RECEIVABLE AT PERIOD PAYMENT DATA

PURCHASED INTEREST

	TYPE OF ENTRY	
	SETTLEMENT DATE	INTEREST DATE
CASH (ASSET ACCOUNT)	(CREDIT)	(DEBIT)
PURCHASED INTEREST RECEIVABLE	(DEBIT)	(CREDIT)

INTEREST RECEIVABLE

	TYPE OF ENTRY	
	ACCRUAL DATE	INTEREST DATE
COUPON INTEREST RECEIVABLE	(DEBIT)	(CREDIT)
COUPON INTEREST INCOME	(CREDIT)	
CASH (ASSET ACCOUNT)		(DEBIT)

* * *

When the buyer purchases a coupon bond, the seller is paid interest accrued to the settlement date. The purchaser has advanced funds (purchased interest) and will be reimbursed when the next coupon interest payment is paid, usually semiannually. The purchased interest receivable is established on the purchase settlement date and reversed or eliminated on the coupon payment or interest date.

As noted above, the bond coupon is usually paid by the borrower semiannually, while the bank managers need to review monthly income results. If the accounting system is a monthly (or daily) accrual of income, a coupon interest receivable will be debited each month (accrual date) until the next coupon interest check (interest date) is received by the bond holder.

P   -   PRINT REPORTS

The following print selection screen is presented below. Depress P, enter, and wait a few seconds for the print option screen to appear.

PRINT SELECTION

THIS PROGRAM PROVIDES A SHORT FORM PRESENTATION TO REFLECT BOTH "STRAIGHTLINE" AND "EFFECTIVE INTEREST" METHODS ON THE SAME PAGE.

THE PROGRAM ALSO PRESENTS A LONG FORM PRESENTATION TO TRACK THE CHANGES IN TIME OF THE ENTRIES UNDER BOTH METHODS. UP TO 72 MONTHS OF DATA MAY BE VIEWED FOR BOTH METHODS.

SELECTION "C" WILL PRINT DATA ENTRY SCREEN AND SAMPLE REQUIRED ENTRIES.

SELECT PRINT DESIRED:

A - SHORT FORM

B - LONG FORM

C - DATA ENTRY AND SAMPLE ENTRIES

One may choose to print the entire report with either the short (A) or long form (B) or to print just the data entry and accounting entries screens (C).

S   -   SAVE TO DISKETTE (REPLACES CURRENT FILE)

This option is made available to enable files to be updated.

BOND ACCOUNTING - - SUMMARY

The accounting for a bond includes the original journal entry at the time of purchase, the periodic accrual of income, the receipt of income from the borrower, and the transactions at maturity. The procedure associated with the entries at the time of bond purchase determines the procedure used to account for premium and discount. The bond may be recorded at cost or at face value. In Table 1 the cost or face value purchase entry is shown for both a discount and a premium bond. Debits are listed as Dr, credits as Cr. The associated income accrual, book value computation, sale before maturity, and maturity entries are provided. This program uses the bond face value as the purchase value. Contra accounts are used rather than merely accreting (writing up) or amortizing (writing down) directly to the bond account. Data analyses, tax management, and external reporting are enhanced with contra record keeping. A separate account is preferred over a direct adjustment to the bond value.

Table 2
Bond Accounting Entries

	Bond Recorded At	
Transaction	Cost	Face
Discounted Bond Purchase	Bond (cost) Dr Cash Cr	Bond (Face) Dr Accum Bond Disc Cr Cash Cr
Monthly Interest Income and Discount Accretion	Accum Bond Accret Dr Disc Accret Cr Coupon Int Rec Dr Coupon Interest Income Cr	Accum Bond Disc Accret Dr Disc Accret Cr Coupon Interest Rec Dr Coupon Interest Income Cr
Book Value Computation	Original Bond Value + Accum Bond Accret	Original Bond Value - Accum Bond Accret
Sale of Bond Before Maturity (Either Gain or Loss)	Cash Dr Loss Dr Bond (cost) Cr Accum Bond Accret Cr Gain Cr	Cash Dr Loss Dr Accum Bond Accret Dr Bond (Face) Cr Gain Cr
Maturity	Cash Dr Bond (Cost) Cr Accum Bond Accret Cr	Cash Dr Bond (Face) Cr
Premium Bond		
Purchase	Bond (Cost) Dr Cash Cr	Bond (Face) Dr Accum Prem Amort Dr Cash Cr
Monthly Interest Income and Premium Amortization	Prem Amort (Exp) Dr Accum Prem Amort Cr Coupon Int Rec Dr Coupon Income Cr	Prem Amort (Exp) Dr Accum Prem Amort Cr Coupon Int Rec Dr Coupon Income Cr
Book Value Computation	Original Bond Value - Accum Prem Amort	Original Bond Value + Accum Prem Amort

Sale of Bond Before Maturity (Either Gain or Loss)	Cash Dr Loss Dr Accum Prem Amort Dr Bond (Cost) Cr Gain Cr	Cash Dr Loss Dr Bond (Face) Cr Accum Prem Amort Cr Gain Cr
Maturity	Cash Dr Accum Prem Amort Dr Bond (Cost) Cr	Cash Dr Bond (Face) Cr

---

SAMPLE PROBLEMS/ASSIGNMENTS

1. Bond prices and interest rates. For any bond with a specific coupon rate and maturity, increase the price and note the decline in the yield to maturity. Decrease the price and note the increase in the calculated yield. At a price equal to the par or face value of the bond, the coupon rate and the market yield are the same. Remember, bond yields vary simultaneously and inversely with changes in bond prices.

2. a. A $100,000, 8%, five-year (sixty-month) Treasury bond is purchased at a price of 88. What is the amount of the first monthly discount accretion on a straightline basis?

    b. With the use of a calculator, prove the monthly income and discount accretion amount for the first month for both the straightline and effective interest methods. Which method is easier to compute? Which provides a more accurate accounting of monthly income?

    c.   Repeat parts (a) and (b) if the bond is selling for 112.

    d.   What is the effective rate change of a transaction fee? Include a $30 brokerage fee in the above problem and note the impact on the yield to maturity? Try a $150 fee.

3.   A four-year zero-coupon bond ($1 million face) is selling for 80. Record in journal entry form (debit/credit) the discount accretion (both straightline and constant yield) for the first month of ownership.

CHAPTER 4

Model B
Money Market Yields, Duration, Forward Rates and Interest Rate Concepts

INTRODUCTION AND CONCEPTS

Model B covers several financial market concepts and serves as a money market calculator. The models include:

1. Yield calculation of money market discount securities.

2. Calculation of the duration of a bond.

3. Calculation of an estimated forward interest rate, given two observed rates at different maturities.

4. A decomposition analysis of nominal interest rates into the real rate, inflation expectations and risk premiums.

The objective of this group of programs is to use the calculating power of the PC to construct a money market calculator with which yield, duration, and forward rate calculations can be both learned and calculated very quickly. While these models are not specifically related to bank management, knowledge of these concepts is an integral part of managing the bank security portfolio. The important financial concepts covered in this chapter are as follows:

1. Money market yields on discounted securities include the bank discount, coupon equivalent, and effective compound interest method. The effective compound rate is the preferred yield for comparison purposes.

2. Security prices vary inversely with interest rates.

3. Yields of shorter-term securities are more volatile than those of longer-term securities for a given price change.

4. Longer-term security prices change more than shorter-term security prices for a given yield change.

29

5. Nominal interest rates observed in the market include the real rate of return, expected inflation (Fisher effect), and premiums for default and interest rate risk.

6. Duration is the holding period which balances price or interest rate risk against the reinvestment risk of a coupon security.

7. For a coupon bond, duration is less than maturity.

8. For a zero coupon bond, duration equals maturity

9. The higher the coupon rate, the shorter the duration-- more cash flows earlier to reinvest.

10. The lower the coupon rate, the longer the duration-- less cash flows in coupon.

11. The higher the interest rate (YTM), the shorter the duration -- reinvestment assumption is more important.

12. The expectations theory of the term structure of interest rates states that long-term interest rates represent the average of current and future short-term rates.

13. Implied expected future short-term rates may be calculated from two observed market rates of different maturities.

Once you are familiar with the models, return to the above list of concepts and test them in the models.

APPLICATIONS

The financial market concepts in this chapter are discussed in a variety of finance courses and textbooks. Usually the concept is emphasized, but here with the money market calculator, application is possible as well. Bank security investment analysis requires yield calculation and knowledge of the duration point. The daily U.S. Treasury yields in the Wall Street Journal provide a future interest rate forecast when using the forward rate calculator. Cases and bank simulation games require yield analysis and interest rate forecasts. Analyze current interest rates. Use these models to estimate the expected inflation rate, as estimated by the financial market. In conclusion, try to use these "concepts" as tools to make business and economic decisions.

MENU AND SCREENS

Model B has the following menus on a two-screen format:

A - TUTORIAL
B - MONEY MARKET YIELD CALCULATIONS
C - INTEREST RATE CONCEPTS
D - DURATION CONCEPT EXPLANATION
E - DURATION CALCULATION
F - VIEW COMPLETE DURATION SCHEDULE
G - CALCULATING FORWARD INTEREST RATES
P - PRINT REPORTS
S - SAVE TO DISKETTE (REPLACES CURRENT FILE CONTENTS)
Q - QUIT PROGRAM

NOTE THE PROGRAM IS SET FOR MANUAL RECALCULATION AND IS PROGRAMMED TO CALCULATE AFTER YOU COMPLETE EACH DATA ENTRY SCREEN.

A - TUTORIAL

The tutorial provides a brief description of each of the models. Note that the programs are set for manual calculation after all data have been entered. The time delay (wait) is between ten and thirty seconds maximum. No data may be entered in the tutorial.

B - MONEY MARKET YIELD CALCULATIONS

The program calculates three yields for discount (no coupon) money market securities up to one year of maturity. A sample screen is as follows:

* * *

MONEY MARKET YIELD CALCULATIONS

FACE VALUE (DOLLAR AMOUNT):	$1,000,000.00
PRICE (% OF FACE VALUE) DECIMAL (i.e. .95 = 95%:	95.0000000%
TRANSACTION COST (DOLLAR AMOUNT):	$0.00
DAYS TO MATURITY (N) (365 MAXIMUM):	270
PRICE (DOLLAR AMOUNT):	$950,000.00
	YIELD %

BANK DISCOUNT
FORMULA: $(((FV - P) / FV) \times (360 / N)) \times 100$ 6.67%

COUPON EQUIVALENT
FORMULA: $(((FV - P) / P) \times (365 / N)) \times 100$ 7.12%

EFFECTIVE INTEREST
FORMULA: $(((1+((FV - P) / P)) \quad (365 / N)) - 1) \times 100$ 7.18%

* * *

The first four lines include the variables to be entered. They are:

1. Enter the face or maturity value of the security in dollars.

2. Enter the price as a percent of face value. Remember, U.S. Treasury bills are often quoted in thirty-seconds, and a decimal conversion must be made. A Treasury bill of 92.18 is an entry of 92.5625.

3. Enter the transaction cost or brokerage fee, if applicable. Transaction costs lower yields.

4. Enter the number of days to maturity up to a maximum of 365.

The formulas for three yield calculations are displayed on the screen. Study the formula differences that produce different yields for the same security.

Bank Discount Method: The traditional central bank yield, assuming a 360-day year and the face value (FV) as the amount invested. The period income (FV-P) divided by the face value gives the period yield, which is then annualized (360/N).

Coupon Equivalent Yield: A yield calculation using a 365-day year and assuming that the price is the amount invested. The N-period yield based on the net invested amount (times) 365/N generates a yield closer to an effective rate, but it still does not consider compounding.

Effective Interest Yield: Calculates the true, effective yield, compounding the N-period yield with the 365/N exponent. The formula is $[1+(FV-P)]^{365/N} - 1 \times 100$. Note that the effective yield is higher than the other two, because of the compounding assumption. Use the effective yield when comparing investment alternatives.

Money market security yields, as observed above, tend to be quoted in a variety of ways. Refer to Instruments of the Money Market, a free publication of the Federal Reserve Bank of Richmond, or any financial markets textbook for details.

C - INTEREST RATE CONCEPTS[1]

Interest rate theory argues that nominal market interest rates include the real rate of interest plus an expected inflation premium and other premiums for other risks assumed.

---

[1] See James VanHorne, Financial Market Rates and Flows, 2nd ed., (Englewood Cliffs, NJ: Prentice Hall, Inc., 1984).

This model provides a computer-based focal point (screen) for analyzing the conceptual components of market interest rates.

The user is requested to enter a loan amount and the components of the market rate of interest. The model simply sums the rate components and calculates the annual dollar amounts of loan interest related to the interest rate components. The value of this simple program is not its "complex" programming, but the insight to be derived from interest rate theory and a visual presentation. The program screen is listed below, followed by a brief overview of interest rate concepts and theories supporting this program.

* * *
* * *

MARKET RATE OF INTEREST CONCEPTS

SAMPLE LOAN REQUEST: $10,000

	COMPONENTS	RELATED ANNUAL INTEREST
REAL RATE OF INTEREST:	3.00%	$300.00
EXPECTED INFLATION RATE:	4.00%	$400.00
DEFAULT-RISK PREMIUM:	3.00%	$300.00
INT. RATE RISK PREMIUM:	2.00%	$200.00
MARKET RATE OF INTEREST:	12.00%	$1,200.00

* * *

The market rate of interest is a function of many variables, some of which are listed on the screen above. The real rate of interest or time value of money is the opportunity cost of consumption or real asset investment benefits. Research for long periods has placed this rate in the 3-4 percent range, consistent with the long-run real growth rate of the U.S. economy. Financial investors in a price-stable, risk-free environment would demand at least the real rate of interest. In the example above, the lender wants 3 percent ($300) to compensate for not having $10,000 available for consumption or real investment, such as real estate or fixed assets.

Financial investors, expecting future inflation, will add a purchasing power premium to the real rate of interest, known as the Fisher effect (Irving Fisher); this premium should approximate investors' (the market) expected average inflation over the term of the loan or security. In the table above, investors foresee a 4 percent rate of inflation in the future and will thus demand a 4 percent ($400) premium for the loss in purchasing power on their $10,000 for the first year.

If the market expects to lose 3 percent of the value of its investment in loans ($300 per $10,000) with similar risk because of default (expected default loss), a default risk premium of 3 percent ($300 per $10,000) will be demanded in order to leave an investment in risk-free securities to make a risky loan. Risk premiums vary with the business cycle, industry life cycles, etc. A U.S. Treasury bond investor will demand a market rate equal to the real rate and expected inflation, but will not likely charge the U.S. Treasury a default risk premium.

Interest rate risk is the risk that varying future interest rates will cause a variation in the future value (price) of the bond. Risk is associated with the variability of future returns. Upward movements in interest rates will cause, or are associated with, a decline in bond values; decreases in interest rates are associated with increasing bond values. A long-term investor faces interest rate risk (future variation in the market value of the bond or loan) and demands a premium sufficient to compensate for the risk taking. Investors, in the example above, want a 2 percent ($200 per 10,000) annually to compensate for future price variability or for the risk of locking in an investment rate when interest returns may go up in the future (prices decline).

After you have read the above brief explanation, answer the following questions by changing the screen inputs and thinking about the concept. Start with the default data and treat each question separately.

1. If inflation were nil and forecasting methods were perfected, what would be the level of market rates?

2. What affects the cost of funds (long term) for the U.S. Treasury? Explain.

3.   If a corporate bond rating is changed from AAA to A, what will happen to the cost of borrowing $10,000?

4.   A variable (weekly) rate loan would likely have what interest rate? Compare to the data above or on the screen. Alternatively, what premiums are charged for a fixed-rate loan? Explain.

5.   If today the market expects inflation to be 8 percent per year, what will be the impact on interest rates? Explain. What does the inflation premium compensate for the investor?

6.   If taxes on investment income are high, what is the impact on interest rates? Why?

7.   If a bond can be called by the issuer at any time, what might happen to the level of interest rates? Why?

D   -   DURATION CONCEPTS EXPLANATION

The duration measure, developed by Frederick Macaulay, is the holding period required to assure the investor the yield to maturity. Duration is the ratio of the sum of the time weighted, discounted future cash flows of the debt security divided by the current price or value. The duration formula is:

$$D = \frac{\displaystyle\sum_{t=1}^{N} \frac{C_t \, (t)}{(1+r)^t}}{\displaystyle\sum_{t=1}^{N} \frac{C_t}{1+r^t}}$$

C_t = interest and/or principal in period t
(t) = length of time until C_t is received
N = final maturity period
r = yield to maturity

A coupon bond investor is faced with both interest rate or price risk and reinvestment risk. The investor can calculate an expected yield to maturity (Model A) at the time of purchase, but the yield to maturity calculation assumes that the periodic coupon receipts received will be reinvested at the yield to maturity. The greater the variation in future interest rates, the greater the variation in the actual yield measured at maturity. Holding the bond until maturity eliminates the interest rate risk or price risk because face value is received, but the reinvestment risk produces a potential distribution of actual yields to maturity depending on the direction and extent of market interest rate variation during the term to maturity. Holding the bond to the duration point assures the yield to maturity to the investor; holding to maturity assures only face value (no price risk) and assumes reinvestment risk. At the duration point, interest rate risk is balanced against reinvestment risk to lock in the yield to maturity to that point.

The duration concept explanation screen lists a general definition of the duration measure, followed by several corollary statements listed below. The duration calculator program (Menu E) is discussed in the next section. Study the duration calculation and test the statements made below. Try to understand the statements from an arithmetic perspective as well as from an economic perspective.

* * *

1. Duration is the maturity point which balances price or interest rate risk against reinvestment risk of a coupon security.

2. For a coupon bond, duration < maturity.

3. For a zero coupon bond, duration = maturity.

4. The higher the coupon rate, the shorter the duration -- more of cash flows earlier to reinvest.

5.   The lower the coupon rate, the longer the duration -- low proportion of cash flows in coupon.

6.   The higher the interest rate (YTM), the shorter the duration -- reinvestment assumption is more important.

* * *

E   -   DURATION CALCULATION

Volatile interest rates and the need for more sophisticated asset/liability management tools have brought renewed interest to the duration concept. Pension fund managers (trust) and bank investment managers with a need to lock in a known rate of return on a coupon bond portfolio have turned to the duration concept for answers. Asset/liability managers have found that matching asset/liability maturities does not eliminate interest rate risk. Matching durations, hard as it is, does.

The duration calculator is designed to enhance the student's understanding of the duration concept. The model calculates and displays the calculations rapidly, without hand cranking, so that concepts can be learned and tested. Memory and calculation time have constrained the flexibility of the model (one year minimum to thirty-period maximum), but not the ability to study and learn the duration concept. In this model, both a coupon bond or loan (coupons followed by face value) and an installment loan (outlay followed by equal installments) duration can be calculated and analyzed. In the following paragraphs the duration calculator screen (sample listed below) will be explained.

* * *

DURATION CALCULATION - 1 YR MIN. AND 15 YRS MAX. MAT. FROM
SETTLEMENT DATE
ENTER TYPE 1=ANNUAL COUPON, 2=SEMIANNUAL COUPON, 3=LOAN: 1
                                          FACE VALUE: 1000
    IF LOAN, ENTER ANNUAL LOAN PAYMENT (IF APPLICABLE): $0
  BOND COUPON RATE (ENTER AS DECIMAL, i.e. .10 = 10%): 7.0000%
 YIELD TO MATURITY (ENTER AS DECIMAL, i.e. .10 = 10%): 8.0000%
                              ENTER MATURITY IN YEARS: 5
                              DURATION IN YEARS: 4.3731
FIVE-PERIOD SAMPLE PRESENTATION: WEIGHTED

	CASH	PRESENT VALUE	PRESENT
PERIOD	FLOW	OF CASH FLOW	VALUE
1	$70.00	$64.81	$64.82
2	$70.00	$60.01	$120.03
3	$70.00	$55.57	$166.71
4	$70.00	$51.45	$205.81
5	$1,070.00	$728.22	$3,641.12

TOTALS FOR ALL PERIODS OF SELECTED MATURITY AS
ENTERED:
	$1,350.00		$960.07		$4,198.48
CALC:	$4,198.48	/	$960.07	=	4.3731

* * *

-   Enter the type of cash flow pattern. One may choose (1)
    annual coupon (face value at maturity); (2) semiannual
    coupons (face value at maturity); or (3) loan
    (installments).

-   Enter the face value (maturity value) of the bond or loan.

-   If a loan, enter the annual (per period) loan payment (if
    applicable). Calculate the annual (monthly) payments on an
    installment loan. See the loan example later in this
    chapter.

-   Enter the bond (loan) coupon rate (as a decimal fraction).

-   Enter the yield to maturity (as a decimal fraction).
    Calculate this value from a calculator or from Menu A. This
    is the discount rate used in the duration calculation. For
    a bond selling at face value, the coupon rate equals the
    YTM. The bond in the above example must be priced at a
    discount because the YTM is greater than the coupon rate.

-   Enter the maturity in years. The program is set up for a
    minimum of one to a maximum of fifteen years. The program

matrix will handle up to thirty periods (fifteen years x semiannual). Other bond (loan) maturity situations may be entered by adjusting the coupon rate and YTM. A five-year loan with interest paid quarterly, principal at maturity, is a twenty-period (five times four) annual coupon calculation. Divide the coupon and YTM by four before entry. Remember to adjust the percent inputs to compute the percent per period and to remember the thirty-period maximum.

The duration in years (or periods) is then calculated with up to thirty seconds of waiting time. A five-period sample presentation is displayed for your analysis. In the example above, the $70.00 annual interest coupon discounted at the YTM of 8 percent is 64.81 times the number of the period (1) equals the weighted present value. In the fifth (and final year of the example) the face value and coupon are listed, as is the five-year 8 percent present value (PV) and PV x 5 or the weighted PV of $3,641.12.

The sum of the cash flows, PV of cash flows and weighted PVs are then listed, followed by the duration calculation (calc) of $4,198.48/$960.07 = 4.3731 or the sum of the time-weighted PVs divided by the sum of the unweighted PV (market price of the bond). In the example, the duration of the coupon bond is less than the maturity of the bond. If the bond is held for 4.3731 years, the interest rate and reinvestment risk would offset each other and a YTM of 8 percent would be assured if the bond is held to that point.

Duration Calculation Examples: Several examples are presented.

a.   Zero Coupon Bond: Assumes a $1,000 face value zero coupon with a maturity of five years, priced to sell at a YTM (annual compounding) of 8 percent.

* * *

DURATION CALCULATION - 1 YR MIN. AND 15 YRS MAX. MAT. FROM
SETTLEMENT DATE
ENTER TYPE 1=ANNUAL COUPON, 2=SEMI-ANNUAL COUPON, 3=LOAN: 1
                                            FACE VALUE: $1,000
     IF LOAN, ENTER ANNUAL LOAN PAYMENT (IF APPLICABLE): $0
   BOND COUPON RATE (ENTER AS DECIMAL, i.e. .10 = 10%): 0.0000%
  YIELD TO MATURITY (ENTER AS DECIMAL, i.e. .10 = 10%): 8.0000%
                              ENTER MATURITY IN YEARS: 5
                              DURATION IN YEARS: 5.0000
FIVE-PERIOD SAMPLE PRESENTATION:

			WEIGHTED
PERIOD	CASH FLOW	PRESENT VALUE OF CASH FLOW	PRESENT VALUE
1	$0.00	$0.00	$0.00
2	$0.00	$0.00	$0.00
3	$0.00	$0.00	$0.00
4	$0.00	$0.00	$0.00
5	$1,000.00	$680.58	$3,402.92

TOTALS FOR ALL PERIODS OF SELECTED MATURITY AS
ENTERED:

	$1,000.00	$680.58		$3,402.92
CALC:	$3,402.92	$680.58	=	5.0000

* * *

Summary: The duration of a zero coupon bond equals the
maturity.

   b.   Loan Analysis: A $10,000, 12 percent, five year loan,
        solving for payments on a calculator, has annual loan
        payments of $2,774.10. The duration is 2.77.

* * *

DURATION CALCULATION - 1 YR MIN. AND 15 YRS MAX. MAT. FROM
SETTLEMENT DATE
ENTER TYPE 1=ANNUAL COUPON, 2=SEMI-ANNUAL COUPON, 3=LOAN: 3
                                             FACE VALUE: $0
      IF LOAN, ENTER ANNUAL LOAN PAYMENT (IF APPLICABLE): $2,774
      BOND COUPON RATE (ENTER AS DECIMAL, i.e. .10 = 10%): 0.0000%
    YIELD TO MATURITY (ENTER AS DECIMAL, i.e. .10 = 10%):12.0000%
                                 ENTER MATURITY IN YEARS: 5
                                 DURATION IN YEARS: 2.7746
FIVE PERIODS SAMPLE PRESENTATION:

| | | | WEIGHTED |
| | CASH | PRESENT VALUE | PRESENT |
PERIOD	FLOW	OF CASH FLOW	VALUE
1	$2,774.10	$2,476.88	$2,476.88
2	$2,774.10	$2,211.50	$4,422.99
3	$2,774.10	$1,974.55	$5,923.65
4	$2,774.10	$1,762.99	$7,051.96
5	$2,774.10	$1,574.10	$7,870.49

TOTALS FOR ALL PERIODS OF SELECTED MATURITY AS
ENTERED:

	$13,870.50	$10,000.01		$27,745.97
CALC:	$27,745.97 /	$10,000.01	=	2.7746

* * *

Summary: If the above loan were funded with a reasonable spread
by a zero coupon CD of 2.77 years or a coupon CD with a duration
of 2.77 years, the interest rate risk has been eliminated. The
loan yield and deposit cost are known for 2.78 years. Instead of
matching maturities to eliminate interest rate risk, cash flows
have been matched, thus reducing the impact of interest rate
variability more effectively.

   c.   Loan Analysis: A $10,000, five-year loan at a 12
      percent fixed rate paid in equal quarterly installments
      of $672.16. The duration is 9.5229 quarters.

* * *

DURATION CALCULATION - 1 YR MIN. AND 15 YRS MAX. MAT. FROM
SETTLEMENT DATE
ENTER TYPE 1=ANNUAL COUPON, 2=SEMI-ANNUAL COUPON, 3=LOAN: 3
                                           FACE VALUE: $0
      IF LOAN, ENTER ANNUAL LOAN PAYMENT (IF APPLICABLE): $672
   BOND COUPON RATE (ENTER AS DECIMAL, i.e. .10 = 10%): 0.0000%
   YIELD TO MATURITY (ENTER AS DECIMAL, i.e. .10 = 10%): 3.0000%
                                 ENTER MATURITY IN YEARS: 20
                                 DURATION IN YEARS: 9.5229
FIVE-PERIOD SAMPLE PRESENTATION:

| | CASH | PRESENT VALUE | WEIGHTED PRESENT |
PERIOD	FLOW	OF CASH FLOW	VALUE
1	$672.16	$652.58	$652.58
2	$672.16	$633.57	$1,267.15
3	$672.16	$615.12	$1,845.36
4	$672.16	$597.20	$2,388.81
5	$672.16	$579.81	$2,899.04

TOTALS FOR ALL PERIODS OF SELECTED MATURITY AS
ENTERED:

	$13,443.14	$10,000.00		$95,228.61
CALC:	$95,228.61 /	$10,000.00	=	9.5229

* * *

Summary: Solve the quarterly installments problem (PMT) on a
calculator. The quarterly rate is 12/4 = 3 percent.   The first
five periods of the duration calculation are shown above. Menu F
below will display all twenty periods. The summary report prints
only the above screen.

F   -   VIEW COMPLETE DURATION SCHEDULE

    These two screens display all periods of the duration
calculation.

G   -   CALCULATING FORWARD INTEREST RATES

    A business person or student is often asked to predict
future interest rates.   Whether it is predicting future loan or
deposit rates or estimating rates for a simulation game, we are
all called upon to offer a forecast once in a while. If we could
predict future rates consistently, we would easily become rich
and famous. It is not an easy task -- just look at the "success"
rate of economists and econometric models over the last ten
years.

While accurate forecasting is a complicated, multi-step process, this model offers an input to the forecasting process by calculating estimated forward rates using actual, observed market interest rates that one can find in the Wall Street Journal or any other source. (The theoretical basis for using calculated forward rates as an estimate of future interest rates is found in the expectations theory of the term structure of interest rates.)

The expectation theory attempts to explain why interest rates vary by term (maturity). Why are long-term U.S. Treasury bond yields (yield to maturity) higher at times than yields of near-term bonds? Market expectations of future interest rates are thought to have an impact upon bond buyers and sellers and their pricing of bonds across the term structure (maturities). The expectation theory states that long-term rates represent an average of current short-term and expected short-term rates. Assuming you can choose short-term or long-term bonds (default risk constant), which one would you select? A one-year CD yields 5 percent, while a two-year one (annual compounding) yields 6 percent. Which should you take? It depends upon your expectations of one-year rates one year from today. Investing at 5 percent for the first year and reinvesting at 7.01 percent would give the same dollar amount or yield as the two-year CD compounded annually.

$$(1.06)^2 = (1.05)(1.0701) = 1.1236$$

The forward rate on the one-year CD one year from now (second year) was calculated from two actual, observed rates listed at a bank. If one assumes that differences in actual market rates by time are explained mostly by expectations, the market (buyers and sellers) is forecasting one-year CDs to yield 7.01 percent one year from now. The computed forward rate is not my estimate or your estimate. It is the implied market estimate of future short-term interest rates, assuming that term yield differences are explained solely by the expectation theory and that other term structure theories are ignored. To some, this is a heroic assumption.

Changes in market expectations of future interest rates will affect the buying/selling of certain term securities, changing prices and yield differences by time. In the case of the CD above, if the market were to change its estimate of what one-year CDs would yield in one year to 8 percent, the bank would sell very few 6 percent two-year CDs and many one-year 5 percent CDs. Why? Expecting future short-term rates to be 8 percent, and desiring the highest two-year return, investors would buy the one-year 5 percent CD and reinvest at 8 percent in a year.

$$(1.05)(1.08) = 1.134 \text{ estimated two-year return}$$

$$(1.06)^2 = 1.1236 \text{ two-year CD return}$$

What two-year CD rate would make the market indifferent between buying the one-year (5 percent) CD or the two-year CD? Answer = $1.134^{1/2}$ or $\sqrt{1.134} - 1 = 6.4$ percent. At this new two-year rate, investors would achieve the same two-year return. One year at 5 percent followed by an expected one-year rate of 8 percent or 6.49 percent for two years is the same.

$$(1.05)(1.08) = 1.134$$

$$(1.0649)(1.0649) = 1.134$$

Calculating Forward Rates

If interest rate expectations are a significant factor in the buying and selling of short- and long-term securities, then calculating expected forward rates provides a rough estimate of the market forecast of future interest rates. While the thousands of traders of billions of dollars are often wrong (forward rates are not a reliable estimate of future rates), calculated forward rates can serve as an input to the forecaster.

The formula used in this model for calculating the j-period forward rate, f, given any two observed (actual) interest rates, R, of different maturities is:

$$_{t+n}f_{jt} = \sqrt[j]{\frac{(1 + {_t}R_{n+jt})^{n+t}}{(1 + {_t}R_{nt})^n}} - 1$$

where $_{t+n}f_{jt}$ = the j period expected or forward rate <u>beginning</u> at time t+n.

t = 1 if $_{t+n}f_{jt}$ assumes a forward rate beginning at t+n, or, 0 if one assumes a forward rate after the end of the nth year. (t is assumed to be 1 in this model.)

j = time period between two actual observed rates or the term of the computed forward rate.

$_tR_n$ = the actual observed interest rate at time t for an n-period security (years to maturity).

<u>Example</u>: An investor is interested in purchasing one of the following government bonds, each of which yields (annual compounding):

Term	Market Yield
2 year	6.50%
3 year	7.25%

Should the investor buy the two- or three-year bond? Of course it depends on what interest rates will be two years from now. A $100 investment in the three-year bond will yield $(1.0725)^3 = 123.36 in three years. The purchase of the two-year bond would give the investor $(1.065)^2 = 113.42 at the end of the two years and the need to reinvest the proceeds for one more year at what rate to equal a sum of $123.36? We need to solve for the one-year forward rate two years from now that allows a $113.42 investment to grow to $123.36. What are expected (forecasted) one year rates two years from now, as revealed by the current yield structure of interest rates?

Using our formula above, where j = 1

$$_{t+2}f_1 = \sqrt[j=1]{\frac{(1.0725)^3}{(1.065)^2}} - 1 = \frac{(1.0725)^3}{(1.065)^2} - 1 =$$

$$\frac{1.2336}{1.1342} - 1 = 8.76\%$$

The expected one-year interest rate two years from now is 8.76%. Investing $113.42 at 8.76% for one year equals $123.36 at the end of three years. This is the same as the total return from the three-year bond $(1.0725)^3 = 123.36. The one-year forward rate of 8.76 percent is the forecasted or expected one-year rate two years from now, as indicated by today's actual market rates.

Using the Model

In this decision model, one has the ability to calculate annual forward rates covering any j-year period, or one may compute quarterly forward rates from observed, actual Treasury bill rates, CD rates, or any quarterly money market securities.

Annual Forward Rates

The data entry screen requests that you enter the rates (yields) and maturities (in even years) of two actual, observed rates found in the market. The two securities should be similar, except for maturity. For example, two banks' CDs, two U.S. Treasury bonds, or two GMAC bonds have similar default risks and other characteristics, except maturity.

Enter the rate and maturity of the near-term (shortest-maturity) security and then the rate and term of the longest maturity. For example, if you wish to compute the one-year forward rate one year from today implied by a one-year Treasury bill yielding 5.50% and a two-year Treasury bill yielding 6.00%, input (in decimal form):

```
Enter rate of near term security:        5.50      percent
Enter maturity of security:                1       years

Enter rate of longest term security:     6.00      percent
Enter maturity of Security:                2       years
```

The model then calculates and presents the following:

The __1__ period expected forward rate beginning after year __1__ from today through year __2__ is __6.50__ percent, rounded to hundreds.

To prove the solution:

first year		second year		Two years, comp. annually
(1.055)	x	(1.065)	=	1.1236
(1.06)	x	(1.06)	=	1.1236

In another example, using the following actual rates from the _Wall Street Journal_, what is the expected two-year rate two years $t+_2f_2$ from today?

Table 1

Maturity	Yield%[1]
1	6.00
2	7.00
3	7.50
4	8.00
5	9.00

To make it easier, draw a time line:

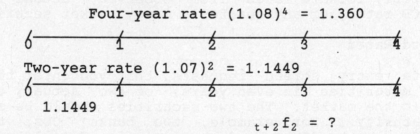

Four-year rate $(1.08)^4 = 1.360$

Two-year rate $(1.07)^2 = 1.1449$

1.1449

$t+_2f_2 = ?$

Input:

```
Enter rate of near-term security:        7.00      percent
Enter maturity of security:                2       years

Enter rate of longest-term security:     8.00      percent
Enter maturity of security:                4       years
```

The __2__ period expected forward rate beginning after year __2__ from today through year __4__ is __9.01__ percent.

Proof:

$$(1.08)^4 = 1.360$$

$$(1.07)^2(1.0900935)^2 = 1.360$$

The market expects two-year security rates to be 9.01 in two years.   Right now, two-year yields are 7.00 percent.   The market is forecasting an increase in interest rates.

Computing Quarterly Forward Rates

Money market securities are often issued quarterly for 91, 182, 274, and 365 days. To estimate future annualized rates at quarterly intervals out to a year, input the near-term (shortest) rate and the number of quarters (entered as a decimal fraction of a year, such as .25, .50, .75) to maturity, followed by the yield and maturity of the longer-term security. The yields are assumed to be annual effective yields, compounded quarterly, not a bank discount yield or coupon equivalent yields.

Example: If the following yields are observed today, what are the estimated one-quarter interest rates for the next three quarters?

Table 2

Quarter	Days	Yield (Comp. Effective Rates)
1 (.25)	91	9.49%
2 (.50)	182	9.39
3 (.75)	274	9.20
4 (1.00)	365	9.00

With reference to the formula discussed in the previous section, j refers to one quarter, and the three estimated one-quarter security rates implied by actual market rates are:

[1] Annual compounding assumed. One can adjust for compounding more than once a year by dividing the yield by the number of compounding periods in the year and multiplying the number of years to maturity by the same amount.

Second-quarter estimated rates:

$$^1\sqrt{\frac{(1.0939)^{2/4}}{(1.0949)^{1/4}}} - 1 = (1.02248)^4 - 1 = 9.30\%$$

(Using a calculator, solving for $1.0939^{.5}$, enter 1.0939, y^x, .5 = 1.0459)

Input:

Enter rate of near-term security   9.49   percent
Enter maturity of security   .25   years

Enter rate of longest-term security   9.39   percent
Enter maturity of security   .50   years

     The ___.25___ period expected forward rate beginning after ___.25___ years from today through year ___.5___ is _9.29_ percent.

Third Quarter Estimated Rates:

$$^1\sqrt{\frac{(1.0920)^{.75}}{(1.0939)^{.5}}} - 1 = \frac{1.0682}{1.0459} = (1.02132)^4 - 1 = 8.82\%$$

When J = 1, disregard the root sign. If J = 2 for a two-period forward rate, find the square root.

The $(1.02132)^4$ is a quarterly rate annualized (to the fourth power); it is 8.82 percent.

Input:

Enter rate of near-term security   9.39   percent
Enter maturity of security   .50   years

Enter rate of longest-term security   9.20   percent
Enter maturity of security   .75   years

     The ___.25___ period expected forward rate beginning after year ___.50___ from today through year ___.75___ is _8.82_ percent.

Fourth Quarter Estimated Rates

$$^1\sqrt{\frac{(1.0900)^1}{(1.0920)^{.75}}} - 1 = \frac{1.090}{1.0682} - 1 = (1.02037)^4 - 1 = 8.40\%$$

Input:

Enter rate of near-term security   9.20   percent
Enter maturity of security   .75   years

Enter rate of longest-term security   9.00   percent
Enter maturity of security   1.00   years

The __.25__ period expected forward rate beginning after year __.75__ from today through year __1.00__ is __8.40__ percent.

The estimated one-quarter interest rates for the next year are:

Quarter 1	9.49%	actual
Quarter 2	9.29%	estimated
Quarter 3	8.82%	estimated
Quarter 4	8.40%	estimated

Short-term rates are expected to decline based on the current market rates (see Table 2).

If one-quarter future rates are as expected (calculated), the investor would be indifferent between a four-quarter security (9.00%), four one-quarter securities at the expected rate, or any combination of quarterly investments out to a year.

Proof:

$$(1.0949)(1.093)(1.0881)(1.084) = (1.4115)^{.25} = 1.09$$

$$(1.0939 \text{ Two qtr rate})^2 (1.0881)(1.084) = (1.4115)^{.25} = 1.09$$

P   -   PRINT REPORTS

A complete report of the latest data entry in each of the above models is printed and saved to the diskette. If you are working several problems and need print copies, it may be easier just to print the screen for each problem solved.

S   -   SAVE TO DISKETTES (REPLACES CURRENT FILE)

SAMPLE PROBLEMS/ASSIGNMENTS

Several practice problems are listed below, organized by the specific model studied. If there is difficulty with using the model or understanding the concept, return to the previous section. Working the problem is a minor goal; understanding the concept is important!

Money Market Yield Calculations

1. Calculate the yields of a 182-day Treasury bill
    purchased at 96.10 (96 and 10/32) with a $1 million
    face value. Why is the coupon equivalent and the
    compounded, effective interest yield higher than the
    traditional bank discount yield?

2. A $10,000 Treasury bill maturing in 10 days is priced
    at 99.26 or 99-26/32 and can be purchased with a $50
    transaction cost. Does the transaction cost affect the
    yield? At what size investment and/or term does the
    transaction cost affect the yields? Explain.

Interest Rate Concepts

1. Look up the approximate yield on 20-year Treasury bonds
    today (the U.S. Treasury securities column in the Wall
    Street Journal). Analyze the makeup of this yield,
    using the interest rate concepts (Menu C). Support
    your position. (Hint: enter the components so that
    they sum to your yield figure.)

2. What is the yield on a 90-day Treasury bill today?
    Analyze this yield as you did in problem 1.

Duration Calculation

1. Calculate the duration of a ten-year $1,000-face corporate bond with a coupon rate of 9 percent. The bond is priced to yield (semiannual compounding) 9.5 percent today.

2. With reference to the bond above, if it is held for the duration and then sold, what are the implications for the investor who purchased and held it?

3. What is the duration of a $1,000 face, zero coupon, 10-year bond yielding (annual) 8.5 percent? Why is the duration equal to the maturity? What might be the advantage of zeros over coupon bonds to the pension fund manager?

Calculating Forward Rates

1. Look up the U.S. Treasury securities listing of securities and yields in the Wall Street Journal. What are the expected one-year interest rates over the next four years? (Hint: list the yields of Treasury bonds maturity approximately one year, two years, three years, four years, and five years from now.) Are interest rates expected to increase or decrease over the next five years? What economic factors might explain the market's estimate of future short-term (one-year) rates?

2.   If you are using a bank simulation game this term, does
     the game give you a yield curve or listing of market
     yields by time? If so, forecast the expected future
     short-term rates as implied by the yield curve.

CHAPTER 5

Model C
Capital Budgeting Analysis

INTRODUCTION AND CONCEPTS

The investment in equipment, real estate and buildings involves decisions that not only entail large amounts of funds but affect the bank for a long time. The careful evaluation of capital assets is an integral part of bank management today. Bankers who used to ask how tall the building would be, must now, in this competitive environment, carefully plot the income, cash flow, and shareholder returns of such a venture. This model provides an opportunity (1) to learn or reinforce the basic concepts of capital budgeting analysis and (2) to practice capital decision planning quickly, using a rather straight-forward model.

Capital investments in equipment, buildings, etc. traditionally were made very infrequently in depository institutions. It was a labor intensive business. Although this is still true, the size of the proposed capital expenditures has increased significantly. Also significant is the impact that allocated capital costs have on the income statement and returns to shareholders.

With the shareholder's perspective in mind, every capital expenditure should be evaluated by studying (1) the expected future net cash flows, (2) the timing of the cash flows, and (3) the riskiness or variability of the cash flows. All three considerations are included in the net present value and internal rate of return methods used in this model. The payback period, the length of time needed to recoup the capital investment, is also calculated.

The net present value (NPV) method discounts expected after-tax cash flows at the target (minimum) rate of return. The sum of the discounted cash flows, which is the maximum the bank should pay to yield its minimally acceptable rate of return, minus the net capital outlay, equals the NPV. If the cost of the project (outlay) is less than the maximum the bank would pay (present value), making the investment would increase the value of the bank (and shareholders' investment) by the amount of the

NPV. If the NPV is less than zero (negative), the cost of the project has exceeded the present value of the future cash flows. If the expected NPV is negative, the investment will decrease shareholder value by that amount. When considering alternative, similar-sized investments, the project with the higher NPV should be selected.

The internal rate of return (IRR) is the annual compound interest rate that equates the net outlay with the expected annual cash flows. If the IRR exceeds the cost of capital (required rate of return), the project is acceptable. Why? If the IRR is realized, the project would provide a return greater than the minimum demanded or required by shareholders. If all bank projects, capital and financial, had a return (economic value) greater than the minimum required (book), bank stock prices would trade above book value. If all investment IRRs turn out to be less than the minimum required (cost of capital), the economic value of bank assets would be less than asset book values. The bank stock would trade below book or accounting value.

APPLICATIONS

This model is useful in demonstrating the importance of the capital purchase decision in the bank. It provides an opportunity to study the concepts related to cash flow determination, financial planning, and project evaluation. Further, the model provides, with some limitations, a decision analysis tool for new product (service) evaluation, the equipment replacement decision and other decisions requiring an outlay followed by future inflows. If a borrower can only pay X amount per year, how much can the bank lend the business at a certain rate? The model has many other uses: debt refunding decisions, lease/borrow decisions, and even merger analyses.

MENU AND SCREENS

Model C has the following menus:

* * *

```
A    -    TUTORIAL
B    -    PURCHASE DECISION MODEL
P    -    PRINT REPORT
S    -    SAVE TO DISKETTE (REPLACES CURRENT FILE CONTENTS)
Q    -    QUIT PROGRAM
```

* * *

A   -   TUTORIAL

   The ten-page tutorial provides a descriptive overview and the screens of the Purchase Decision Model.   No data may be entered in the tutorial.

B   -   PURCHASE DECISION MODEL

   Data are entered on the first screen, followed by four analysis screens. The model enables the user to consider a new purchase or replacement decision for up to fifteen periods and calculates the NPV, IRR, and payback period.   Capital budgeting is an incremental analysis -- added dollars invested for added dollar returns. All the screens present the incremental data, given the decision to purchase (replace) the asset.

   The data entry screen requests up to eleven inputs. These are discussed below, along with the assumptions of each.   A sample screen is now presented.

* * *

PURCHASE DECISION
ENTER PERCENTAGES AS DECIMAL (i.e., .10 = 10%)
****ENTER THE FOLLOWING DATA****

(MAX.   PURCHASE,   DELIVERY   AND   INSTALLATION   COST   OF $999,999,999,999)

$100,000	1.	PURCHASE PRICE OF NEW ASSET
$2,000	2.	DELIVERY AND INSTALLATION EXPENSES OF NEW ASSET
$2,500	3.	WORKING CAPITAL INVESTMENT
$0	4.	REMAINING BOOK VALUE OF OLD ASSET
$0	5.	SALE OF OLD ASSET, NET OF TAXES
$28,000	6.	ADDED ANNUAL OPERATING PROFIT
$4,000	7.	SALVAGE VALUE
12.00%	8.	COST OF CAPITAL (ENTER AS DECIMAL)
34.00%	9.	MARGINAL INCOME TAX RATE (ENTER AS DECIMAL)
6.00%	10.	INVESTMENT TAX CREDIT (%) (ENTER AS DECIMAL)
4	11.	USEFUL LIFE (1 TO 15 YEARS)

* * *

1.   Purchase Price of New Asset: The amount of the cash outlay to acquire the new asset.

2.   Delivery and Installation Expenses of New Asset: The depreciable cash expenses of positioning and conditioning the asset for use.

3.   Working Capital Investment: The added nondepreciable investment in supplies, inventory, etc. at the start of the

investment resulting from the decision to purchase the asset. The amount is assumed to be recaptured at the end of the investment period.

4. Remaining Book Value of Old Asset: The book value of the asset replaced if a replacement decision is made. It is assumed that the remaining life of the old asset matches the useful life of the new one.

5. Sale of Old Asset, Net of Taxes: The amount of cash realized, net of taxes paid on sale or taxes saved if sold at a value less than book value. See the two examples below at a 34 percent marginal tax rate.

```
Sold for  (1) More Than Book        (2) Less Than Book
             $50,000  Sale             $50,000  Sale
            - 40,000  Book            - 60,000  Book
              10,000  Gain            (10,000)  Loss
               3,400  Tax               3,400  Tax Saved
             $46,600  Net Sale        $53,400  Net Sale
```

6. Added Annual Operating Profit: The combination of added cash revenue less the cost of producing revenue plus any cash expense saving per year. The model assumes equal annual pre-tax operating profits over the useful life of the investment.

7. Salvage Value: Input the final sale value of the asset, net of taxes. Salvage value is ignored in computing annual depreciation, so the book value is assumed to be zero at the end of the investment period. With a ten-year useful life limitation, several investment situations (bank branch) may have significant salvage values which represent the present value of cash flows extending beyond year ten.

8. Cost of Capital: The minimum rate of return required on incremental investments to provide a competitive rate of return to shareholders. See the Marginal Cost of Funds model (G). The cost of capital is the discount rate in the NPV method and the hurdle, comparison rate in the decision rule of the IRR method.

9. Marginal Income Tax Rate: The tax rate on incremental gains/losses associated with the investment.

10. Investment Tax Credit (ITC): A percent of the purchase price of the asset credited (deducted) from current period taxes owed. The ITC was repealed by the Tax Reform Act of 1986 but may be relevant to certain decisions today, as well as serving as a public policy discussion point in the classroom.

11. Useful Life (1 to 15 Years): Enter the useful life from one
     to fifteen years (whole integers).

     The second screen reviews the incremental depreciation
expense per year.   Added depreciation, a noncash expense, is
important because it affects added taxable income and added taxes
paid.   The screen displays, for a replacement decision, the new,
old, and net change in annual depreciation expense and the tax
shield associated with the annual change in depreciation. In the
sample screen below, the incremental noncash depreciation expense
of $20,400 yields a $8,670 tax reduction each year. The $20,400
times (1-.4) equals $8,670.

* * *

DEPRECIATION SUMMARY

(SALVAGE VALUE IS NOT CONSIDERED IN DEPRECIATION IN
THIS MODEL, BUT IS RECOVERED AT THE END OF THE LAST PERIOD)

    $25,500   ANNUAL DEPRECIATION (NEW)
        $0   ANNUAL DEPRECIATION (OLD) *

    $25,500   NET ANNUAL DEPRECIATION

     $8,670   NET ANNUAL DEPRECIATION TAX SHIELD @ 34.00% TAX
               RATE

* RELEVANT IN REPLACEMENT DECISION ONLY

* * *

     The cash flow analyses follow on the next four screens. The
first screen details the components of the net cash outlay. See
the sample screen below associated with the purchase decision
input above.

* * *

CASH FLOWS ANALYSIS

NET OUTLAY:

($100,000)   -   PURCHASE PRICE OF NEW ASSET
   (2,000)   -   DELIVERY & INSTALLATION EXPENSES OF NEW ASSET
   (2,500)   -   WORKING CAPITAL INVESTMENT
        0   +   SALE OF OLD, NET OF TAXES
    6,120   +   INVESTMENT TAX CREDIT

 ($98,380)   -   NET INVESTMENT OUTLAY

* * *

The purchase price, delivery and installation expenses, and working capital investments are outlays, signified by bracketed figures. The sale of the old asset, net of taxes (gain or loss compared to book value) and investment tax credit are then combined to determine the net investment outlay. The net outlay are the zero period, initial cash outlay necessary to generate the future cash inflows. The next screen reviews the incremental annual cash inflows after taxes. The incremental income statement approach is utilized, with noncash depreciation added to net income to determine net cash flows per period. Note the return of working capital and salvage value in the last year.

* * *

NET ANNUAL AFTER TAX CASH INFLOWS:

YEAR	1	2	3	4
ADDED OPERATING PROFIT (REV-EXP)	$28,000	$28,000	$28,000	$28,000
SALVAGE VALUE	0	0	0	4,000
TOTAL CASH INFLOWS BEFORE TAXES	28,000	28,000	28,000	32,000
NET ANNUAL DEPRECIATION CHANGE	(25,500)	(25,500)	(25,500)	(25,500)
ADDED TAXABLE INCOME	2,500	2,500	2,500	6,500
ADDED TAX CASH FLOW	850	850	850	2,210
ADDED NET INCOME	1,650	1,650	1,650	4,290
PLUS DEPRECIATION	25,500	25,500	25,500	25,500
NET CASH FLOW AFTER TAX	27,150	27,150	27,150	29,790
RECOVERY OF WORKING CAPITAL	0	0	0	2,500
TOTAL ANNUAL ATX CASH FLOW	$27,150	$27,150	$27,150	$32,290

* * *

The investment analysis and evaluation screen summarizes the data input, cash flows, and decision rules associated with the capital plan. The cash flows are displayed at the upper left of the sample screen below. The sum of the cash flows, discounted at 12 percent, equals the present value of $85,731. Subtracting the outlay ($98,380) from the PV equals an NPV of -$12,649. The project does not return the minimum (12 percent) sought by investors. If the NPV were positive, the actual cost (outlay) would have been less than the maximum the firm should pay (PV), and the investment as planned would be acceptable.

* * *

INVESTMENT ANALYSIS AND EVALUATION

($98,380)	NET OUTLAY		IF INTERNAL RATE OF RETURN IS
27,150	YEAR 1	NET CASH	"ERR", CHANGE THE FOLLOWING
27,150	YEAR 2	FLOWS	ESTIMATED RATE OF RETURN USED
27,150	YEAR 3		BY PROGRAM: 20.00%
32,290	YEAR 4		(DEFAULT SHOULD BE 20.00%)
0	YEAR 5		
0	YEAR 6		DECISION RULE: IF NPV
0	YEAR 7		POSITIVE AND IF IRR >
0	YEAR 8		12.00%, ACCEPT.
0	YEAR 9		IF NOT, REJECT.
0	YEAR 10		
0	YEAR 11	$85,731	PRESENT VALUE SUM AT 12.00%
0	YEAR 12	(98,380)	NET OUTLAY
0	YEAR 13	(12,649)	NET PRESENT VALUE
0	YEAR 14	5.90%	INTERNAL RATE OF RETURN
0	YEAR 15	3.62	PAYBACK PERIOD (YEARS)

* * *

The annual compounded discount rate, which equates the cash outlay with the sum of the discounted cash flows, is called the internal rate of return (IRR).   If the IRR is greater than the cost of capital, the project should be accepted or compared with other competing projects. The expected return would then exceed the minimum required return. If the IRR is less than the minimum rate required, reject the project.   Why?   The expected return will not provide a competitive rate of return for shareholders.

The calculation of the IRR with LOTUS 1-2-3 requires that a first estimation of the IRR be entered.   The program then iterates to the correct value.   If "err" appears as an answer, return to the screen and change the IRR estimator.

The payback period is the length of time needed to recapture the original investment. The fraction of a year is the number of months needed for payback divided by the annual cash flows expected during the year.   The payback method is a project liquidity measure but ignores the time value of money. In the above case, a decision rule stating three years as a minimum payback period would cause the above capital plan to be rejected.

SAMPLE PROBLEMS/ASSIGNMENTS

First Bank - ATM Evaluation

First Bank is considering the purchase and installation of their first automatic teller machine (ATM) for the main office lobby.   The ATM costs $31,000, and delivery and installation costs are estimated to be $3,500.   Added working capital for supplies and forms will be $750. First Bank expects the ATM to reduce part-time teller expenses and generate fee income totaling $8,900 per year over the useful life of six years. The salvage value of the machine is estimated (worst case) to be $4,000 net of taxes and the marginal cost of capital is estimated to be 12 percent. The marginal tax rate of First Bank is 34 percent.

1. Enter the above data in the Purchase Decision Model (Menu B). Review the outlay and annual expected cash flows.

2. Should First Bank purchase the ATM, based on the NPV and IRR methods of evaluation? What are the implications associated with proceeding with the ATM investment under these circumstances? Include both a profits analysis and shareholder consideration.

3. What combination of price cuts, picking up delivery expenses, and installation credits from the ATM manufacturer would make this project acceptable from a shareholder perspective?

CHAPTER 6

Model D
Deposit Pricing Model

INTRODUCTION AND CONCEPTS

Pricing financial services is an ongoing and challenging decision for financial institutions today. Pricing depository services is especially difficult. Traditionally, depositors were attracted by a combination of implicit interest (services) and relatively low, regulated, explicit interest rates. With the demise of regulated deposit interest ceilings (Regulation Q), depository institutions must consider a number of variables when designing a depository service. In a competitive environment, the rate of interest paid for deposits looms as the dominant, but not the only, variable for the banker to consider when designing a deposit service. The price paid (interest rate) must be related to the bank asset earnings rate, the proportion of the deposit not available for investment (reserve requirements or float), operating costs, and the return on asset (ROA) goal of the bank.

Service charging of deposit accounts is a major pricing variable related to the deposit service, and for many banks this has become an important source of revenue. Service charging (1) may be used to influence customer behavior, e.g. NSF check charges; (2) may be used to direct customers to more efficient bank transactions, e.g., ATMs; and (3) may be used to offset costs and improve deposit service profitability. In this model, service charge levels enable the analyst to achieve ROA goals.

The Deposit Pricing Model enables one to analyze the relationship of several pricing variables and to observe their impact upon profit and profitability (ROA). The banker who offers what the competition offers is sometimes offering a loss to the bottom line. This model enables one to consider various deposit pricing strategies and their impact upon profits and ROA. Remember, implicit costs (service) must appear as explicit costs somewhere in your analysis! Data from the Federal Reserve Bank's Functional Cost Analysis are provided for your cost analyses.

APPLICATIONS

The Deposit Pricing Model is an excellent sensitivity analysis tool. After the deposit rate, minimum balance, float, earnings rate, and service charges are entered, one can observe the impact upon profits. Set the target ROA, and the service charges, if necessary, to attain the goal will be computed. This program is useful when analyzing the level of deposit interest rates to pay, or pricing deposits in a simulation game or case analysis.

MENU AND SCREENS

This default program lists five different deposit accounts offered by most banks in 1987. They were the inventions of (1) the highly regulated deposit banking environment of the past (demand deposit and savings account) and of (2) the deregulation countdown from 1980 to 1986 (NOW account, money market deposit account, money market deposit account (MMDA), and the super-NOW account). In the deregulated years to come, some variations of these five accounts will probably emerge. Most likely banks will encourage either transaction accounts (payment services) or savings (investment) accounts. Transaction accounts will probably have higher reserve requirements, greater float, and lower interest rates (higher service charges), whereas investment accounts will have little or no reserve requirements, little float, and higher interest rates. In this model one may name, develop, and price a deposit service.

Once the variables have been established, the "book" balance analysis illustrates the revenue, expense and profits expected from a specific account. A second screen compares the ROA results of the previous screen and indicates what (1) asset earnings rate, (2) interest expense rate, or (3) annual service charge level is needed to achieve the stated ROA goal. The same analysis is then repeated based on the "collected" balance (book balance less float).

Model D has the following menus on two screens:

```
A    -    TUTORIAL
B    -    SET INTEREST AND SERVICE CHARGE TABLE
C    -    SET TITLES AND ANNUAL SERVICING COST TABLE
D    -    SET INTEREST RATE CALCULATION OPTION
E    -    SET RESERVE REQUIREMENTS AND TAX RATE
F    -    ENTER ACCOUNT TEST DATA
P    -    PRINT REPORT
S    -    SAVE TO DISKETTE (REPLACES CURRENT FILE CONTENTS)
Q    -    QUIT PROGRAM
```

A   -   TUTORIAL

The tutorial provides a two-screen description of the model, including data analysis screens. Review the tutorial briefly and then return to the analyses of the specific menus. No data may be entered in the tutorial.

B   -   SET INTEREST AND SERVICE CHARGE TABLE

This menu option is used only if selected in Menu D. It provides a tiered balance/rate deposit account to analyze. Below is a sample screen listing the high balance for each of five possible tiers, the interest rate to be paid on each of the tiers, and the annual service charge to be levied on the account if its average or minimum balance falls in a specific tier range. Many banks are using this option to encourage higher balances and the consolidation of several small accounts that the customer might have.

* * *

OPTION 2 INTEREST CALCULATION TABLE

	HIGH BALANCE FOR RANGE	INTEREST RATE FOR RANGE	ANNUAL SERVICE CHARGE
USE ONLY IF 5 TIERS	500	0.00%	$5
USE ONLY IF 4 TIERS OR MORE	1,000	5.25%	$0
USE ONLY IF 3 TIERS OR MORE	2,500	7.00%	$0
USE ONLY IF 2 TIERS OR MORE	5,000	8.00%	$0
USE FOR HIGHEST TIER	999,999,999,999	9.00%	$0

* * *

The table above assumes that the bank will pay no interest on an account with a minimum or average balance of $500 or less and will charge an annual service charge of $5.00. Balances between $500 and $1,000 will earn 5.25 percent with no service charge. Five tiers are possible. See the figure below.

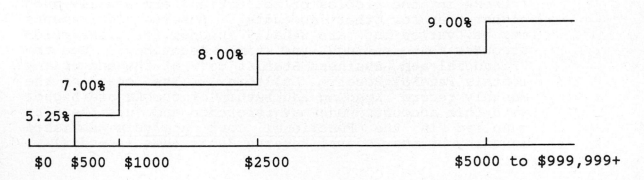

Another example is shown below with a two-tier balance/rate system. It is a product of the bank marketing department and is designed as a high-interest checking account, paying interest on balances of over $3,000, but charging monthly fees to offset servicing costs.   Note that a two-tier balance/rate account requires one entry of $3,000 on the fourth entry line.

* * *

OPTION 2 INTEREST CALCULATION TABLE

	HIGH BALANCE FOR RANGE	INTEREST RATE FOR RANGE	ANNUAL SERVICE CHARGE
USE ONLY IF 5 TIERS	0	0.00%	$0
USE ONLY IF 4 TIERS OR MORE	0	0.00%	$0
USE ONLY IF 3 TIERS OR MORE	0	0.00%	$0
USE ONLY IF 2 TIERS OR MORE	3,000	3.00%	$24
USE FOR HIGHEST TIER	999,999,999,999	6.50%	$12

* * *

C   -   SET TITLES AND ANNUAL SERVICING COST TABLE

In Menu C you may choose one of several deposit accounts offered by depository institutions today or plan and create your own deposit account by entering another name.   The annual costs of servicing a specific account are entered to the right of each account. Data from the Federal Reserve Bank's Functional Cost Analysis have been included in the appendix of this chapter. Study the pages related to the account analyzed or similar to the account created and be ready to support the estimated servicing costs of the various accounts.

Several traditional deposit accounts are discussed below, but you may name your own.

1)   Demand Deposit Account: No explicit interest may be paid on this account at this time.   You may deregulate the account (pay interest) and see the result. Further, reserve requirements and float balances (checks in the process of collection) are usually much higher than for other accounts.   Reserve requirements may be varied but are usually higher for transaction accounts than savings and time deposits.   See the "Financial and Business Statistics" at the end of any monthly Federal Reserve Bulletin.   The cost of the monthly record keeping and return of checks are higher with this account. One may reference and use the data supplied in the Functional Cost Analysis published annually by the Federal Reserve Banks (see appendix).

2)   NOW Deposit: This interest-paying checking account was first approved in the New England states. Analyze this account later.   What variables create a breakeven profit level or meet an ROA goal?

3)   Super NOW Account: A high-interest transaction account permitted during the Regulation Q phaseout period of the early 1980s.   Banks were allowed to pay market rates, but usually service charged for high activity (many checks) and paid interest on collected funds (balance less float).   Some banks have tiered balance/rate accounts.

4)   Money Market Deposit Account: Depository institutions were permitted to offer MMDAs at the same time as the Super NOW was introduced. In an effort to compete with money market mutual funds, institutions were permitted to pay market rates, but transfers and withdrawals were limited.

5)   Savings Deposit: The traditional Regulation Q fixed-rate account. Market rates were paid after March 1986, some on a tiered balance/rate basis.

D   -   SET INTEREST RATE CALCULATION OPTION

Menu D offers two options related to how interest is paid on deposit accounts.   Option one pays (if interest is to be paid) a fixed rate on the entire account balance. The interest rate paid is entered in Menu F.

Option two is the tiered balance/rate account inputted in Menu B.

E   -   SET RESERVE REQUIREMENTS AND TAX RATE

Menu E enters the reserve requirements of each of the deposit accounts listed in Menu C. The Monetary Control Act of 1980 established uniform reserve requirements, after a lengthy phase-in period, for all depository financial institutions. See the "Business and Financial Statistics" in any Federal Reserve Bulletin.   Transaction accounts have traditionally had higher reserve requirements than savings or long-term deposit agreements.   Reserve requirements reduce the proportion of the deposit account balance available for loan or security investment and the revenue generated on the account. Currently the Federal Reserve Banks do not pay interest on reserve deposit balances.

An example of the screen for Menu E is listed below, with the names (code) of the accounts listed previously under Menu C.

* * *

RESERVE REQUIREMENTS AND TAX RATE

NOTE: ENTER ALL RATES AS DECIMALS (i.e., 25% as .25)

DESCRIPTION	CODE	RESERVE RATE
CHECKING DEPOSITS	1	12.00%
NOW DEPOSITS	2	12.00%
SUPER-NOW DEPOSITS	3	12.00%
MONEY MARKET DEPOSIT ACCOUNT	4	3.00%
SAVINGS DEPOSITS	5	3.00%
EXTRA TAX RATE TO BE USED FOR CALCULATIONS:		34.00%

* * *

The tax rate must also be entered on the Menu E screen. It is used in the profitability analysis. Should the marginal or average tax be used? For an incremental, new deposit service consideration, the added taxable revenue would be taxed at the marginal rate. For general analysis, and depending on the size of the bank taxable income, an average tax rate below the marginal rate might be used.

F   -   ENTER ACCOUNT TEST DATA

Once the data for Menus B, C, D, and E have been entered, return to this section for added input entries and analyses of the deposit accounts. This section contains five screens including the data input screen, two profitability analysis screens (both for book and collected balance), and two goal/challenge screens. Using the screen data below, study the variables to be entered.

* * *

TYPE OF ACCOUNT

DESCRIPTION	CODE
CHECKING DEPOSITS	1
NOW DEPOSITS	2
SUPER-NOW DEPOSITS	3
MONEY MARKET DEPOSITS	4
SAVINGS DEPOSITS	5

ENTER CODE FOR ACCOUNT TYPE:	3
ENTER EXPECTED AVERAGE BALANCE:	$4,500
ENTER ESTIMATED % FLOAT BALANCE:	8.00%
ENTER YOUR EXPECTED EARNINGS RATE ON THESE FUNDS:	12.50%
IF OPTION (1), ENTER RATE YOU ARE PLANNING TO PAY:	8.00%
ENTER YOUR RETURN ON ASSET GOAL:	1.00%

* * *

Enter the following:

Account Type: Select the code related to the accounts listed in
                Menu C, and listed above.

Expected Average Balance:

                The average-balance customers are expected to
                maintain the account selected above.

Estimated Percent Float Balance:

                The   proportion   of   the average balance not
                available for bank investment because of checks in
                the process of collections (CIPC) or other delays
                caused by the check clearing system.   Transaction
                accounts will have higher float proportions than
                other accounts. The float situation is the reason
                for paying deposit interest on the collected
                balance in the account. While definitions vary by
                bank, a general definition of collected balance is
                book (deposit subsidiary ledger) deposit balance
                less float (CIPC).

Expected Earnings Rate on These Funds:

                The gross interest yield expected on invested
                funds derived from a deposit source.   It may
                relate to a specific asset area (e.g., loans) or
                be a general, weighted asset yield.

IF OPTION 1, ENTER RATE YOU ARE PLANNING TO PAY:

                The interest rate to be paid if you have chosen
                option 1 in Menu D. Option 1 pays a single rate
                on all funds. If option 2 is selected and a
                tiered balance/rate structure is developed in Menu
                B, this input is zero.

Enter Your ROA Goal:

                Set a target ROA for the deposit service and later
                review the input changes needed to meet the goal.

     The deposit account data entered above are now analyzed,
first in a book balance analysis and then in a collected balance
analysis.   The deposit account analysis screen is defined below.
Each of the formulas behind the numbers on the screen can be
reviewed at the top of the screen by moving the cursor to a
specific number (line) with the arrow keys.

	Line	
$4,500	1	AVERAGE BALANCE OF ACCOUNT - entered (Menu F)
$360	2	UNCOLLECTED BALANCE (FLOAT) - Line 1 x float % (Menu F)
$540	3	RESERVE REQUIREMENTS - line 1 x res. req. (Menu E)
$3,600	4	INVESTABLE BALANCE - line 1 - (2+3)
12.50%	5	EARNINGS RATE - entered (Menu F)
$450	6	GROSS EARNINGS EXPECTED - line 5 x 4
$4,500	7	AVERAGE BALANCE OF ACCOUNT - entered (Menu F) (used in book analysis)
8.00%	8	INTEREST RATE OPTION 2 - highest rate entered (Menu B or F)
$360	9	INTEREST EXPENSE - line 7 x 8
$450	10	GROSS EARNINGS - line 4 x 5
$0	11	SERVICE CHARGE - entered (Menu B)
$360	12	INTEREST EXPENSE - line 7 x 8
$56	13	SERVICING COSTS - entered Menu C
$34	14	NET EARNINGS BEFORE TAX - line (10+11)-(12+13)
$12	15	APPLICABLE TAX - entered Menu E X-line 14
$22	16	NET EARNINGS AFTER TAX - line 14-15

Prove the numbers at the left of the accounts above. Line 7 will be the average collected balance (lines 1-2) in the collected balance analysis.

The last screen in Menu F provides a comparison of the expected ROA with the ROA goal, followed by a challenge analysis. The challenge analysis lists three deposit account variables, the new input rate or amount needed to meet the challenge or ROA goal, and the changes needed in the variable to reach the ROA goal.

* * *

1.00%   RETURN ON ASSET GOAL

0.50%   RETURN ON ASSET ACTUAL

***** CHALLENGE *****
CHANGES THAT COULD BE CONSIDERED

	NEW RATE	CHANGE
EARNINGS RATE:	13.45%	0.95%

***** OR *****

INTEREST EXPENSE RATE:	7.24%	-0.76%

***** OR *****

SERVICE CHARGE: $41.78 NO SERVICE CHARGE IF GOAL ATTAINED

* * *

In the example above, the account analysis indicates that the expected ROA is below the goal level of 1 percent. The goal could be met if the investable funds earning rate were .95% higher or set at 13.45 percent, or if the interest rate paid on the account were .76% lower or 7.24 percent, or if service charges were increased by $41.78 a year. In your examples, input the recommended changes and return to this screen. Some combination of changes in input variables will also produce a goal ROA level. Competition often hinders changes in the interest rate or possibly in the service charges. The analyst must then consider other variables, cost reduction, tiered balance/rate methods of paying interest, etc. to find a competitive combination or deposit account package that achieves the goal. Let marketing name the account, but make sure that the financial analyst has a say in pricing it.

SAMPLE PROBLEMS/ASSIGNMENTS

Muncie Trust is considering a new savings deposit service for retail customers called Super Saver. Muncie is hoping to combine the traditional savings account and MMDA in a tiered interest rate setting, where the saver is paid higher rates and service charged less for ever-increasing average deposit balances. A monthly statement will be mailed to the customer, and Muncie estimates the annual operating cost per account to be $4.00/month. This includes a maximum of four transfers or withdrawal transactions per month. Muncie has set a goal of a 1 percent return on assets and has estimated the following parameters and data for analysis. The reserve requirements on the account will be 3 percent and Muncie's marginal tax rate is 34 percent. The average float balance is estimated to be 3 percent, but Muncie wants to continue to pay interest on book balance, for it is easier to understand for both employees and customers. The estimated earnings rate on deposits is currently 10.50 percent.

INTEREST PAID ON TIERED BALANCES

		Rate	Service Charge
Balance less than	$300.00	0.00%	24.00
Balances over	800.00	5.00%	0
Balances over	2,000.00	6.25%	0
Balances over	5,000.00	6.50%	0
Above	5,000.00	6.75%	0

Suggestion: Enter interest rates in decimal form. With the tiered rate, enter 2 under Menu D and a zero interest rate at the data entry screen, Menu F.

1. What is the expected level of annual profit and ROA at the following book balances? (Hint: Input the above data, and then change balances in Menu F and note the book balance

profit and ROA on the next two screens. See if your data entry is correct by checking the first row with the $1,000 balance.)

Book Balance	Rate Paid	Profit Level	ROA	Service Charges Needed for Goal
$1,000	6.25%	($8.00)	-.78%	$32.94
$1,500	6.25%			
$2,000	6.25%			
$2,500	6.50%			
$3,000	6.50%			
$6,000	6.75%			

(See the first iteration for the $1,000 balance, question 4.)

2. Muncie estimates that customers will keep an average balance of $2700 in this account, which will meet the ROA goal of 1 percent. What alternative pricing incentives might Muncie consider to make their accounts with low balances at least break even or be profitable? Muncie is willing to accept a low ROA for any balances that may, in time, increase to the ROA goal level but insists that all accounts cover expenses or break even. (Hint: Set the ROA goal to zero and note the reduction in rate paid or service charges needed.)

3. If Muncie Trust finds that this deposit service provides positive dollar profits but fails to meet their goal of 1 percent over time, what should they do? What determined the ROA goal of 1 percent? What are the implications for shareholders? Discuss this issue in an essay.

4. Design a profitable deposit account of the future that would be acceptable to the general public. Detail your assumptions, the target market and other relevant factors. Present a most likely situation (plan), attaching the printed report and your written report.

Problem I Solution
Super-Saver -- First Iteration
DEPOSIT PRICING SIMULATION MODEL

TYPE OF ACCOUNT

DESCRIPTION	CODE
CHECKING DEPOSITS	1
NOW DEPOSITS	2
SUPER-NOW DEPOSIT	3
SUPER-SAVER	4
SAVINGS DEPOSITS	5

ENTER CODE FOR ACCOUNT TYPE:	4
ENTER EXPECTED AVERAGE BALANCE:	$1,000
ENTER ESTIMATED % FLOAT BALANCE:	3.00%
ENTER YOUR EXPECTED EARNINGS RATE ON THESE FUNDS:	10.50%
IF OPTION 1, ENTER RATE YOU ARE PLANNING TO PAY:	0.00%
ENTER YOUR RETURN ON ASSET GOAL:	1.00%

DESCRIPTION	CODE	ANNUAL SERVICING COST
CHECKING DEPOSITS	1	84.00
NOW DEPOSITS	2	85.00
SUPER-NOW DEPOSIT	3	56.00
SUPER-SAVER	4	48.00
SAVINGS DEPOSITS	5	28.00

CALCULATION BASIS: 2
OPTION (2) INTEREST CALCULATION TABLE

SERVICE	HIGH BALANCE FOR RANGE	INTEREST RATE FOR RANGE	ANNUAL CHARGE
USE ONLY IF 5 TIERS	300	0.00%	$24
USE ONLY IF 4 TIERS OR MORE	800	5.00%	$0
USE ONLY IF 3 TIERS OR MORE	2,000	6.25%	$0
USE ONLY IF 2 TIERS OR MORE	5,000	6.50%	$0
USE FOR HIGHEST TIER	999,999,999,999	6.75%	$0

RESERVE REQUIREMENTS AND TAX RATE
NOTE: ENTER ALL RATES AS DECIMALS (i.e., 25% as .25)

DESCRIPTION	CODE	RESERVE RATE
CHECKING DEPOSITS	1	12.00%
NOW DEPOSITS	2	12.00%
SUPER-NOW DEPOSIT	3	3.00%
SUPER-SAVER	4	3.00%
SAVINGS DEPOSITS	5	3.00%

ENTER TAX RATE TO BE USED FOR CALCULATIONS: 34.00%

DEPOSIT PRICING SIMULATION MODEL

BASED ON INTEREST PAID ON BOOK BALANCE

$1,000	AVERAGE BALANCE OF ACCOUNT
$30	UNCOLLECTED BALANCE (FLOAT)
$30	RESERVE REQUIREMENTS
$940	INVESTABLE BALANCE
10.50%	EARNINGS RATE
$99	GROSS EARNINGS EXPECTED

$1,000	AVERAGE BALANCE OF ACCOUNT	
6.25%	INTEREST RATE	OPTION - 2
$63	INTEREST EXPENSE	

$99	GROSS EARNINGS
$0	SERVICE CHARGE
$63	INTEREST EXPENSE
$48	SERVICING COSTS
($12)	NET EARNINGS BEFORE TAX
($4)	APPLICABLE TAX
($8)	NET EARNINGS AFTER TAX

1.00%	RETURN ON ASSET GOAL
-0.78%	RETURN ON ASSET ACTUAL

***** CHALLENGE *****
CHANGES THAT COULD BE CONSIDERED

	NEW RATE	CHANGE
EARNINGS RATE:	13.37%	2.87%

** OR **

	NEW RATE	CHANGE
INTEREST EXPENSE RATE:	3.55%	-2.70%

** OR **

SERVICE CHARGE: $32.94 NO SERVICE CHARGE
IF GOAL ATTAINED

DEPOSIT PRICING SIMULATION MODEL

BASED ON INTEREST PAID ON COLLECTED BALANCE ONLY

$1,000	AVERAGE BALANCE OF ACCOUNT
$30	UNCOLLECTED BALANCE (FLOAT)
$30	RESERVE REQUIREMENTS
$940	INVESTABLE BALANCE
10.50%	EARNINGS RATE
$99	GROSS EARNINGS EXPECTED
$970	AVERAGE COLLECTED BALANCE
6.25%	INTEREST RATE OPTION - 2
$61	INTEREST EXPENSE
$99	GROSS EARNINGS
$0	SERVICE CHARGE
$61	INTEREST EXPENSE
$48	SERVICING COSTS
($10)	NET EARNINGS BEFORE TAX
($3)	APPLICABLE TAX
($7)	NET EARNINGS AFTER TAX
1.00%	RETURN ON ASSET GOAL
-0.66%	RETURN ON ASSET ACTUAL

***** CHALLENGE *****
CHANGES THAT COULD BE CONSIDERED

	NEW RATE	CHANGE
EARNINGS RATE:	13.17%	2.67%

** OR **

INTEREST EXPENSE RATE:	3.66%	-2.59%

** OR **

SERVICE CHARGE: $30.65 NO SERVICE CHARGE
                                         IF GOAL ATTAINED

CHAPTER 7

Model E
Depreciation/Tax Accounting

INTRODUCTION AND CONCEPTS

This program provides the user the opportunity to input certain data from a property account (equipment) transaction. The program then calculates tax and book depreciation based on the useful life selected. The deferred tax is reflected, if applicable, at the rate inputted by the user. The user may then select different life terms and view the results of the depreciation schedules. Sample entries to record the annual depreciation expense and the deferred taxes for the first year and for the last year are then displayed. These entries are presented on an annual basis for presentation purposes, but it is suggested that they be prorated and recorded on a monthly basis at the bank.

The purpose of this program is to illustrate the difference between book accounting and tax accounting. Tax accounting is based upon tax laws designed to impact economic issues. Book accounting attempts to allocate expense over the useful life of the asset. Separate depreciation rates between tax and book accounting generate timing differences in recording depreciation expenses and impact the timing of taxes paid. These timing differences create what is called deferred tax. In this program, note the changes in the deferred tax recordings in each period.

APPLICATION

This program assists in understanding the concept of depreciation, the accounting for depreciation, and the concept of deferred taxes that occurs when tax and accounting (book) depreciation schedules are different. The model allows one to vary the rate of depreciation, perhaps as tax laws change, and to analyze the tax depreciation and book depreciation differences.

74

MENU AND SCREENS

Model E has the following menus on two screens:

A   -   TUTORIAL

B   -   SET DEFERRED TAX RATE

C   -   SET ACRS DEPRECIATION RATE TABLE

D   -   DATA ENTRY FOR NEW PURCHASE

E   -   VIEW COMPARATIVE SCHEDULE

F   -   VIEW SAMPLE DEPRECIATION ENTRIES

P   -   PRINT REPORT

S   -   SAVE TO DISKETTE (REPLACES CURRENT FILE CONTENTS)

Q   -   QUIT PROGRAM

A   -   TUTORIAL

The tutorial provides an introduction to the concepts and an opportunity to scroll through the screens in the model.

B   -   SET DEFERRED TAX RATE

Enter the marginal tax rate at which the deferred tax is to be calculated. Enter as a decimal.

C   -   SET ACRS DEPRECIATION RATE TABLE

The Accelerated Cost Recovery System (1981) prescribed, statutorily, the depreciation rates over a set recovery period that equipment and real estate could be expensed for tax purposes. The 1986 tax law prescribes six ACRS equipment depreciation schedules and two real estate depreciation schedules, depending on the type of equipment or real estate involved. This model provides three of the ACRS schedules: the three-, five- and ten-year schedules. Enter the percentage cost allocation for each of the years, not exceeding 100 percent. The percent times the cost of the equipment is the amount of tax depreciation expense for that particular year. These are not tax rates, but represent the rate of tax depreciation per year.

D   -   DATA ENTRY FOR NEW PURCHASE

Enter the following four data entry items:

1.   The depreciable cost of the equipment or real estate.

2. The month of the year when the equipment was purchased. The model assumes that you purchased the item at the beginning of the month so noted and later assigns a portion of the first year's depreciation. If 4 is entered, 12-3/12 of the annual depreciation or 75 percent is allocated in year one.
3. Enter the year the asset is acquired.
4. Enter the financial (book or accounting) method of depreciating the asset. Enter (1) for ACRS and (2) for straightline, which is proportional over the years and months.

E   -   VIEW COMPARATIVE SCHEDULE

The yearly tax book difference, if present, is presented in this section. A sample screen is presented and discussed below. The input data (Menu D) include a $1,000 cost, purchased in August 1987, to be depreciated straightline for book purposes. Enter the depreciation life (three, five, or ten years) of the asset, and the program calculates the following columns:

* * *

ENTER DEPRECIATION LIFE (3, 5 OR 10):   10
(YOU MAY CHANGE THE LIFE AT THIS TIME AND VIEW THE RESULTS)
BOOK DEPRECIATION SCHEDULE PER METHOD SELECTED   ON DATA ENTRY SCREEN

TAX BOOKS		FINANCIAL BOOKS		TIMING DIFF.			DEFERRED TAX
1987	$80	1987	$42	$38	X	34.00% =	$12.92
1988	$140	1988	$100	$40	X	34.00% =	$13.60
1989	$120	1989	$100	$20	X	34.00% =	$6.80
1990	$100	1990	$100	$0	X	34.00% =	$0.00
1991	$100	1991	$100	$0	X	34.00% =	$0.00
1992	$100	1992	$100	$0	X	34.00% =	$0.00
1993	$90	1993	$100	($10)	X	34.00% =	($3.40)
1994	$90	1994	$100	($10)	X	34.00% =	($3.40)
1995	$90	1995	$100	($10)	X	34.00% =	($3.40)
1996	$90	1996	$100	($10)	X	34.00% =	($3.40)
1997	$0	1997	$58	($58)	X	34.00% =	($19.72)
TOTAL $1,000		TOTAL $1,000		$0	X	34.00% =	$0.00

* * *

Date: Up to ten years from purchase date.

Tax Books: The annual ACRS depreciation rate (inputted in Menu C) times the depreciable cost of the asset. For example, in the first year, $80 of depreciation expense is included for tax reporting.

Financial Books: Includes, in this case, the straightline
                      financial accounting depreciation allocation
                      for each year. The first and last year's
                      depreciation is proportional to the number of
                      months the asset was owned. In this example,
                      the asset was purchased in August 1987 and
                      5/12ths of $100 (annual full-year
                      depreciation) is $42. The remaining 7/12ths
                      ($58) is deducted in 1997.

Timing Difference: Subtracting the financial books amount from
                      the tax books amount gives the amount of tax
                      deduction over (positive number) or under
                      (negative) book deduction for the year.

Deferred Tax: The timing difference times the marginal tax
                      rate equals the annual amount of deferred tax
                      associated with the tax/book depreciation
                      differentials, or the added annual amount of
                      taxes deferred because the amount of tax
                      depreciation exceeded the book depreciation.
                      In the table above, the $80 of noncash, tax-
                      deductible expense saved $80 (.34) = $27.20
                      in tax outlays, whereas the shareholders'
                      annual report (books) noted a $42 deduction
                      and a tax shield of $42 (.34) = $14.28. The
                      actual taxes paid in 1987 was $27.20 - 14.28,
                      or $12.92 less than that reported in the
                      financial accounting records (provision for
                      income taxes). The $12.92 would appear as a
                      deferred tax liability in 1987, noting that
                      the firm actually paid less taxes than
                      recorded in the shareholder financial
                      statements. Later in the life of the asset,
                      the firm must pay more taxes than book
                      records indicate, and the prior deferred tax
                      liability is reduced to zero. Add the annual
                      deferred tax amounts. They sum to zero. The
                      total amount of depreciation is identical for
                      tax and book accounting. The timing
                      differences or differing depreciation
                      schedules between tax and book cause a
                      differential between taxable income and book
                      income and a differential between the actual
                      taxes paid and the book provision for income
                      taxes. The deferred tax liability account
                      reconciles the actual tax payments/book
                      amount timing differences over the life of
                      the asset.

F   -   VIEW SAMPLE DEPRECIATION ENTRIES

The first- and last-year accounting journal entries associated with the comparative schedule (Menu E) are presented in two screens. Both the expense accrual and deferred tax entries are presented. The first expense accrual notes the depreciation expense debit and accumulated depreciation credit of $42. The deferred tax expense debit is an amount added to the total book federal income tax expense. Instead of crediting cash or paying the taxes, a deferred credit (long term liability) is established. Remember, in the early years of the example, the tax depreciation exceeded the book amount, so the actual taxes paid were less than the book.

* * *

GENERAL LEDGER ENTRIES TO RECORD ANNUAL ACCOUNTING

(ENTRY AMOUNTS ARE FOR FIRST YEAR DEPRECIATION)

EXPENSE ACCRUAL

DEBIT: DEPRECIATION EXPENSE (BOOK) $42.00

CREDIT: ACCUMULATED DEPRECIATION $42.00
          (CONTRA ASSET ACCOUNT)

DEFERRED TAX

DEBIT: DEFERRED FEDERAL TAX EXPENSE $12.92

CREDIT: ACCRUED DEFERRED FEDERAL TAX $12.92

* * *

In the final year, the actual taxes paid will exceed the book amount by $19.72. This is noted by crediting or reducing (negative debit) the book tax expense by $19.72. The cumulative deferred tax account associated with this asset is reduced to zero because the timing differences have balanced out. The asset is fully depreciated.

* * *

FINAL YEAR

EXPENSE ACCRUAL

DEBIT: DEPRECIATION EXPENSE (BOOK) $58.00

CREDIT: ACCUMULATED DEPRECIATION $58.00
           (CONTRA ASSET ACCOUNT)

DEFERRED TAX

DEBIT: DEFERRED FEDERAL TAX EXPENSE   ($19.72)

CREDIT: ACCRUED DEFERRED FEDERAL TAX   ($19.72)

* * *

P   -   PRINT REPORT

A compact single-page report is generated, listing the details of the asset, the annual comparative schedule, and journal entries.

S   -   SAVE TO DISKETTE (REPLACES CURRENT FILE)

SAMPLE PROBLEMS/ASSIGNMENTS

1. First Bank acquired a $25,000 ATM in June 1987. The machine was depreciated straightline for book purposes and was a five year asset for ACRS tax depreciation. Using the default ACRS data (with the program), calculate and answer the following questions.

    a. With reference to the ATM, will the bank actually pay more or less in federal taxes than the annual report indicates? Explain.

b. How much book depreciation is allocated to 1987? Prove this answer.

c. Explain the tax timing difference for the first year.

2. If the five-year ACRS schedule were 20 percent per year (Menu C) and the ATM were purchased in January 1987 (Menu D), what tax-book timing differences would there be? If the bank used ACRS depreciation for book purposes (Menu D) and ACRS for tax purposes (original), what would the timing differences be?

CHAPTER 8

Model F
Loan Pricing Concepts

INTRODUCTION AND CONCEPTS

This model studies several different loan pricing techniques used by banks and discussed in commercial bank management texts and seminars. The emphasis of this model is on concepts rather than on providing a model for industry use. The program covers prime plus, prime times, and market-based methods of rate structuring. Each method allows adjustment for the credit risk level of the customer.

In addition to presenting rate structuring techniques, the model provides the opportunity to study target pricing concepts based upon a target rate of return on equity. The "what if" capability of LOTUS 1-2-3 is used extensively.

APPLICATION

This model is very supportive of loan management concepts developed in major textbooks. Loan pricing concepts are generally covered descriptively or with static, single-example illustrations. This model provides the capability to introduce many varied concepts, assignments, and alternative iterations. The pricing objective in this model is focused on the bank's shareholders. Loans are investments that should provide returns sufficient to give a competitive return on shareholder capital without taking undue risk. This model emphasizes target return on equity (ROE) pricing and includes an opportunity to make adjustments for significant risk variation in loans. Other loan-pricing methods include:

1. Competitive pricing: meeting competition. Often necessary, but this model allows the loan officer to review the loan from a shareholder perspective.

2. Markup or cost-plus pricing: provides a stated spread over the marginal cost of funds. The marginal cost of funds is a single input in this model but may be derived in the next model, Model G. Increased

commercial loan fees and expenses today tend to outdate single-markup pricing techniques.

3.　Market share or penetration pricing:　pricing for volume or　market share without a profitability or risk analysis may provide short-term　bonuses for loan officers but varied results for long-term profitability and shareholder returns.　Will this　loan increase the value of the bank and the shareholder's investment?

The emphasis　in this　model is　on the lending function and not necessarily on the other services/costs related to a specific customer.　A later model, H, covers total customer profitability concepts.

MENU AND SCREENS

Model F has the following menus on two screens:

A　-　TUTORIAL
B　-　SET CREDIT RISK LEVEL
C　-　SET PRIME RATE
D　-　SET MARKET-BASED RATES
E　-　MARKET-BASED RATE METHOD - SELECT MATURITY
F　-　LOAN PRICING MODEL
P　-　PRINT REPORT
S　-　SAVE TO DISKETTE (REPLACES CURRENT FILE CONTENTS)
Q　-　QUIT PROGRAM

A　-　TUTORIAL

The tutorial provides ten screens of explanatory text　and a sample of　screens used　in the model.　No data may be entered in the tutorial.

B　-　SET CREDIT RISK LEVEL

This and the three menu items that follow are input preparation for the Loan Pricing Model (F).　Four risk levels may be created by the analyst, and three rate　adjustment methods may be entered for each of　the increasing risk levels.　The rate adjustment methods include:

1.　Prime Plus: each risk category may　be assigned an absolute markup (or markdown) from　the prime rate. Increased risk would　require greater　increments over prime.　In the example below, risk level 1 is prime and risk level 2 is "one over" prime.

2.　Prime Times: each risk category may　be assigned a multiple which, times prime, would equal the loan rate. A prime rate of 8 percent in a　prime-times category of 1.2 would assign a loan rate of 8 (1.2) = 9.6 percent.

3.   Market-Based Rate: each risk category may be assigned an absolute markup (or markdown) from a market-determined interest rate entered in Menu E. A 1.50 percent over a Treasury bill rate of 7 percent would generate a loan rate of 8.50 percent.

* * *

RISK DETERMINATION
NOTE ENTER ALL PERCENTAGES AS DECIMAL (i.e., .01 is 1.00%)
ENTER ADJUSTMENTS TO PRIME OR BASE RATES IN EACH RISK LEVEL.

	CODE	PRIME PLUS	PRIME TIMES	MARKET-BASED RATE
RISK LEVEL	1	0.000%	1.00	0.750%
RISK LEVEL	2	1.000%	1.10	1.000%
RISK LEVEL	3	1.500%	1.15	1.250%
RISK LEVEL	4	2.000%	1.20	1.500%

CUSTOMER RISK LEVEL IS DETERMINED FROM CREDIT REVIEW
BY LOAN OFFICER.

(LOWEST CREDIT RISK LEVEL IS 1, HIGHEST RISK LEVEL IS 4)

* * *

C   -   SET PRIME RATE

Enter the prime rate to be charged for fixed-rate loans one month to one year. See example below.

* * *

PRIME RATE METHOD

NOTE ENTER ALL PERCENTAGES AS DECIMAL (i.e., .01 is 1.00%)

MATURITY TERM	RATE	EFFECTIVE RATES PRIME PLUS	PRIME TIMES
1 MONTH	9.750%	10.750%	10.725%
2 MONTHS	10.000%	11.000%	11.000%
3 MONTHS	10.250%	11.250%	11.275%
6 MONTHS	11.250%	12.250%	12.375%
1 YEAR	11.750%	12.750%	12.925%

EFFECTIVE RATES HAVE BEEN ESTABLISHED BASED ON RISK LEVEL.
CURRENT RISK LEVEL IS 2 AND IS SET IN THE PRICING MODEL.

* * *

In the example above, the term structure of interest rates is upward sloping, indicating an expectation of higher future short-term rates.   The rate structure may be flat (the same rate for each maturity) or downward sloping with time.

The risk level assumed in the above screen has been set in the Loan Pricing Model (Menu F).   With a risk level of 2, the rate charged for a one-month prime plus loan is 10.75 percent (9.75 + 1.00) and the prime times rate is 10.725 percent (9.75 x 1.1).

D   -   SET MARKET-BASED RATES

Three open market rates over ten maturities are available for market-based loan pricing.   The rates include the London Interbank Offered Rate (LIBOR), large, negotiable certificates of deposit and U.S. Treasury bills.   These rates will be used for any market-based loan pricing analysis.   Due to screen limitations, not all maturities are listed for each money market security.   The quoted rates represent the yields on the securities, while the effective rates include the risk adjustment.   A quoted three-month Treasury bill rate of 9.99 percent priced at "one over" adjusts to a 10.99 effective rate for risk level 2, selected in the Loan Pricing Model (Menu F).

* * *

MARKET BASED RATE METHOD
NOTE ENTER ALL PERCENTAGES AS DECIMAL (i.e., .01 is 1.00%)

BASE RATE	TERM	QUOTE	EFFECTIVE RATE
LIBOR	3 MONTHS	11.625%	12.625%
LIBOR	6 MONTHS	12.000%	13.000%
LIBOR	1 YEAR	12.625%	13.625%
CD	1 MONTH	10.400%	11.400%
CD	2 MONTHS	10.950%	11.950%
CD	3 MONTHS	11.100%	12.100%
CD	6 MONTHS	11.200%	12.200%
CD	1 YEAR	11.650%	12.650%
T-BILLS	13 WEEKS/3 MONTHS	9.990%	10.990%
T-BILLS	26 WEEKS/6 MONTHS	10.270%	11.270%

EFFECTIVE RATES HAVE BEEN ESTABLISHED BASED ON RISK LEVEL.
CURRENT RISK LEVEL IS 2 AND IS SET IN THE PRICING MODEL.

* * *

E   -   MARKET-BASED RATE METHOD -- SELECT MATURITY

Enter the desired maturity code. In the example below, if market-based pricing is selected, the loan maturity matching the money market security is a three-month maturity.   This information is carried forward to the Loan Pricing Model.   If a market-based rate is not available at the selected maturity, the

rates that appear will be listed as zero. The rates listed have
been adjusted for the risk category selected in the Loan Pricing
Model, in this case, 2.

* * *

MATURITY SELECTION - MARKET BASED RATE BASIS

MATURITY	CODE
1 MONTH	1
2 MONTHS	2
3 MONTHS	3
6 MONTHS	4
1 YEAR	5

ENTER DESIRED MATURITY TERM CODE: 3
AVAILABLE RATES:

LIBOR	12.625%
CD	12.100%
T-BILL	10.990%

NOTE IF AVAILABLE RATE IS ZERO, RATE IS NOT AVAILABLE
FOR THAT BASE.

EFFECTIVE RATES HAVE BEEN ESTABLISHED BASED ON RISK LEVEL.
CURRENT RISK LEVEL IS 2 AND IS SET IN THE PRICING MODEL.

* * *

F   -   LOAN PRICING MODEL

The Loan Pricing Model is the focal point of this program.
All of the other preparatory input screens are funneled into this
model. In addition to the risk and rate structure developed
earlier, one may now enter the following variables into this
three-screen model:

1.   Capital-to-loan ratio of the bank.
2.   Effective interest expense rate of the bank.
3.   Other loan fees collected.
4.   Servicing expense of the bank.
5.   Return on equity goal of the bank.
6.   Marginal tax rate of the bank.

The model generates an annualized profitability analysis and
a loan pricing challenge which indicates changes needed in input
variables in order to achieve the target rate of return on
equity. Each screen is now analyzed.

The first screen is the Loan Pricing Model input screen, an
example of which is presented below.

* * *

```
                    LOAN PRICING MODEL
               CUSTOMER LOAN REQUESTED AMOUNT:        $500,000
           COMPENSATING BALANCE LEVEL PERCENTAGE:       10.00%
           (ENTER 0% IF USING DOLLAR LEVEL)  *OR*
                                   DOLLAR LEVEL:             $0
         ENTER MATURITY IN MONTHS (1,2,3,6, OR 12):         2
              ENTER RISK LEVEL (1,2,3, OR 4):     2    RATE QUOTES
              ** NOTE **              1       PRIME PLUS     11.000%
    IF RATE REFLECTED FOR A           2       PRIME TIMES    11.000%
    METHOD IS .00%, THAT METHOD       3            LIBOR      0.000%
    DOES NOT OFFER A QUOTE FOR        4               CD     11.950%
    YOUR LOAN MATURITY.               5           T-BILL      0.000%
 ENTER NUMBER ABOVE FOR PRICING METHOD:           1          11.000%
 FOR TERM OF LOAN: LOAN FEES (ALL REV. EXCEPT INT.):          $100
   FOR TERM OF LOAN: OPERATIONS EXP. (PROC., SERV.):          $300
                    INTEREST COST OF FUNDS RATE:             9.75%
                    EQUITY CAPITAL TO LOAN RATIO:           12.00%
                          MARGINAL TAX RATE:                34.00%
                          RETURN ON EQUITY GOAL:            15.00%
```

* * *

Customer Loan Requested Amount: Enter the amount of the loan
needed by the customer, plus any amount of compensating balance.

Compensating Balance Level Percentage: The percent of the loan
balance (enter as decimal) or dollar amount of added deposit
account balances kept idle as a result of this loan. If 500,000
is the level of proceeds needed, the customer must request a loan
of $500,000/1-.1 or $555,555 if the percentage compensating
balance is 10 percent. The effect of the compensating balance is
to raise the yield of the loan (customer unable to use entire
loan) or to increase the amount borrowed.

Maturity in Months: Select from loan maturities of one, two,
three, six, or twelve months.

Risk Level: Enter the assigned risk level of the customer, with
one the lowest and four the highest risk rating. Risk evaluation
is a complicated process entailing evaluation of the "C's" of
credit, credit-scoring models, etc. Selection of the appropriate
risk level and rate structure (Menu B) is critical. Competitive
pressures tend to lower loan rates below the yields needed to
compensate for the risk assumed. Evaluate the loan under varied
risk levels.   Higher risk levels may entail more bank service
costs (loan review, monitoring and loan officer time). Loan fees
might be charged to compensate when rates cannot be raised
because of competition.

Rate Quotes: Up to five rate quotes associated with the risk level of customers derived from earlier inputs (Menus C, D, and E) are displayed on the screen.   In cases where a specific maturity does not have a market-based rate, zeros appear. No input is available here; it was determined earlier.

Pricing Method: Enter one of the five rate pricing methods above. Let the pricing method become a variable and review the profitability of several pricing methods.

Loan Fees: Includes total ($) revenues associated with the loan (except interest) for the entire term of the loan. Loan fees may include commitment fees, points, or specific loan servicing and origination fees.

Loan Operations Expense: Includes total noninterest expenses associated with the loan, including officer salaries, data services, occupancy, legal fees, etc. associated with commercial loans.   These would be considered if a full-cost inclusion is made vs. a direct, variable-cost analysis.   See the Federal Reserve Bank's Functional Cost Analysis pages in the appendix at the end of the text.

Interest Cost of Funds Rate: The marginal cost of nonequity (debt) funds.   The analysis is organized for later review of the return to allocated equity capital, so only a debt funds rate should be included here. This rate times the net amount of funds advanced by the bank will equal the total interest costs.

Equity to Capital to Loan Ratio: Enter the proportion of the loan supported by bank equity capital.   This may be a past average or, better, a target (intended) for all loans, or it may be directly related to the riskiness of the loan; the more risk involved, the greater the proportion of equity allocated.   A $500,000 loan with an equity to capital loan ratio would assume that $60,000 ($500,000 x .12) of the loan would be funded by equity.   In the next screen, the return on equity evaluation would be based on the $60,000.

Marginal Tax Rate: Enter the marginal tax rate of the bank. The marginal tax rate, not average, is the appropriate decision analysis input.

Return on Equity Goal: Enter the desired ROE level (enter as decimal).   This target minimally acceptable return, or cost of equity capital, is compared with the actual return in the following screens. The basis for determining the ROE goal is the consideration of bank shareholders.   What equity return is needed, commensurate with the risk assumed, to please existing shareholders and attract new ones?   What is the current opportunity rate for investors? Historical equity returns might be reviewed, for perspective, but the analyst must consider what risks and opportunities bank shareholders are facing today, not yesterday. This concept is expanded in Model G.

After all inputs have been made, the user may "Y" to change any input data or "N" to the next screen.

The second screen in the Loan Pricing Model is the loan pricing review. Each of the following items on the screen will now be reviewed.

* * *

LOAN PRICING REVIEW
(ANNUALIZED)

LOAN REVENUE	INTEREST	$55,000.00
	FEES	$600.00
	TOTAL REVENUE	$55,600.00
LOAN EXPENSES	INTEREST	$43,875.00
	EXPENSES	$1,800.00
	TOTAL EXPENSES	$45,675.00
	PRE-TAX INCOME ON LOAN	$9,925.00
	APPLICABLE TAX	$3,374.50
	NET INCOME ON LOAN	$6,550.50
	PRE-TAX RATE OF RETURN ON EQUITY	16.54%
	AFTER-TAX RATE OF RETURN ON EQUITY	10.92%

DEPRESS "ENTER" KEY TO CONTINUE

* * *

Loan Revenue: The loan of $500,000 times the loan rate of 11 percent. Note that annualized (as if the loan had a one year maturity) data are presented here. Annualizing provides a common denominator comparison for varied loan maturities and ROE analyses.

Fees: The amount of loan fees annualized. For the two-month loan above with a $100 loan fee, the annualized amount is $100 times 6, the number of two-month loans in a year.

Total Revenue: The sum of interest income and fee income.

Interest Expense: The amount of bank debt funds contributed (loan less compensating balance) times the interest cost of funds rate. In the above case, ($500,000 - 50,000) x .0975 = $43,875. This is an annualized amount; the customer was only charged two months' interest of 2/12 x $43,875.00 = $7,312.50.

Loan Expenses: The amount of loan expenses annualized. Loan expenses above were $300 for a two-month loan or $300 x 6 = $1,800 annualized.

Total Expenses: The sum of loan expenses.

Pre-Tax Income on Loan: The difference between total loan revenue and loan expenses.

Applicable Tax: The product of the pre-tax income and the marginal tax rate inputted in the Loan Pricing Model, or $9,925 (.34) = $3,374.50.

Net Income on Loan: The difference between the pre-tax income and income taxes.

Pre-Tax Rate of Return on Equity: The pre-tax income ($9,925) divided by the allocated equity ($500,000 x .12) or $60,000 equals 16.54%.

After-Tax Rate of Return on Equity: The net income ($6,500.50) divided by the allocated equity of $60,000 equals 10.92 percent. The pre-tax return of 16.54% (1-.34) = 10.92%. This ROE value is compared to the ROE goal in the next screen.

The last screen in the Loan Pricing Model is the challenge: loan pricing evaluation listed below.

* * *

```
        ** CHALLENGE: LOAN PRICING EVALUATION **
             RETURN ON EQUITY GOAL OF BANK:      15.00%
          ESTIMATED RETURN ON EQUITY OF LOAN:    10.92%
```

NOW ONE MAY FINE TUNE OUR PRICING APPROACH. BELOW ARE CHANGES THAT WOULD ATTAIN THE ROE GOAL. YOU MAY USE A COMBINATION OF EACH.

                                                POSSIBLE CHANGES
THINGS TO DO IF GOAL NOT ATTAINED:
      1. INCREASE LOAN RATE   0.742%
OR 2. INCREASE OR OBTAIN COMPENSATING BALANCE $38,041.96
OR 3. INCREASE FEES $618.18

THINGS TO DO IF LOAN OVERPRICED AND NOT COMPETITIVE:
      1. DECREASE LOAN RATE   0.000%
OR 2. LOWER COMPENSATING BALANCE REQ (IF USED) $0.00
OR 3. DECREASE FEES (IF USED) $0.00

* * *

The goal or target ROE and the actual ROE are displayed at the top of the page, along with individual variable changes that would bring the actual ROE to the goal level. Raising the interest rate on the loan by .742 percent from 11 to 11.742 percent would provide $3,710 more annual interest revenue ($2448.60 after tax), increasing net income to $6,550 + $2,448.60 = $9,000/$60,000 = 15.00% ROE. Each of the other two variables, increasing the compensating balance and increasing noninterest loans fees, would also produce a target ROE of 15 percent. If the actual ROE of the loan exceeds the target, the program would list the changes in any one of the same three variables that would bring the actual down to the target level. If the loan were not competitive in the market price, any one of three changes might be made and still meet the ROE goal. If the expected ROE on the loan exceeds the target, shareholder wealth is increased. If the expected ROE is below the goal level, making the loan may increase total profits but, incrementally, not enough to adequately compensate the equity allocated to the loan. Shareholders will be receiving a return less than their minimally acceptable rate of return, and shareholders' wealth will decline. It is assumed that the target (goal) ROE is set at the level commensurate with the incremental risk assumed on the loan.

The challenge screen is an excellent spreadsheet tool for decision analysis. Study the formulas by placing the cursor over the values on the screen and printing the screen. The formulas may be traced to the variables by printing the screens of the various menu items. Refer to any Lotus 1-2-3 manual for the definition of the formula symbols.

If the ROE goal is not met, return to the Loan Pricing Model, inputting any one of the "challenge" variable changes or find a competitive combination that will meet the ROE goal.

P   -   PRINT REPORT

The program prints a complete report of all screens associated with the Loan Pricing Model.

S   -   SAVE TO DISKETTE

The diskette will be updated with the latest inputs. SAVE replaces the default data.

SAMPLE PROBLEMS/ASSIGNMENTS

1.   First Bank has received a loan request for a $50,000 six-month loan from Ace Supplies, a retailer of seasonal furniture. The loan would finance the seasonal buildup of a new line of seasonal patio furniture and would be paid off from the sale of the inventory. Ace has been a deposit customer of the bank for four years but has never applied for a line of credit. Review the financial statements of Ace Supplies below and assign an appropriate risk category.

Please defend your risk category (1, 2, 3, or 4) selected, citing ratios and other factors.

* * *

Ace Supplies
Year ended December 31
($000) 1986

	1986	1987	Estimated 1988
Cash	$ 3.1	$ 4.5	$ 5.0
Accounts receivable	15.1	22.4	44.2
Total inventories	21.4	31.8	50.8
Total current assets	$ 39.6	$ 58.7	$100.0
Fixed assets	34.7	51.5	60.0
Total assets	$ 74.3	$110.2	$160.0
Accounts payable	$ 16.6	$ 32.4	$ 69.3
Notes payable	0	0	0
Total current liabilities	16.6	32.4	69.3
Long-term debt (attorney)	11.0	25.0	30.0
Net worth	46.7	52.8	60.7
Total liabilities and net worth	$ 74.3	$110.2	$160.0
Sales	$147	$218	$323

	1986	1987	Estimated 1988	Industry Average 1987
Collection period	37 days	37 days	49 days	40 days
Current ratio	2.4 times	1.8 times	1.4 times	2.0 times
Quick ratio	1.1 times	0.8 time	0.7 times	1.0 times
Debt ratio	37.1%	52.1%	62.1%	40.0%
Profit margin on sales	5.1%	4.8%	4.3%	4.0%
Rate of return on assets	10.1%	9.5%	8.7%	9.0%
Rate of return on net worth	16.0%	19.8%	22.9%	15.0%

2.   First Bank has assigned the following variables relative to
the four risk categories, the effective prime rate for
varied maturities, and market-based rates.   Input these
rates in Menus B, C, and D.

* * *

RISK DETERMINATION
NOTE ENTER ALL PERCENTAGES AS DECIMAL (i.e., .01 is 1.00%)
ENTER ADJUSTMENTS TO PRIME OR BASE RATES IN EACH RISK LEVEL.

	CODE	PRIME PLUS	PRIME TIMES	MARKET-BASED RATE
RISK LEVEL	1	0.000%	1.00	0.750%
RISK LEVEL	2	1.000%	1.10	1.000%
RISK LEVEL	3	1.500%	1.15	1.250%
RISK LEVEL	4	2.000%	1.20	1.500%

CUSTOMER RISK LEVEL IS DETERMINED FROM CREDIT REVIEW BY LOAN
OFFICER.

(LOWEST CREDIT RISK LEVEL IS 1, HIGHEST RISK LEVEL IS 4)

* * *

MATURITY TERM	RATE	PRIME PLUS	PRIME TIMES
1 MONTH	8.250%		
2 MONTHS	8.250%		
3 MONTHS	8.250%		
6 MONTHS	8.500%		
1 YEAR	8.750%		

* * *

MARKET-BASED RATE METHOD

BASE RATE	TERM	QUOTE	EFFECTIVE RATE
LIBOR	3 MONTHS	8.750%	
LIBOR	6 MONTHS	8.800%	
LIBOR	1 YEAR	9.000%	
CD	1 MONTH	6.750%	
CD	2 MONTHS	6.800%	
CD	3 MONTHS	6.850%	
CD	6 MONTHS	6.920%	
CD	1 YEAR	7.100%	
T-BILLS	13 WEEKS/3 MONTHS	6.250%	
T-BILLS	26 WEEKS/6 MONTHS	6.300%	

* * *

First Bank is considering the following loan variables for Ace Supplies. Input the following in the Loan Pricing Model (Menu F).

Compensating Balance	–	none
Maturity		6 months
Risk Level		?
Loan Fees		$200
Loan Expenses		$400
Interest Cost of Funds		7%
Equity Cap./Loan Ratio		12%
Marginal Tax Rate		34%
ROE Goal		?

Based on your analysis of the risk level of Ace Supplies, what is an appropriate rate of return on capital goal to use in this evaluation? Support your suggestions.

3. Evaluate the loan in the Loan Pricing Model, using the data above and your risk evaluation and ROE goal. Print your output and summarize the results with a cover sheet attached to the output.

4. Return to the Loan Pricing Model and, for discussion purposes, assign a risk category of 3 and a ROE goal of 18%.

    a. Will total bank profits be increased if this loan is made and is paid as agreed?

b. If First Bank made more loans like this one, what might happen to the market value of the bank's common shares? Why? Describe your reasons in detail.

c. What changes could First Bank most likely make with this loan to meet its ROE goal of 18 percent? Which areas might be acceptable to Ace Supplies?

d. Second Bank down the street is willing to make the loan at a rate 0.5 percent lower than that of First Bank. What specific assumptions and variables must be present (those entered in the Loan Pricing Model) at Second Bank for it to make the loan? Study each of the input variables. Input the lower prime rate in Menu C. Write your analysis.

CHAPTER 9

Model G
Marginal Cost of Funds

INTRODUCTION AND CONCEPTS

The cost of funds is an important input variable in many bank decisions and BFDA models. In this model, the cost of funds is the dependent variable. The goal of Model G is to estimate the marginal cost of funds for a depository institution. The model is designed (1) to serve as a method for teaching/learning marginal cost of funds concepts and (2) to provide a decision analysis tool to calculate the marginal cost of funds for use in other decision models, cases and bank simulation games.

The marginal cost of funds is an important financial planning and decision variable. It is usually referenced when an added or incremental investment is being considered, so the cost of funds analysis should, consistently, consider the cost of incremental (marginal) funds if they were obtained today. Historical, imbedded costs of capital are irrelevant. The question should be, "If I had to raise funds today, what rate of return must be earned on new investments to satisfy investors?"

The term cost of funds or cost of capital implies that the bank has a cost of funds independent of where the funds are invested. This is not the case. The riskiness of assets (business risk) and the debt/equity financing mix (financial risk) are directly related to the cost of funds. Other terms which can be used interchangeably with cost of funds are minimum acceptable rate of return, target rate of return, or required rate of return. The emphasis of these terms is on where the funds are to be invested. The cost of funds then serves as the minimum rate of return required on investments (loans, securities, fixed assets) in order to satisfy suppliers of capital. Opportunity costs or alternative investor uses must then be considered.

The cost of funds concept, then, is an analysis from the perspective of the supplier of funds, especially the shareholder. The shareholder is the residual or last claimant on returns earned on asset investments. The proper cost of funds analysis must then include not only an analysis of what contract (debt or

95

deposit) funds cost if raised today, but also a difficult subjective analysis of the minimum rate of return required on added equity capital needed to satisfy shareholders. This cost of equity can be related to historical returns, current alternative returns available (opportunity costs), and the level of risk involved in the new asset investments under consideration.

This model provides an opportunity to study and compute the marginal cost of funds (1) from a single funding source such as CDs or (2) on a weighted average basis. If a single source basis is used, the real marginal cost of funds is the sum of the explicit marginal cost plus an implicit spillover cost of equity required by shareholders because the deposits/capital ratio (financial risk) has increased.

Real Marginal Cost	=	Explicit Marginal Cost	+	Implicit Marginal Cost

The explicit marginal cost is the interest cost of funds (percent) plus other percentage cost additions associated with obtaining and maintaining the specific source, whether negotiable CDs, subordinated notes, etc. The sum of the percentage cost factors divided by one minus the reserve requirements and/or the proportion of non-earning assets associated with the specific source (if applicable) is the explicit marginal rate (cost). The reserve requirement/non-earning asset adjustment is considered because a proportion of the funds raised must be kept in a non-interest-earning reserve asset.

$$\text{Explicit Marginal Cost} = \frac{\text{Interest Cost} + \text{Acquisition Cost} + \text{Servicing Cost} + \text{FDIC Insurance Premium}}{1 - \text{Reserve Requirement (\%)}}$$

An alternative cost of funds method is the weighted average method. Each dollar of funds raised is assumed to be composed of a given proportional mix of debt funds (deposits) and equity. The capital/asset ratio and other relative proportions of funds are assumed to be constant. The financial risk does not change as funds are raised because the financing mix (capital/assets ratio) does not change. If an asset returns the weighted marginal cost of funds, all suppliers of capital, including the residual shareholders, are provided their after-tax required rate of return on marginal funds contributed.

In both the specific source and weighted average cost of funds methods, several summary points should be emphasized.

1. Historical, past costs of funds are irrelevant. The cost of funds analysis requires a current perspective: "If I had to raise funds today . . ."

2. Both cost methods correctly take a shareholder perspective in decision analysis. What is the impact of a change in the capital/asset ratio or a higher than average risk investment? Management is the agent of shareholders, and must not only consider the expected dollar profit implications of asset and funding decisions but be sensitive to any changes in business or financial risk.

3. The cost of funds is a constant evaluation of the depository institutions by the financial markets. Monitoring the opinions of funding sources is an important management function.

APPLICATION

Model G is useful both as a teaching/learning medium and as a cost of funds calculator for case and bank simulation game analyses. Student analysts often do not consider the shareholder cost of equity in pricing/costing case or simulation decisions. Many times loans are underpriced and share price values decline. Almost all texts and courses cover this concept. Not all may take this shareholder's equity approach, but the student should be exposed to the varied approaches and arguments of financial structure theory. The model also provides an analysis of shareholder returns if investment returns are above or below the cost of funds. Refer to the Functional Cost Analysis in the appendix.

MENU AND SCREENS

Model G has the following menus on two screens:

A   -   TUTORIAL
B   -   ENTER FUNDS ACQUISITION PLANNING DATA
C   -   ENTER ACQUISITION AND SERVICING EXPENSES
D   -   VIEW SINGLE SOURCE PRESENTATION
E   -   VIEW WEIGHTED AVERAGE PRESENTATION
F   -   DECISION-MAKING EXERCISE
P   -   PRINT REPORT
S   -   SAVE TO DISKETTE (REPLACES CURRENT FILE CONTENTS)
Q   -   QUIT PROGRAM

A   -   TUTORIAL

The four tutorial screens provide a summary of the concepts and input instructions for later use. No data may be entered in the tutorial.

B   -   ENTER FUNDS ACQUISITION PLANNING DATA

Using the sample screen below as an example, the line items are defined and discussed.

* * *

FUNDS ACQUISITION PLANNING DATA

AMOUNT OF FUNDS TO BE RAISED: $100,000
BANK AFTER-TAX REQUIRED RETURN ON PREFERRED: 00.00%
BANK AFTER-TAX REQUIRED RETURN ON EQUITY: 14.00%
BANK MARGINAL TAX RATE: 34.00%

ENTER NUMBER INDICATING SOURCE FUNDS USED IN ANALYSIS: 3

	MARKET RATE	RESERVE %	ADJ RATE
1 - TRANSACTION ACCOUNTS	6.500%	3.0%	6.701%
2 - OTHER DEPOSITS (EXC. CD'S)	8.000%	0.0%	8.000%
3 - CD'S	9.000%	3.0%	9.278%
4 - OTHER	0.000%	0.0%	0.000%
5 - CAPITAL NOTES	14.000%	NA	14.000%
6 - PREFERRED STOCK	0.000%	NA	0.000%
7 - COMMON STOCK (PRE-TAX)	21.212%	NA	21.212%

ENTER RISK SPILLOVER FACTOR (COMPENSATES INVESTORS FOR THE ADDITIONAL RISK RESULTING FROM AN INCREASE IN LEVERAGE): 0.4800%

* * *

Amount of Funds to Be Raised: Input the amount of funds to be raised in the market.

Bank Required Return on Preferred and Common Equity: The cost of preferred and equity or the minimum rate of return needed on equity financed investments to maintain the shareholder's market value. The preferred stock stated dividend divided by the current price or current dividend rates on new issues is a good proxy rate. The common equity return is not a contractual rate found in the Wall Street Journal, but must be estimated. The level of business and financial risk and opportunity costs (alternative returns available in the market) are major factors to consider. Historical returns on equity are relevant only for a past perspective. The required return today is the correct orientation. The model then converts the after-tax preferred and common returns to pre-tax, by dividing by one minus the marginal tax rate.

Bank Marginal Tax Rate: Enter the marginal tax rate. Added returns imply added, incremental taxes. Debt funds are tax deductible; equity funds are not.

Enter Number Indicating Source Funds Used in Analysis: Input the number of the source of funds (listed below) that will be used in the single source analysis. The four debt sources listed are commonly used in a "single source cost of funds" analysis, and the model is set up under the assumption that one of the debt sources will be selected. The common stock(s) may be entered and analyzed, even though it does not quite fit the analysis in single source analysis (Menu D).

Enter the Market Rate and Reserve Requirements/Non-Earning Asset Percentage: Enter the pre-tax current market rate on the specific sources of funds plus any processing and acquisition costs (%) if applicable, and the reserve requirements and/or non-earning proportion of each, if applicable. The preferred and common stock required rate of return is a calculated value in the program. The required rate of return divided by one minus the marginal tax rate equals the pre-tax required return (14%/1 - .34 = 21.2%).

Enter the Risk Spillover Factor: Add the increment to be added to the marginal cost of specific sources of funds to compensate for the increase in financial risk if specific debt funds are increased and capital funds remain constant. The decline in the capital/assets ratio increases the risk to shareholders and may require added returns. If the incremental debt funds added is not thought to increase shareholder risk, enter a zero. The required rate of return on equity above assumes a constant capital/asset ratio.

C   -   ENTER ACQUISITION AND SERVICING EXPENSES

Input the non-interest incremental expenses of raising added funds. Enter as dollars or as a percentage (proportion of the total funds raised) on an annualized basis. If 90-day CD funds cost $500 per quarter or 2 percent in non-interest expenses, the annualized inputs would be $2,000 (dollars) and .02 (2 percent). Acquisition, servicing, and FDIC insurance premium expenses are entered separately. If percentages (entered as decimals) are used, enter a zero in the dollar input. See the Functional Cost Analysis statistics in the appendix.

D   -   VIEW SINGLE SOURCE PRESENTATION

The inputs from Menus B and C are summarized in a percentage and dollar presentation of the effective marginal cost of funds. The sum of the explicit interest, acquisition, servicing and FDIC premium, adjusted for reserve requirements, equals the marginal cost of funds. In the screen presentation below, the sum of the percentage costs totals 9.70%. Dividing by one minus the idle funds proportion equals the marginal pre-tax cost of funds. The non-earning asset adjustment is the difference between the adjusted rate of 10 percent (9.7/.97) and the 9.7 percent or .3 percent. If dollar acquisition, servicing, and other expenses have been entered, each is converted to a percentage display, just as a percentage entry is displayed on a dollar basis.

The implicit spillover increment of .48 percent is added to the marginal cost of funds to give the effective marginal pre-tax cost of funds of a single funding source. In the example below, an annual asset return of 10.48 percent is required in order to cover explicit costs of funds and other expenses, as well as to provide an increment (.48% or $480) to shareholders to compensate them for added financial risk. Compare this "cost" to pre-tax asset "returns."

* * *

SINGLE SOURCE RATE

MARGINAL COST OF FUNDS PRESENTATION

		DOLLAR
EXPLICIT MARGINAL COST	PERCENTAGE	VALUES
INTEREST COST	9.0000%	$9,000
ACQUISITION COST	0.4000%	$400
SERVICING COSTS	0.2600%	$260
FDIC INSURANCE PREMIUM	0.0400%	$40
	9.7000%	$9,700
RESERVE REQ/NON-EARNING ADJUST.[a]	.3000%	$300
MARGINAL COST OF FUNDS	10.0000%	$10,000
IMPLICIT EQUITY MARGINAL COST	0.4800%	$480
EFFECTIVE MARGINAL COST OF FUNDS	10.4800%	$10,480

* * *

E   -   VIEW WEIGHTED AVERAGE PRESENTATION

The weighted average analysis assumes that incremental funds are raised in pre-determined proportions of debt/equity funds. The weighted average pre-tax cost of incremental funds is calculated on this screen. The paragraph below and the sample screen explain the presentation.

The explicit cost of funds, the reserve requirements and/or non-earning asset adjustment, and estimated required return to shareholders (entered in Menu B) are combined to calculate a pre-tax weighted average.

---

[a] $\dfrac{9.700\%}{1-.03} = 10.000\% - 9.700\% = .300\%$

* * *

WEIGHTED AVERAGE MARGINAL COST OF FUNDS PRESENTATION

SOURCE OF FUNDS	% COMP	INCREMENTAL FUNDS	PRE-TAX ADJUSTED COST	PRE-TAX COMPONENT COST
TRANSACTION ACCOUNTS	25.0%	$25,000	6.701%	1.675%
OTHER DEPOSITS (EXC CD'S)	30.0%	$30,000	8.000%	2.400%
CD'S	25.0%	$25,000	9.278%	2.320%
OTHER	00.0%	0	0.000%	0
CAPITAL NOTES	10.0%	$10,000	14.000%	1.400%
PREFERRED STOCK	00.0%	0	0.000%	0
COMMON STOCK	10.0%	$10,000	21.212%	2.121%
	100.0%	$100,000		9.916%

WEIGHTED AVERAGE MARGINAL COST OF FUNDS: 9.916%

* * *

The percentage composition column (% comp) must be entered and must total 100 percent. This proportion may be determined by (1) historical averages, (2) market determined proportions, or, better, by (3) the optimal financing mix necessary to minimize the cost of funds. Book accounting values may be used to compute the total and components, but market values are theoretically correct. The explicit rates have been adjusted upward to reflect non-earning proportions of funds (6.50%/1-.03 = 6.701%). Compare this pre-tax weighted average cost of incremental funds to the expected pre-tax return on investments. This pre-tax analysis is extended to an after-tax analysis in the decision-making exercise with Menu F.

F   -   DECISION-MAKING EXERCISE

Two screens analyze the marginal weighted cost of funds and calculate the expected incremental return on incremental equity from an asset investment. There are only two input variables in these two screens: the asset investment (funds needed) amount and the expected return on the funds raised. The input data from prior menu areas are combined to present a pre-tax weighted marginal cost of funds.

* * *

DECISION-MAKING EXERCISE

SOURCES	% COMP	INCREMENTAL FUNDS	PRE-TAX EXPLICIT RATE	PRE-TAX NOMINAL EXPENSE	ADDED NON-EARNING ADJ. EXP.
TRANS ACCTS	25.0%	$25,000	6.500%	$1,625	50
OTHER DEP.	30.0%	$30,000	8.000%	$2,400	0
CD'S	25.0%	$25,000	9.000%	$2,250	70
OTHER	00.0%	0	0.000%	0	0
CAP. NOTES	10.0%	$10,000	14.000%	$1,400	120
PREF. STOCK	00.0%	0	0.000%	0	0
COMMON STOCK	10.0%	$10,000	21.212%	$2,121	0
	100.0%	$100,000		$9,796	

Added Non-Earning Adjustment Expense $ 120
Effective Marginal Dollar Cost $9,916

$9,916/100,000 = 9.916% Effective Weighted Avg. Cost

* * *

In the first row of screen one above, transaction accounts will support (25 percent) or $25,000 of the loan, with an explicit cost of 6.5 percent or $1,625.   An added imputed cost for reserve requirements (non-earning assets) is added in the column to the right.   The adjustment is calculated as the difference between the effective, adjusted rate and the actual rate paid times the amount of funds (6.701% - 6.500% = .201% x $25,000 = $50). The effective dollar, marginal cost of $100,000 of new funds is the sum of the actual interest paid, the required rate of return on preferred and common stock, and the added cost adjustment for idle funds.

* * *

DECISION-MAKING EXERCISE: EARNINGS AND RETURNS

ENTER ASSET AMOUNT: $100,000   ENTER RATE: 9.916%

INTEREST INCOME:	9,916
EXPLICIT COST OF DEBT:	-7,675
NON-EARNING ADJ. EXP.:	-120
PRE-TAX EARNINGS:	2,121
TAXES:	-721
EARNINGS AFTER TAXES:	1,400
PREFERRED DIVIDEND:	0
EARNINGS AVAILABLE COMMON:	1,400

AFTER-TAX RETURN ON ADDED:

PREFERRED STOCK   0.00%
COMMON EQUITY   14.00%

* * *

An incremental dollar/rate analysis, given an expected asset return, is then calculated in the second screen. The interest income ($100,000 x .09916) less the explicit, actual interest expense (sum of pre-tax nominal interest expense) the non-earning asset imputed cost, and taxes (34 percent) equals earnings after taxes of $1,400. The expected after-tax return of $1,400 divided by the incremental equity of $10,000 forecasts a 14 percent after-tax return on equity, equal to the 14 percent after-tax required rate of return entered in Menu B. Investing incremental funds at the weighted average cost of funds of 9.916 percent will provide the minimum rate of return on equity of 14 percent Expected pre-tax returns above 9.916 percent will provide returns to equity above the 14 percent required rate, attract equity investors and increase shareholder value. Pre-tax investment returns below 9.916 percent will generate equity returns below the 14 percent required rate and cause some investors at the margin to sell, thus reducing shareholder value.

P   -   PRINT REPORT

The report generated is a concise analysis of the single source and weighted average marginal cost of funds.

S   -   SAVE TO DISKETTE (REPLACES CURRENT FILE)

SAMPLE PROBLEMS/ASSIGNMENTS

1. Input 11 percent as the earnings rate in the Menu F decision-making exercise. What is the expected return on equity? Compare it with the required equity return (Menu B). What are the implications for shareholders when investment returns exceed or fall below the marginal cost of funds? What happens to the bank stock price and why?

2. If Bank A's market value per share exceeds its book value, what can be said about its actual investment returns relative to its marginal cost of funds?

3. If the bank began to invest heavily in high risk construction loans, how could this be reflected in your decision analysis?

4. Describe an economic setting and conditions in which a shift from loans to Treasury bills causes an increase in the market value of the bank stock. Explain, using this model supported by a short discussion.

5. What are the marginal cost of funds implications of regulatory authorities requiring increased bank capital/asset ratios?

CHAPTER 10

Model H
Customer Profitability Analysis

INTRODUCTION AND CONCEPTS

The goal of this model is to analyze the profitability of a specific customer deposit/loan relationship with the bank. Deposits and lending have always been related, but until recently, lending and deposit service pricing had been bundled together. Deregulation and increased competition have encouraged banks to evaluate specific loan and deposit services in order to achieve an adequate or target profit return. Costing and pricing is now an important middle management activity in most banks.

While the banks are unbundling, so are many customers, seeking specific services from various banks. Most banks, however, still attempt to provide a full range of loan/deposit services for their business and retail customers. They should regularly analyze the deposit/loan profitability of specific customers. While not a total profitability analysis, this model provides the student analyst the opportunity to study a deposit/loan service-oriented customer profit-ability analysis (CPA) model which focuses on shareholder profitability and other commonly used profitability measures. In addition, one can review the many pricing variables and the role each plays in achieving targeted customer profitability. Review the tutorial, and then return to each of the sequential menu areas. Finally, review the profitability in Menu G and answer the questions at the end of the chapter.

APPLICATION

This model provides a dynamic, decision-making orientation to the CPA presentations of most banking textbooks. The student can now practice CPA, either in a historical evaluation or in a planning (new customer or new service relationship) mode. What added services, priced how, will achieve targeted profitability? How does item pricing affect total return? If spreads or loan/interest margins are narrowing, can service charging and item pricing not only make the customer relationship profitable (positive dollar profits) but achieve a targeted return on allocated capital?

MENU AND SCREENS

Model H has the following menus on two screens, cumulating in a concluding customer profitability analysis.

```
A    -    TUTORIAL
B    -    ENTER CUSTOMER FUNDS USED DATA
C    -    ENTER CUSTOMER FUNDS PROVIDED DATA
D    -    ENTER GENERAL BANK DATA
E    -    ENTER MISCELLANEOUS CUSTOMER REVENUE DATA
F    -    ENTER MISCELLANEOUS CUSTOMER EXPENSE DATA
G    -    CUSTOMER PROFITABILITY MODEL
P    -    PRINT REPORT
S    -    SAVE TO DISKETTE (REPLACES CURRENT FILE CONTENTS)
Q    -    QUIT PROGRAM
```

A   -   TUTORIAL

The tutorial presents a two-screen summary of the program, followed by a review of the screens utilized in the menus that follow. No data input is permitted in the tutorial.

B   -   ENTER CUSTOMER FUNDS USED DATA

Funds used refers to the amount of customer loans outstanding and the current interest rate on each loan. Enter up to six loans. The interest rate and balance are variables in CPA. Reduced borrowing levels and/or changes in the rate structure affect customer profitability.

C   -   ENTER CUSTOMER FUNDS PROVIDED DATA

The average deposit accounts (maximum of six), the interest rate paid on these accounts, and the specific reserve requirements may be inputted. If interest is paid on the collected balance, enter under the column title. If interest is paid on the ledger balance (book), enter one line down at the right of the "A:" prompt.

The deposit (funds provided) variables affect customer profitability. The larger the deposit and the lower the reserve requirements (see Federal Reserve Bulletin), the greater the amount of loan funds contributed by the customer. Of course, the interest rate paid relative to the loan rate (spread) is a very important factor affecting profitability.

In the screen below, the customer has one deposit account, probably a demand deposit account, with an average balance of $150,000 and two others: $50,000 and $15,000 which earn interest (ledger balance).

* * *

CUSTOMER FUNDS PROVIDED
NOTE ENTER ALL PERCENTAGES AS DECIMAL (i.e., .01 is 1.00%)

ENTER AVERAGE LEDGER
BALANCE AT A: IF INTEREST

	AVERAGE COLLECTED BALANCE	REQUIRED RESERVE	INTEREST RATE
PAID ON LEDGER BALANCE			
DEPOSIT ACCOUNT #1	$150,000	12.00%	0.00%
A: $0			
DEPOSIT ACCOUNT #2	$44,000	3.00%	7.00%
A: $50,000			
DEPOSIT ACCOUNT #3	$12,000	3.00%	7.50%
A: $15,000			
DEPOSIT ACCOUNT #4	$0	0.00%	0.00%
A: $0			
DEPOSIT ACCOUNT #5	$0	0.00%	0.00%
A: $0			
DEPOSIT ACCOUNT #6	$0	0.00%	0.00%
A:			

* * *

D   -   ENTER GENERAL BANK DATA

Specific variables are entered, to be used later in the CPA.
A sample screen and discussion of each variable follow.

* * *

GENERAL BANK DATA
NOTE ENTER ALL PERCENTAGES AS DECIMALS (i.e., .01 is 1.00%)

CAPITAL TO LOAN RATIO   12.00%

MARGINAL COST OF FUNDS RATE
    MAY BE SPECIFIC DEBT SOURCE OR
    WEIGHTED AVERAGE OF PRE-TAX DEBT
    COST.   8.00%

RETURN ON EQUITY GOAL   15.00%

MARGINAL TAX RATE   34.00%

* * *

Capital to Loan Ratio: The target or optimum proportion of
equity capital to loan. The amount of equity funds allocated to
support the loan or keep the capital/loan ratio constant is
entered. This input times the loan balance determines the equity
amount used in the ROE profitability analysis in the CPA (Menu

G). The customer's deposits and/or other residual funds plus the allocated equity equals the total loan amount.

Marginal Cost of Funds: The specific debt source rate or the weighted average pre-tax debt cost of funds (Model G) used to cost the residual debt funds contributed by the bank (loans minus customer deposits).

Return on Equity Goal: The targeted or desired return on allocated capital. Each customer is supported by an amount of equity with an assumed minimum or required rate of return.

Marginal Tax Rate: The marginal tax rate of the bank in an analysis of a new customer. One could argue the use of the average tax rate in a periodic review of bank customers. In a larger, profitable bank, the average and marginal tax are the same.

E   -   ENTER MISCELLANEOUS CUSTOMER REVENUE DATA

Other customer revenue sources are analyzed and entered in Menu E. In the screen below, note the first entry item.   Enter the time period considered when entering miscellaneous revenue and expense data. The variables are then annualized in the CPA.

* * *

MISCELLANEOUS CUSTOMER REVENUE
ENTER NUMBER OF MONTHS COVERED IN ANALYSIS PERIOD: 1
    (PROGRAM ACCEPTS MONTHLY PERIODS OF 1, 3, 6 OR 12 MONTHS)
NOTE PROGRAM WILL ANNUALIZE THE REVENUE ENTERED ON THIS SCREEN AND ALSO EXPENSES ENTERED ON THE MISCELLANEOUS EXPENSE SCREEN WHEN COMPLETING THE CUSTOMER PROFITABILITY MODEL.

SERVICE CHARGES ON DEPOSIT ACCOUNTS $8.00

ALL OTHER FEES ON DEPOSIT ACCOUNTS $10.00

LOAN COMMITMENT FEES $0.00

ALL OTHER FEES ON LOAN ACCOUNTS $15.00

DATA PROCESSING FEES $56.00

ALL OTHER MISCELLANEOUS FEES $0.00

* * *

In the above case, the figures are monthly and relate to several specific noninterest loan and deposit services provided that have been (will be) priced and billed (collected). The data processing fees relate possibly to payroll accounting, reconciliation services, etc. Each service has been priced using a variety of methods: cost plus, competitive, target rate of return, etc.

F - ENTER MISCELLANEOUS CUSTOMER EXPENSE DATA

Other noninterest customer expenses are analyzed and entered based on the time period entered under Menu E. For example, if a monthly period was selected, enter monthly data here. Most of the miscellaneous expenses below are related to deposit account activity. Each of the items is defined briefly below. The number of items, the price per item, and the total are listed.

* * *

MISCELLANEOUS CUSTOMER EXPENSES

PROGRAM WILL ANNUALIZE THE FOLLOWING 1 MONTH(S) DATA IN THE MODEL.

ANALYSIS OF EXPENSES

ACCOUNT MAINTENANCE	3	@	$6.00	$18.00
DEBITS POSTED	1245	@	$0.10	$124.50
DEPOSITS POSTED	15	@	$0.25	$3.75
CHECKS DEPOSITED	335	@	$0.05	$16.75
CHECKS SORTED	1245	@	$0.05	$62.25
RETURNED ITEMS	20	@	$0.50	$10.00
WIRE TRANSFERS	10	@	$5.00	$50.00
ROLLS OF COINS	300	@	$0.03	$9.00
LOAN HANDLING COST	0	@	$0.00	$0.00
DATA PROCESSING	10	@	$50.00	$500.00
ALL OTHERS: (ITEMIZE)				
	0	@	$0.00	$0.00
	0	@	$0.00	$0.00
	0	@	$0.00	$0.00

* * *

Account Maintenance: The number of statements or reports sent to the customer in the period (month). The customer has three deposit accounts.

Debits Posted: Reductions in or debits to the deposit (credit) accounts, mostly checks.

Deposits Posted: The number of deposits made in the period.

Checks Deposited: The deposits posted above probably included checks, currency, and coins. Each check deposited by the company must be processed in the bank operations center (proof machine) and be prepared (MICR encoded) to continue the check clearing process.

Checks Sorted: The checks written by the customer may be sorted (sequenced) and prepared for statement mailing.

Returned Items: The checks deposited by the customer are returned to the bank, most because of insufficient funds.

Wire Transfers: The interbank transfer of funds.

Rolls of Coins: The preparation of loose coins for the customer.

Loan Handling Cost: Fees for loan origination, processing, etc.

Data Processing: Billing for CPU time used (or other measures) in providing data services to the customer, such as payroll check preparation, etc.

All Others: Enter customer expenses not included above per the time period at the top of the screen.

G - CUSTOMER PROFITABILITY MODEL

Data entries in the earlier menu items are now combined in a three-screen summary analysis. The first screen, shown below, presents a summary of the sources and uses of funds for the customer, including the total annualized average loan balances, the net investable funds provided by the customer, the amount of capital supporting the loan (loan amount times the capital/loan ratio), and the residual funds needed from other deposit sources to support the loan (loan amount minus investable funds and allocated capital).

* * *

SOURCE AND USE OF FUNDS
(ANNUALIZED)

FUNDS USED

AVERAGE LOAN BALANCES $600,000

SOURCE OF FUNDS

INVESTABLE FUNDS
  PROVIDED BY CUSTOMER $186,320
  (NET OR UNCOLLECTED BALANCES
  AND REQUIRED RESERVES)

ALLOCATED CAPITAL $72,000

RESIDUAL FUNDS $341,680

* * *

The next CPA screen is an annualized revenue expense analysis of the customer. Revenues include loan interest revenues plus miscellaneous revenues (Menu E), while expenses include customer deposit interest, bank expenses incurred in servicing the deposit accounts (Menu F), and the dollar cost of residual funds needed to support the customer loan.

* * *

INCOME STATEMENT

REVENUES:
INTEREST ON LOANS	$54,500.00
MISCELLANEOUS CUSTOMER REVENUES	$1,068.00
TOTAL REVENUE	$55,568.00

EXPENSES:
INTEREST ON DEPOSITS	$4,625.00
MISCELLANEOUS CUSTOMER EXPENSES	$9,531.00
COST OF RESIDUAL FUNDS	$27,334.40
TOTAL EXPENSES	$41,490.40

NET INCOME BEFORE TAXES	$14,077.60
APPLICABLE TAX	$4,786.38
NET AVAILABLE FOR ROE	$9,291.22

COST OF CAPITAL FUNDS ALLOCATED	$10,800.00
RETURN ON EQUITY GOAL:	15.00%
RETURN ON EQUITY ACTUAL:	12.90%

* * *

The annualized net income available for ROE is the difference between revenues and expenses. Is the account profitable? On a dollar profit basis it is, using the example above, but does the customer provide a return compatible with the ROE goal? The account above would need $10,800 in net income (cost of capital funds allocated) to provide a 15.00 percent ROE. The $9,291.22 divided by $72,000 allocated capital provides a return of 12.90 percent, below the target ROE of 15 percent. This customer contributes to total dollar profits but, incrementally, does not provide a competitive return on allocated capital. Other profitability measures often used are net income/residual funds and net income to total borrowed funds. These ratios are not shareholder specific or applicable to all bank/customer relationships. The funds base to use in the CPA is discussed below.

The last screen of the CPA analyzes the net income return relative to three commonly used measures of the amount of funds that the bank must provide to support the customer: allocated equity, net residual funds used, and total borrowed funds. The net income/allocated equity takes a shareholder and specific customer perspective, but the amount of equity is a function of the size or riskiness of the loan.

The ratio of pre-tax income to net or residual funds is a spread measure of the customer relationship. The revenues (net of overhead) less the cost of residual funds equals the spread (pre-tax income) associated with the customer. A figure of zero would be a breakeven level on net funds used but would not provide any return on allocated capital.

The pre-tax profits/total loans or borrowed funds is applicable only to borrowing customers. A target return on total loans must be established. Zero indicates a breakeven level; and a shareholder perspective is not included.

* * *

NET RETURN ON ALLOCATED CAPITAL ABOVE EQUITY GOAL   -2.10%
    A VALUE GREATER THAN ZERO INDICATES THAT THE BANK'S
    RETURN ON CAPITAL IS ABOVE THE TARGET RATE. A
    VALUE LESS THAN ZERO SUGGESTS THAT THE CUSTOMER
    RELATIONSHIP HAS BEEN INCORRECTLY PRICED AND
    SHOULD BE REVIEWED.

SPREAD ON NET BANK FUNDS USED   4.12%
    MEASURES THE PRE-TAX NET INCOME ON THE
    RESIDUAL FUNDS USED.

RETURN ON TOTAL BORROWED FUNDS   2.35%
    MEASURES THE PRE-TAX PROFIT
    AS RELATED TO THE CUSTOMER'S LOAN RELATIONSHIP.

* * *

If the CPA indicates that the profit goals are not or will not be met, consider anyone or a combination of the following:

1. Increase customer loan balances.
2. Increase loan rates.
3. Increase compensating balances on transaction accounts.
4. Analyze the customer's account activity and expenses relative to service charges, etc.
5. Unbundle and explicitly price loan/deposit-related services or value added for customers not yet priced apart from the loan or deposit.
6. Sell added bank services, priced to provide reasonable returns.
7. Continue to search for ways to reduce the cost of providing bank services through automation, etc.

P   -   PRINT REPORT

S   -   SAVE TO DISKETTE (REPLACES CURRENT FILE)

Sample Problems and Assignments

Hargrove Hardware and Supply has had a deposit and loan relationship with the First Bank of Monroe for years. Periodic analysis has indicated that the account is profitable -- it earns positive profits. The data from Hargrove Hardware and Supply have been entered as the default data on the BFDA diskette and were included as sample screens in this chapter. Review the printed report or the various screens and answer the following questions.

1.   Is the Hargrove Hardware and Supply relationship profitable for First Bank? Discuss.

2.   Has First Bank priced its account activity fees at a reasonable level? Analyze and discuss.

3. Hargrove Hardware and Supply has many suppliers' accounts and is considering an affiliation with a national hardware supplier, which would reduce the number of monthly checks written to less than 200. Is this a relevant variable in the company's analysis of the new hardware affiliation?

4. What combination of changed customer relationships would meet the First Bank target ROE of 15 percent? As the customer account manager, what combination of changes would you consider reasonable for both Hargrove Hardware and Supply and First Bank?

CHAPTER 11

Model I
Bank Financial Statement
Analysis

INTRODUCTION AND CONCEPTS

This chapter and the associated BFDA model enable the student analyst to generate twenty-five popular bank financial ratios for five years by entering only seventeen annual financial data items from bank financial statements. The program will generate a five-year trend analysis and averages for a single bank or a comparative analysis for up to five banks for a five-year period. The interpretation and analysis, of course, are left to the analyst, but this number-crunching model saves computation time and frees up more time for analysis.

This chapter will offer direction and definitions in support of the software. The user is encouraged to (1) review the data input instructions prior to inputting data and, later, (2) review the ratio definition section, which defines each ratio and classifies its use for financial analyses. The purpose of this model is (1) to cover the areas and concepts of bank financial analysis and (2) to provide an efficient tool which quickly moves the student to analyses and away from ratio computation.

APPLICATIONS

This model is very useful in case analyses which require a bank financial analysis. The three-page output provides an efficient tool for trend analysis and answering questions rather than spending a lot of time generating ratios. In addition, the printed output is an excellent table to support case analyses and conclusions.

The model generates five years of ratios for a single bank or an analysis of up to five different banks for a five-year period. Averages for each ratio are also generated. The ratios provide the opportunity to study areas such as profitability, capital adequacy, net interest margins, asset quality, and bank overhead. The profitability/growth analysis provides a decomposition analysis of the ROE and links profitability, the dividend decision and internal capital growth. The ROA and ROE are graphed for your analysis. The student is advised to graph other ratios when studying a five-year trend. Figures and graphs reveal trends and relationships that tables hide.

MENU AND SCREENS

Model I has the following menus on two screens:

A   -   TUTORIAL PROGRAM

B   -   DATE/NUMBER HEADINGS ENTRY

C   -   PERFORMANCE DATA INPUT

D   -   ROLLS LAST FOUR YEARS DATA

E   -   BANK RATIO ANALYSIS

F   -   PROFITABILITY/GROWTH ANALYSIS

G   -   VIEW GRAPH (REQUIRES GRAPHIC ABILITY)

P   -   PRINT REPORT

S   -   SAVE TO DISKETTE (REPLACES CURRENT FILE CONTENTS)

Q   -   QUIT PROGRAM

A   -   TUTORIAL PROGRAM

The tutorial program provides a narrative description of the program and a reminder to depress the numlock key and use the ten-key pad later when entering financial data. This menu will be an effective tool if the user understands the components of each ratio and is able to relate the level and trends to the economic climate and management's decisions in the period. When you see a trend or major shift in the direction of a ratio, noting so is not enough. Why did it change? What factors may explain what happened? Graph all the ratios on a large sheet of paper (or your computer), study them together, and always keep saying "why?" and looking for the reasons.

B   -   DATE/NUMBER HEADINGS ENTRY

In this sub-routine, the last year of your data must be identified for the tabular columns listed later. A five-year bank analysis <u>ending</u> in 1986 would require that one enter 1986 at this point. If a peer group comparison is to be made, enter the number of banks that will be compared (maximum of five). Assign a number to each bank and note it in your records. Later, when inputting, the data will be entered beginning with the latest year or highest-numbered bank first.

C   -   PERFORMANCE DATA INPUT

This program uses macro commands to walk the user through the data input phase. Here is where the old adage "garbage in, garbage out" applies. Make sure you have the correct data, year, etc. Definitions of each data item and its financial statement source are listed below. It is suggested that the user assemble the data, using the attached Data Input Sheet, and then enter them in the program. Make a copy of the Data Input Sheet and retain the master. Enter the latest year or the highest-numbered bank first, etc. Organize your data in this order. You may select the cursor movement, allowing it to move either vertically or horizontally. If errors are made, you may return to the same screen by using the Ctrl-Break, Alt C sequence. If you must turn off the computer and finish the inputting later, make sure you have "saved" (Menu S) before cancelling the program. After you have inputted, carefully proof your data. (Hint: For very large banks with billion dollar entries, round off three zeros. Your ratio will not be affected. After data entry, check the calculated net income to make sure your inputs are correct.

The data needed for the performance review are listed below, along with a brief explanation of each.

Data Entry Item	Explanation
Average Loans (Adjusted)	Total average gross loans less unearned income. See the Average Balance Sheet presentation.
Average Total Assets	Represents total assets found in the Average Balance Sheet in the annual report. May be an average of beginning (prior year) and ending total assets from the year-end balance sheet.
Average Earning Assets	Also found in Average Balance Sheet presentation or by estimating. Subtract average nonearning assets from total assets.

Average Total Equity	Total common equity or as modified by analyst. Located in Average Balance Sheet or by averaging the beginning and ending common equity from the year-end balance sheet.
Number of Full-Time Equivalent Employees	Usually in the Financial Highlights or Operating Summary of the Annual Report (10K report)
Interest Income-FTE	Total interest income on a fully tax equivalent basis. See the Average Balance Sheet report. Tax-free income (income statement) may be adjusted upward per the marginal tax rate to a pre-tax equivalent level. Tax-free income of $100 will be an FTE level of (100/1 -tax rate).
Interest Expense	Total interest expense located in the Average Balance/Interest presentation or from the income statement.
Other Income	Total noninterest income (revenue) from the income statement, excluding security gains (losses).
Other Expense	Total noninterest operating expenses, excluding federal income taxes. Usually a totaled item in the income statement.
Security Gains, Net or Security Losses, Net	Total annual security gains (losses) net of tax effect-- found in the income statement under other income or revenue.
Salary and Employee Benefits	Total employee compensation from the income statement.
Net Occupancy - Equipment Expense	Total expenses of bank, building, equipment, etc., net of rental income. Usually an income statement line item.

Loan Loss Provision	The total annual expense provision for loan losses from the income statement.
FTE Adjustment	The total added to the tax-free interest income to determine the total interest income - FTE. Also found in Average Balance Sheet and rates analysis in the annual report. The difference between interest income-FTE and interest income from the income statement.
Federal Tax Provision	The total book federal income tax expense -- income statement.
Dividends Paid	The total common cash dividends paid during the year. See the Financial Highlights or the Statement of Changes in Financial Position. Not found in the balance sheet or income statement.
Net Loan Chargeoffs	Found in the Loan Loss Reserve reconciliation in the footnotes to the balance sheet.

D   -   ROLLS LAST FOUR YEARS DATA

This option provides room to add the latest year's data to the model. The earliest year's data (low-numbered bank) are, of course, removed from the file. The option can also be used to remove all the program default data before inputting actual bank data. Four iterations of Menu D are needed to clear default data.

* * *

NOTE THE FOLLOWING IMPORTANT INFORMATION
BEFORE ENTERING YOUR SELECTION.

****

YES   -   EARLIEST YEAR (LOWEST NUMBER BANK) DATA WILL BE
REMOVED FROM FILE TO MAKE ROOM FOR LATEST YEAR
(HIGHEST NUMBER BANK).   MOVES EACH YEARS (BANK) DATA
ONE YEAR (BANK) TO THE RIGHT.   MAY BE USED TO CLEAR
DEFAULT DATA BY USING THIS FUNCTION THE REQUIRED
NUMBER OF TIMES TO CLEAR DESIRED FIELDS.

NO   -   CANCELS COMMAND AND RETURNS TO MENU.   RETAINS DATA
PREVIOUSLY ENTERED.   IF   UNSURE   OF   THE   DESIRED
SELECTION, USE THIS ALTERNATIVE UNTIL DATA FIELDS HAVE
BEEN REVIEWED.

* * *

E   -   PERFORMANCE RATIO REVIEW

Once the input data are loaded in Menu C, you can scroll
through the calculated output in this section. Two years or two
banks may be reviewed at one time. To move to the next screen,
depress the enter key. The formula and description of the
calculated amounts and ratios are presented below. The formula
numbers relate to the row numbers associated with the data entry
items below, and to several of the calculated amounts such as
total revenue (67) and net income (72). The formula for the
ratios may be read from the screen by placing the cursor (use the
arrow key) on any calculated ratio number. To return to the
program macro, depress Ctrl-Break and Alt-C.

<u>DATA ENTRY ITEMS</u>

43   AVERAGE LOANS
44   AVERAGE TOTAL ASSETS
45   AVERAGE EARNING ASSETS
46   AVERAGE TOTAL EQUITY
47   NO. FULL-TIME EQUIV EMPLOYEES
48   INTEREST INCOME-FTE
49   INTEREST EXPENSE
50   OTHER INCOME
51   OTHER EXPENSE
52   SECURITIES GAINS-NET **OR**
53   SECURITIES LOSSES-NET
54   SALARIES & EMPLOYEES BENEFITS
55   NET OCCUPANCY-EQUIPMENT EXPENSES
56   LOAN LOSS PROVISION

57   FULLY TAX EQUIVALENT ADJUSTMENT
58   FEDERAL TAX PROVISION
59   DIVIDENDS PAID
60   NET LOAN CHARGE OFFS

Line	Performance Analysis Items	Formula	Brief Description
65	Total Revenue (Exc. Sec. Gains)	48+50−57	Total revenue from operations-- excludes security gains
67	Total Revenue	48+50+52−57	Total revenue including security gains
70	Total Expenses Exc. Fed. Inc. Tax	49+51+53+56	Amount of revenue needed to break even
72	Net Income	67−70−58	See bank income statement: total revenues- total expenses
74	Earning Assets to Average Assets	45/44	Level of earning assets as it relates to profitability
76	Equity Capital to Avg. Assets	46/44	A traditional capital adequacy measure
78	Net Chargeoffs to Average Loans	60/43	Actual net losses in period relative to average loan investment

80	Loan Loss Prov. to Net Chargeoffs	56/60	Book credit losses relative to actual net losses in period
84	Int. Inc.- FTE to Avg. Assets	48/44	A gross yield rate per total assets. The gross yield less the interest cost (86) equals the net interest margin (88)
86	Interest Expense to Average Assets	49/44	Interest cost of funds per dollar of total assets
88	Net Interest - FTE to Avg. Assets	48-49/44	The net interest margin per total asset dollar. Concerned with the level and stability. Reflects spread management performance. Serves as a "gross profit margin" available for expenses and profit.
91	FTE Adjustment to Avg. Assets	57/44	The yield added to (84) and (88) to adjust tax-free revenue to an "as if it were taxable" level

94	Interest Inc - FTE to Earning Assets	48/45	Gross yield now stated per dollar of earning assets. Relates yields per amount of earning assets to total assets.
96	Int Exp. to Earning Assets	49/45	Interest cost per earning assets
98	Net Interest - FTE to Earning Assets	48-49/45	The traditional net interest margin (NIM). Analyzes the level and stability of the NIM
102	FTE Adjustment to Earning Assets	57/45	The yield added to the gross yield and NIM to enable a period-to-period comparison. Removes the bias in the yield from portfolio shifts from taxable to tax-free securities

104	Breakeven Yield	70-50-52/45	The gross revenue yield on earning assets needed to break even (to earn zero net income). Compare actual yield with breakeven to note cushion
106	Other Income to Avg. Assets	50/44	Noninterest revenue per dollar of assets excludes capital gains. Off-balance-sheet-noninterest revenues are becoming more important to banks
108	Other Expenses to Avg. Assets	51/44	Total noninterest expenses (overhead) per dollar of assets. The level and trend of overhead are important contributors to profitability
110	Other Income to Other Expenses	50/51	Measures the extent to which noninterest revenue (fees, etc.) contributes to overhead (personnel and plant expense)

113	Other Income to Salary/ Benefits Expenses	50/54	Noninterest revenue relative to the major overhead expense. Notes other revenue per dollar of personnel costs
116	Salary/ Benefits Expense to Avg. Assets	54/44	Personnel costs per dollar of assets
120	Net Occupancy and Equipment Expense to Avg. Assets	55/44	Building and equipment expense per dollar of assets
123	Loan Loss Provision to Avg. Assets	56/44	The annual <u>expense</u> provision per dollar of assets
125	Total Revenue to Average Assets	67/44	Also called the <u>asset utilization ratio</u>. Measures the revenue generated per dollar of assets. A component of ROA
127	Return on Assets -- Net Income	72/44	A classic profitability ratio (ROA). Measures net income per dollar of assets

129	Return on Equity -- Net Income	72/46	Net profit per dollar of shareholder's equity
131	Personnel Expense per Employee	54/47	Salary/-benefits costs per full-time employee
133	Million Assets per Employee	(44/$1mil)/47	A productivity ratio comparing people to assets managed

The data input and the ratio calculation are only the preliminary steps in a financial analysis. The ratios are relationships (numerator to denominator) that indicate performance or position. The interpretation related to whether the number (ratio level) is high, low, okay, or not okay is up to the analyst. To do this analysis, one must establish a standard, an ideal, a level where concern is raised, etc. Further, a single value at a point in time is static and does not relate movement (trend and direction). Trend analysis adds a dynamic element, for the analyst is usually extrapolating, extending, or predicting future position (balance sheet) or performance (income statement). Graphing the ratios (see the graphic example listed in menu G) assists in finding trends in data far better than tabular material. Use the graphing capability of Lotus 1-2-3 to see its value.

Once ratios have been calculated and trends and comparisons have been made, the analysis has just begun! What is responsible for the trend, the decline, or the improvement? Why? Asking "why?" at every turn is the key to identifying economic factors, management decisions, competitor actions, etc. that may explain the trend. Most ratios are but red flags or indicators. By themselves, they do not explain why certain things are happening. One must decompose or break down the general ratio into subcomponents to isolate the specific problem area from the ten or so possible factors that might have produced the same movement in the ratio.

The Performance Ratio Review also calculates the arithmetic, mean average for up to five years (or five banks). Averages relate to the middle ground. They do not always represent the ideal, optimum, goal, or where the bank should be. The analyst must establish this criterion, which is another important part of the financial analysis process. From a manager's perspective, ratio standards, ideals, or minimum points are compared to the actual situation in the planning/control cycle. Using ratio analysis in the planning process and later in the review/control process provides the opportunity to perform the full management cycle: the establishment of a standard; decisions needed to achieve the goal; and finally, review, analysis, and the actions needed to get back on course.

F - PROFITABILITY/GROWTH ANALYSIS

This model includes the following ratios and relationships:

```
Profit   Asset   Return  Equity  Return  Retention  Internal
Margin X Utili- =  On   X Multi- =  On   X Rate    = Capital
         zation  Assets  plier   Equity            Genera-
                                                    tion Rate
```

This menu combines three important financial concepts-- profitability, dividend policy, and bank capital -- in a single model. By inputting only five annual data items (previously entered in Menu C) from the financial statements, the model calculates and displays a table and graph of seven ratios for up to five years. The model is an extension of the traditional ROA analysis and, when used in conjunction with Model J, Income Statement as a Percent of Average Assets, provides the opportunity for an extensive decomposition analysis. In the following paragraph, the seven ratios of the model are defined and discussed. Note the connection and relationship of the ratios and especially, the economic factors and management decisions embodied in the ratios. This model is useful not only for historical, after-the-fact financial analysis but also in a financial planning format. Given the stability of ratios into the future (or assuming so) and forecasts of future asset growth, particular components (ratios or amounts) can be forecast. Use your Lotus 1-2-3 capability to generate a forecasting model.

Ratio Definition and Discussion

The following data items used for the ratios in this section were entered and discussed under Menu C. They include:

Data Entry Item	Line
Total Revenue	48+50+52-57
Net Income	67-70-58
Dividends	59
Average Total Equity	46
Average Total Assets	44

The seven ratios in the model are presented below. As each is reviewed, defined, and discussed, note (1) the data components; (2) the decision areas affecting the data components;

and (3) the level of management where decisions regarding the ratio are made.

<u>Profit Margin</u>. The ratio of net income divided by total revenue, the profit or net margin measures the profit per dollar of revenue. For every dollar of bank revenue, what accrues to shareholders after expenses? A decomposition analysis of the profit margin would entail a study of the income statement ledger items divided by total revenue. This is often called a percentage composition, using total revenue as 100 percent. Changes in the margin are revealed by changes in specific expense areas. The profit margin by itself indicates little about profitability or return per dollar invested.

<u>Asset Utilization</u> (AU). The ratio of total revenue divided by total average assets measures the extent to which revenues are generated per dollar of asset investment. Average total assets, rather than ending total assets, are preferred because bank assets tend to vary considerably. Asset utilization times the profit margin equals the return on assets. The average ratio will generally vary with interest rates and with the level of earning assets in the bank. Off-balance-sheet bank services generate more revenue per dollar of assets for the bank. The ratio is a rough gross yield ratio. Decomposing this gross yield would include a study of the yields and yield changes on specific asset categories, such as loans and securities.

<u>Return on Assets</u> (ROA). The ratio of net income divided by total average assets is a traditional bank profitability ratio measuring income per dollar of asset invested. Model J of BFDA provides a decomposition of this ratio and is a useful model for studying the changes in ROA from period to period.

<u>Equity Multiplier</u> (EM). The ratio of total average assets to total average common equity is a measure of the extent of financial leverage in the bank. This ratio is the reciprocal of the classic capital ratio, capital/assets. This ratio reflects a major top management financing decision: the proportion of debt and equity. It serves as a measure of financial risk. The ROA times the EM equals the return on equity (ROE).

<u>Return on Equity</u> (ROE). The ratio of net income to common stockholder's equity is the classic shareholder profitability ratio. The ROE is the product of the profit margin (profit per dollar of revenue) times the asset utilization (revenue-generating ability of assets) times the EM (how the bank is financed). Changes in the ROE may be explained by decomposing and analyzing the three component ratios. One must also consider risk in the analysis of ROA and ROE. Increases in ROE may have come from increased risk taking (loans, leverage) rather than from more efficiency. Separate the source of ROA and ROE into efficiency factors and risk change (assumption) factors in your analysis.

<u>Retention Rate</u> (RR). The ratio of net income retained relative to net income in the period is the RR. It is the complement of the payout ratio, the proportion of net income paid in dividends. The important top management dividend decision is reflected in this ratio. What proportion of net income should be kept for future growth distributed as cash dividends? An analysis of the dividend policy of the bank should include an appraisal of the level and trend of this ratio. Is the level of dividends a function of current period earnings (payout ratio) or are dividends constant, buffering shareholders from short-term variations in earnings? The ROE times the retention rate equals the internal capital generation rate. The RR (dividend policy) changes the "profitability" model into a "capital" model. The ROE is also a capital ratio, measuring the growth of equity capital from income sources. The RR splits the income between dividends paid and the level retained.

<u>Internal Capital Generation Rate</u> (ICGR). The ratio of net income retained in the period relative to common equity measures the growth in bank capital from internal earning sources. The ICGR is a rough measure of the ability of the bank to grow (assets) from internal capital sources without changing its capital/asset or financial leverage ratio. The ICGR is the product of (is affected by) the margin, asset utilization, EM, and the RR. The ability of a bank to fund capital growth from earnings sources is then a function of (1) how much they make per dollar of revenue (margin); (2) how well they generate revenue per dollar of assets (AU); (3) how they finance their bank (EM); and finally, (4) what portion of earnings is kept in the bank.

G   -   VIEW GRAPH (REQUIRES GRAPHIC ABILITY)

The following calculations from the Profitability/Growth Analysis are plotted for up to a five-year period.

```
           Profit Margin          (PM)
           Asset Utilization      (AU)
           Return on Assets       (ROA)
           Equity Multiplier      (EM)
           Return on Equity       (ROE)
           Internal Capital Generation Rate (ICGR)
```

Note the trends and variation in the return on equity and internal capital generation rate. Study the trends and variation in the components of the ROE and ICGR. What factors explain the trends and variation in the ROE and ICGR? Note: The ROA ratio has been multiplied by 10 to enhance its visibility on the screen.

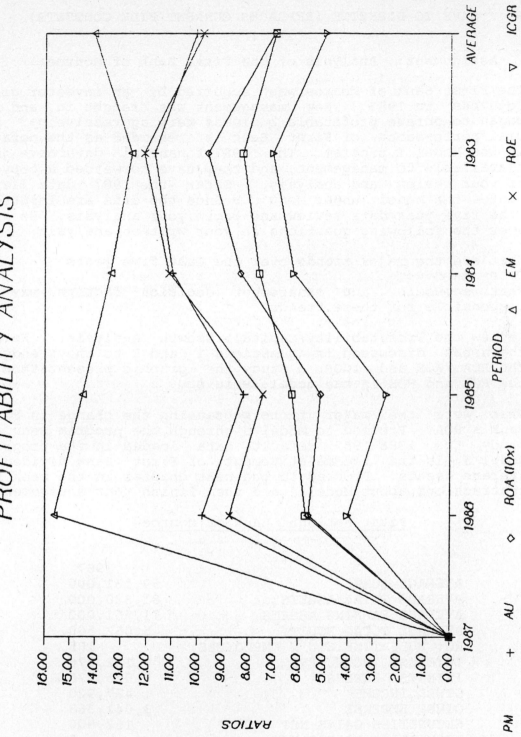

P - PRINT REPORT

S - SAVE TO DISKETTE (REPLACES CURRENT FILE CONTENTS)

Assignment: Analysis of the First Bank of Monroe

The First Bank of Monroe was acquired by an investor group from Columbus in 1983. New management was brought in, and the bank began to pursue profitable business very aggressively. The financial performance of First Bank is recorded as the default data in the Model I program. The 1987 financial data have just become available to management, and they have forwarded a copy to you for your review and analysis. Enter the 1987 data listed below into the model under Menu C. Once the data are inputted, print the five-year data review and begin your analysis. Be sure to answer the following questions in your written analysis:

1. What are the major trends over the last five years?

2. What economic and management decision factors may be responsible for these trends?

3. Review the Profitability/Capital Growth Analysis. Relate the areas discussed in questions 1 and 2 to the trends in the ROA, ROE and ICGR. Study the graphic presentation of the ROA and ROE in the model, Menu G.

4. What were the major factors causing the change in First Bank's ROA? Proceed to Model J through the program menu and study the 1986-1987 default data loaded in the program. Model J is the income statement of First Bank divided by average assets. Proceed to the next chapter in the book for instructions about Model J and then finish your assignment.

First National Bank of Monroe

	1987
AVERAGE LOANS	59,131,000
AVERAGE TOTAL ASSETS	81,320,000
AVERAGE EARNING ASSETS	71,561,000
AVERAGE TOTAL EQUITY	5,082,500
NO. FULL-TIME EQUIV EMPLOYEES	105
INTEREST INCOME-FTE	9,132,276
INTEREST EXPENSE	5,025,576
OTHER INCOME	487,920
OTHER EXPENSE	3,041,368
SECURITIES GAINS-NET **OR**	162,600
SECURITIES LOSSES-NET	0
SALARIES & EMPLOYEES BENEFITS	2,276,000
NET OCCUPANCY-EQUIPMENT EXPENSES	672,480

LOAN LOSS PROVISION	609,900
FULLY TAX EQUIVALENT ADJUSTMENT	642,428
FEDERAL TAX PROVISION	81,320
DIVIDENDS PAID	210,040
NET LOAN CHARGEOFFS	727,400

MODEL I

Data Input Sheet*

1988

Period/Bank

Line

43 AVERAGE LOANS	22,394	19332	16386		
44 AVG TOTAL ASSETS	37025	32567	26652		
45 AVG EARNING ASSETS	34034	29,664	24,832		
46 AVG TOTAL EQUITY	2331	2,095	1,779		
47 NO. EMPLOYEES	14200	12800	12400		
48 INT INCOME-FTE	3405654	2775978	2501947		
49 INT EXPENSE	2,144,457	1670,194	1478483		
50 OTHER INCOME	489884	430807	413514		
51 OTHER EXPENSE	930,609	847,464	794304		
52 SEC GAINS-NET *OR*	26,029	71478	112689		
53 SEC LOSSES-NET					
54 SAL & BENEFITS	472808	437053	403432		
55 NET OCCUP/EQUIP EXP	146649	134458	131723		
56 LOAN LOSS PROVISION	162114	325382	155900		
57 FULLY TAX EQUIV ADJ	94365	125,461	187,569		
58 FED TAX PROV	147300	54,055	72,443		
59 DIVIDENDS PAID	155973	133,127	107,137		
60 NET LOAN CHARGEOFFS	148834	104,388	82,248		

Exc →

T → (by line 51)

reported the item under tax. (by line 57)

on the Δ in S.E. (by line 58)

assest of Loan Loss (by line 59)

*Use the first column for the latest year or highest-numbered
bank. The titles have been abbreviated. See text definitions.

CHAPTER 12

Model J
Income Statement as a
Percent of Average Assets

INTRODUCTION AND CONCEPTS

Model J provides an opportunity to extend the ROA analysis of the previous model (I) via a decomposition analysis of ROA. Changes in ROA (net income/average assets) may be explained by changes in specific income statement areas. The model involves inputting the ledger amounts for two income statements. The model then computes the percentage change, displays the income statement as a percent of total assets, and lists the changes in the ledger accounts as a percent of total assets. Each computed change indicates the ROA impact (positive or negative) of the particular ledger account. The net change of all revenue/expense ledger accounts, of course, represents the change in the ROA of the bank.

APPLICATIONS

This model complements Model I by providing a detailed analysis of the changes in the income statement. Period-to-period review of changes in financial data may be analyzed by (1) dollar change, (2) percentage change, or (3) impact on the return on assets (ROA) of the bank. This model enables the user to input two periods of bank income statements and calculates the percentage change in the ledger accounts from period to period and the impact on ROA. This model provides an alternative method of decomposing ROA and ROA changes. Traditionally ROA is broken down into margin variables and asset utilization variables. This model divides the income statement ledger accounts by average assets and details the income statement as a percent of average assets. Period-to-period changes in ROA are then explained by changes in the specific accounts. The analyst then must explain the reasons for the changes in ROA.

This model is an excellent tool when there are significant changes in ROA from period to period. Was it revenue or expense changes that caused the wide swing in bank ROA? On the other hand, perhaps the bank maintained its ROA from year to year, but application of this model indicates significant changes in the revenue/expense ledger areas. Students are often perplexed when a bank generates five years of consistent ROA. "Nothing's happening!" Analyze your bank with this model and you will see the dramatic changes that took place to generate that stable ROA bottom line.

Menu and Screens   **MENU AND SCREENS**

Model J has the following menus:

A   -   TUTORIAL

B   -   SET INCOME PERIOD DATES TO BE ENTERED

C   -   FINANCIAL DATA ENTRY

D   -   VIEW COMPARATIVE INFORMATION

P   -   PRINT REPORT

S   -   SAVE TO DISKETTE (REPLACES CURRENT FILE CONTENTS)

Q   -   QUIT PROGRAM

A   -   TUTORIAL

The tutorial provides a brief explanation of the program and a walk through of the screens that follow. You will be asked to input (Menu C) two bank income statements and the program will (1) compute the percentage change in each ledger account, (2) present the income statement as a percent of average assets, and, finally, (3) calculate the difference in basis points (1/100th of a percent). The basis point change for each ledger item represents the impact on the ROA (net income/average assets) if the particular ledger item in question were the only item that changed.

B   -   SET INCOME PERIOD DATES TO BE ENTERED

The user has the opportunity to establish a year associated with the latest data entered. If 1987 is entered, the model will compare 1986 and 1987 income statements. If the income periods are not sequential or do not represent a year, enter a 2 in the input and the model will compare period 1 with period 2.

C   -   FINANCIAL DATA ENTRY

The model provides a rather standard bank income statement. Organize and rearrange your bank income statements to fit this standard format. Use the Data Input Sheet provided at the end of this chapter. Make sure that all of the income statement data have been assigned (combined in some cases). Total average assets can be located in the "Average Balance" table in the footnotes of the bank annual report or by averaging year-end (period-end) statements. The macro model will move the cursor down the screen, beginning with the latest period. If an error is made before entering, back spacing will remove the entry. If an error (omission) is entered, return to the top of the screen by the Ctrl-Break, Alt C sequence. As the second column is entered, the percentage change (change in dollars divided by the earliest year base) appears at the right of the screen. Check the totals of the columns entered as you pace down the screen to see if they match those on your Data Input Sheet. If everything has been entered correctly, the net income figure will match your Data Input Sheet figure.

D -   VIEW COMPARATIVE INFORMATION

Once the data have been inputted correctly, the individual screens can be studied. The data entry and percentage change columns are reviewed first, followed by the data items per average assets and the changes. The interpretation of the change in data items per average assets is tricky at first, but read carefully for the next few lines. Below is a partial bank output. Note the basis point changes at the right of the table. Total interest revenue/average assets increased from 9.05 percent to 10.44 percent, an increase of 1.39 percent or 139 basis points. If total interest revenue alone had changed in the period, the ROA would have increased by 139 basis points or 1.39 percent. Most of the increase in net interest revenue came from increases in loan interest and fees of 1.59 percent (higher yields, greater proportions of loans). In this analysis, positive numbers (basis change) represent increases in ROA, while negative numbers represent reductions in ROA. The decline in U.S. Treasury revenue (yield or volume), if considered by itself, would have reduced ROA by 37 basis points between periods 1 and 2.

INCOME STATEMENT AS A PERCENT OF TOTAL AVERAGE ASSETS

	INCOME AS A % OF TOTAL AVG. ASSETS		BASIS CHANGE IMPACT ON ROA
YEARS	2	1	
DAILY AVERAGE ASSETS	100.00%	100.00%	
INTEREST INCOME			
INT & FEES ON LOANS/LEASES	9.45%	7.86%	1.59
INT ON DUE FOR BANKS	0.01%	0.03%	-0.02
INT ON FUNDS SOLD	0.00%	0.02%	-0.02
US TREASURY SECURITIES	0.11%	0.48%	-0.37
US GOV'T AGENCIES	0.34%	0.48%	-0.14
STATE/MUNI SECURITIES	0.44%	0.14%	0.30
OTHER INTEREST INCOME	0.08%	0.03%	0.05
TOTAL INTEREST REVENUE	10.44%	9.05%	1.39

```
INTEREST EXPENSE
   INT ON DEPOSITS            4.49%        4.85%        0.36
   INT ON FUNDS PURCHASED     0.65%        0.35%       -0.30
   INT ON BORROWED FUNDS      0.89%        0.19%       -0.70
   OTHER INTEREST EXPENSE     0.16%        0.13%       -0.03
      T. INTEREST EXPENSES    6.18%        5.52%       -0.66

   NET INTEREST REVENUE       4.26%        3.53%        0.73
```

The positive or negative signs preceding expense items are interpreted the same way. Positive signs (reduction in expense per average assets) represent contributions to ROA, while negative signs (expense increases) represent ROA reductions. The weighted changes are represented in totals such as net interest revenue. Net interest revenue increased by 73 basis points (100 basis points equals 1 percent), the net of 139 to ROA by interest revenue less an ROA reduction from increased interest expense/average assets of 66. If net interest revenue alone were to be considered, the ROA would have increased 73 basis points between periods 1 and 2. The bottom-line net income change, the change in ROA, thus has been decomposed and explained by each revenue/expense item.

P   -   PRINT REPORT

S   -   SAVE TO DISKETTE (REPLACES CURRENT FILE CONTENTS)

Be sure to save before leaving your work station.

SAMPLE PROBLEM/ASSIGNMENTS

In the last chapter, the data for the First National Bank of Monroe were analyzed. You were asked to input 1987 data and study the five-year trend. Between 1986 and 1987, though net income increased, the ROA declined by nine basis points from .56 to .47 percent. What areas and bank decisions/results caused the decline? To speed your analysis, 1986 and 1987 data for First Bank have been entered as the default data in this program. Print (P) the output and write up your analysis, entitled "Factors Affecting ROA, 1986-87; Reasons and Analysis." Include the analysis (why?) along with the factors that affected the ROA.

MODEL J

Data Input Sheet*
Income Statement as Percentage of Average Assets

PERIOD	2	1
AVERAGE ASSETS	37025	32567
INTEREST INCOME		
INT & FEES ON LOANS & LEASES	2300941	1837533
INT ON DUE FOR BANKS	161783	85115
INT ON FUNDS SOLD	42575	25717
US TREASURY SECURITIES	707079	592859
US GOV'T AGENCIES	71830	81734
STATE/MUNICIPAL SECURITIES		
OTHER INTEREST INCOME	4609	3297
TOTAL INTEREST REVENUE	3311789	2650537
INTEREST EXPENSE		
INT ON DEPOSITS	1443418	
INT ON FUNDS PURCHASED		
INT ON BORROWED FUNDS		
OTHER INTEREST EXPENSE		
TOTAL INTEREST EXPENSE		
NET INTEREST REVENUE		
PROVISION FOR LOAN LOSSES		
NET INT INC AFTER PROV		
OTHER INCOME	439884	430807
TRUST INCOME		
SERVICE CHARGE ON DEPOSITS		
TRADING ACCOUNT PROFITS		
OTHER NONINTEREST INCOME		
SECURITIES GAINS (LOSSES)	26029	71478
TOTAL OTHER INCOME		
OTHER EXPENSE		
SALARIES & WAGES		
PENSION & EMPLOYEE BENEFITS		
OCCUPANCY EXPENSE – NET		
FURNITURE & EQUIPMENT		
DEPRECIATION		
OTHER NONINTEREST EXPENSE		
TOTAL OTHER EXPENSE		
INCOME BEFORE INCOME TAXES		
APPLICABLE INCOME TAXES		
NET INCOME		

*Organize and rearrange your data to fit these ledger accounts.

CHAPTER 13

Model K
Bank Performance Analysis

INTRODUCTION AND CONCEPTS

Model K evaluates selected bank financial ratios compared to peer bank data and assigns an overall evaluation similar to a regulatory CAMEL rating. While highlighting the regulatory evaluation process, the model is an elementary but excellent example of how the very subjective process of assigning a bank rating number might be modeled with Lotus 1-2-3. The user assigns subjective numerical levels ranging from "excellent" to "very poor" and then inputs specific bank and peer group data from the Uniform Bank Performance Report with the goal of rating the bank compared to its peers. The UBPR is generated from quarterly call report data and is made available to each bank. The report is public information and provides an excellent data base for bank self-evaluation and planning. In the classroom setting the UBPR provides data for teaching and studying trend and peer group (cross-sectional) financial analysis techniques. A sample UBPR is attached with a class assignment. The professor or seminar leader is encouraged to obtain a variety of UBPRs from banks or from the regulatory agencies. Varied size performance, geographic areas, etc. provide a good sample for class use. See the order form attached to the sample UBPR.

The Uniform Interagency Bank Rating System (CAMEL) was developed by federal banking regulators to monitor bank performance and to identify problem banks as early as possible. The quarterly call reports, filed by each bank, are analyzed and a UBPR is generated. Specific areas reviewed and analyzed from the CAMEL acronym and include:

C   Capital Adequacy
A   Asset Quality
M   Management Quality
E   Earnings Adequacy
L   Liquidity

Based on the appraisal of each of the above areas, the bank is assigned a Performance Evaluation Rating (PER) from 1 (strong) to 5 (unsatisfactory).

PERFORMANCE EVALUATION

The UBPR and PER accompany the examiner team to the bank. After the examination, the PER and examiner evaluation are used to generate an overall Composite Rating with a range from 1 (financially strong) to 5 (high chance of failure). The low-rated banks are closely watched and examined frequently. The high-rated banks are watched with less rigor.

APPLICATION

This model is a simpler version of the regulatory Performance Evaluation Review. It permits the banker or student to input certain UBPR data and then, based on a pre-assigned, subjective rating system, to evaluate the bank in each of four areas and generate an overall performance rating.

The overall performance rating is an average of each of these four areas:

C   Capital Adequacy
A   Asset Quality
E   Earnings Adequacy
L   Liquidity

This model is useful for a variety of teaching/learning assignments:

1.   Case analyses involving financial analysis and accompanying UBPR data.

2.   Study and evaluation of the UBPR and a specific bank UBPR. Both trend and peer group analyses are available.

3.   The model provides a beginning for the development of a self-analysis model for bankers and bank analysts. Though a bank is not operated solely to satisfy regulators, the data generated by the UBPR is very helpful in competitor and peer group financial analysis. It is important to stress that the analysis be made in each quarter, once performance criteria have been set. Is the bank on target toward its goals relative to its peers?

4.   Student analysts are encouraged to study a sample of bank ratios and to evaluate whether a calculated ratio number signifies good or poor performance. See Menu C.

5.   Student analysts are encouraged to explain the possible
      reasons for significant variation in peer group data.
      Different is not always wrong, and many strategies and
      paths can be used to find effective performance.
      Practice with associating financial ratios and changes
      with economic events and decisions is vital training
      for the developing analyst.

MENU AND SCREENS

Model K has the following menus on two screens:

PROGRAM MENU

A	-	TUTORIAL
B	-	BANK NAME, RATING AND CLASSIFICATION FORMAT
C	-	SET RATING INDICATORS
D	-	DATA ENTRY - ASSET QUALITY
E	-	DATA ENTRY - EARNINGS
F	-	DATA ENTRY - LIQUIDITY
G	-	DATA ENTRY - CAPITAL
H	-	RATING SUMMARY
P	-	PRINT REPORT
S	-	SAVE TO DISKETTE (REPLACES CURRENT FILE CONTENTS)
Q	-	QUIT PROGRAM

A   -   TUTORIAL

The tutorial programs provide an overview of the concepts of
the model and enable the user to scroll through the screens.
After reviewing this material, review the other menu areas.

B   -   BANK NAME, RATING AND CLASSIFICATION FORMAT

In Menu B the bank name may be entered or assigned a date
such as 1-1987, which could represent the first quarter of 1987.
A bank would want to identify the time periods and specific
UBPRs. The next item entered represents the proportion (percent)
of the banks (peer group, state total, or national total) that
fall under each rating format. In the program default data, 10
percent of the banks are estimated to have an excellent rating,
whereas 65 percent of the banks of "some total banks" are
categorized in categories 2 and 3. Fifteen percent of the banks
are below standard and 10 percent are labeled very poor. This
input serves as a standard with which a bank's ratio (peer group
percentage) is compared and assigned a rating (Menus C-F). The
proportion of banks in each rating category may not be widely
known, but will likely become common knowledge in the years to
come as ratings data become more and more a part of the domain of
public information. The analyst may also establish rigid (loose)
standards associated with goal performance, such as low (high)
individual percentages in rating categories 5 and 4 (1 and 2) and

thus be ranked high (low) only if the ratio performance is outstanding (very poor). Thus the percentage assignment can include actual peer or total bank ratings proportions or a subjective comparative rating system for comparing and assessing the bank's ratios later on. See the sample screen below.

* * *

BANK NAME: FIRST BANK

BASIS IS DERIVED BY PERCENTAGE ASSIGNED AND WILL BE USED IN LATER ANALYSIS IN EVALUATING THE BANK TO PEER GROUP PERCENTILE RANKINGS. ("VERY POOR" WILL ADJUST FOR TOTAL TO EQUAL 100.00%)
RATING FORMAT

DESCRIPTION	RATING	BASIS	PCT
EXCELLENT	1	10	10.00%
VERY GOOD	2	15	15.00%
ADEQUATE	3	50	50.00%
BELOW STANDARD	4	15	15.00%
VERY POOR	5	10	10.00%
		TOTAL	100.00%

** NOTE ** ENTER "PCT" AS DECIMAL (i.e. .10 IS 10.00%)

* * *

The next screen permits the analyst to establish numerical ranges within the one to five ranking scale. The percentile ranking of a specific bank ratio, compared to its peer group is assigned a number from one to five based on the table discussed above. The mean average of the sum of the individual ratio percentile ratings is the overall rating of the bank. In the table below, the analyst may establish a subjective numbering system which will later place the bank in a category from excellent (rating of one) to very poor (rating of five). As with the assigned percentiles in the above section, the analyst may vary the ratings brackets, but the important thing is to maintain period-to-period consistency.

* * *

RATING CLASSIFICATION BASIS

ENTER BELOW THE RATING RANGES DESIRED IN THE PROGRAM MODEL WHEN THE UPPER RANGE IS ENTERED THE LOWER RANGE WILL BE SET. THESE RANGES SHOULD REPRESENT A SOUND GRADING SYSTEM. IN COMPARING PERIODS THIS SHOULD BE SET AND NOT ALTERED. UPPER RANGE OF 5.000 AND LOWER RANGE OF 0.001 HAVE BEEN PRESET.

RATING	LOWER RANGE	TO	UPPER RANGE
1	0.001		1.000
2	1.001		2.000
3	2.001		3.000
4	3.001		4.000
5	4.001		5.000

* * *

C   -   SET RATING INDICATORS

In a ratio analysis, the analyst usually interprets a specific ratio value on a scale between good and poor. When comparing a specific ratio value to peer group averages, the analyst must make the same subjective interpretation and, depending on the perspective taken, one may judge a below or above average value as good or poor. For example, if the analyst were emphasizing short-term maximization of ROA and ROE as desirable, a high proportion of liquid, marketable securities (liquidity) might be interpreted as detrimental. A low equity capital to assets may be good for maximizing profitability, but is poor from a risk containment, regulatory perspective.

In this section, the analyst has the opportunity to review the ratio interpretation of the authors and, if desired, change the ratio interpretation. In the screen below, the analyst is given three choices: to leave the default interpretation values as is for later use (Y); to review and/or set ratio indicators (N); or to return to the model menu (M).

* * *

RATING INDICATORS SELECTION

THE RATING INDICATORS CONTROL HOW HIGH OR LOW PERCENTILE LEVELS
ARE INTERPRETED.   DEFAULT VALUES MAY BE STUDIED AND CHANGED IF
DESIRED.   BY   SELECTING "Y" INDICATORS ARE RESET TO DEFAULT
VALUES.   BY   SELECTING "N" ONE MAY REVIEW AND/OR CHANGE THE
INDICATOR FOR EACH INDIVIDUAL RATIO.

IN USING THE RATING INDICATORS THE FOLLOWING RULES ARE TO BE
OBSERVED:

1=LOWER RANGE PERCENTILE IS TO BE CONSIDERED BEST (i.e. 0 TO 50)
5=UPPER RANGE PERCENTILE IS TO BE CONSIDERED BEST (i.e. 51 TO 99)

TO RESET DEFAULT VALUES, ENTER Y.
TO REVIEW AND/OR SET RATIO INDICATORS, ENTER N.
TO RETURN TO THE MODEL MENU, ENTER M.

* * *

The bank's ratio values are compared to peer averages and
are assigned a percentile ranking.   Based on the percentile
ranking, the analyst then must determine if a low or high
percentile ranking is good or poor.   In the exercise which
follows, the analyst will assign a ratio interpretation (good or
poor) to a percentile ranking, inputting a one if a percentile
ranking between zero and fifty is considered good and a five if a
percentile ranking between 51 and 99 is considered good.

On the next six screens, the analyst may review and/or
change the interpretation of the thirty-five bank ratios used in
this model. These ratios are defined and discussed in the next
section, and, for the inexperienced analyst, a review of the
ratio definitions is suggested before proceeding.   The default
data ratio interpretations assumes the bank is attempting to
achieve reasonable profitability but, with modest risk
assumption, a general goal with which many bank managers and
regulators can identify.

In the Asset Analysis screen below, the first ratio, total
earning assets, is assigned a value of five, which indicates that
if the ratio percentile ranking is above fifty percent or above
average, the bank performance, based on this ratio, is good. If
the bank loan ratios and loan growth ratio are less than the
fifty percentile level, the ratio is interpreted as better than
if the bank ratio were above the peer average (a percentile over
fifty). If the analyst feels that above average loan proportions
are consistent with favorable bank performance, replace the ones
with fives.   Review all the ratio categories of asset, earnings,

liquidity and capital analyses. If the ratios are not familiar to you, turn to the next section, where the ratios are defined.

* * *

(TO RESTART AT FIRST LINE, DEPRESS "CTRL" & "BREAK", THEN "ALT" AND "N")

PERCENTILE RATING INDICATOR

ENTER 1 IF LOWER RANGE PERCENTILE IS CONSIDERED BEST
(i.e. 0 TO 50)

ENTER 5 IF UPPER RANGE PERCENTILE IS CONSIDERED BEST
(i.e. 51 TO 99)

	INDICATOR	IND. = 1	IND. = 5
ASSET ANALYSIS			
TOTAL EARNING ASSETS	5	2	4
TOTAL LOANS TO AVG ASSETS	1	3	3
COMMERCIAL & INDUSTRIAL LOANS	1	3	3
1 - 4 FAMILY RESIDENTIAL LOANS	1	3	3
LOANS TO INDIVIDUALS	1	3	3
LOAN GROWTH	1	2	4

* * *

The two columns to the right of the ratio indicator represent the calculated ranking of the ratio based on the one or a five entry in the first column. The bank will be assigned a composite overall performance evaluation ranging from a one (excellent) to five (very poor) in the Menu H section.   The composite value is an average of the individual rankings (one to five) assigned each ratio. In the above screen a total earnings assets to total assets ratio above average (50 to 99 percentile) is considered good and was assigned a 5.   Based on the distribution of bank ratings (Menu B), the ratio level (percentile ranking) was assigned a value of four, indicating a below-standard performance.   Changing the "one" or "five" indicator will shift the ratio ranking the opposite way, except when in the mid-range (three).

Review the default indicators assigned by the authors in the table below. Do you agree with each?   Were we consistent? Later, after completing this chapter and software review, redefine an extremely low risk or a high risk, profit maximizing bank and then change the indicators as needed.

* * *

PERCENTILE RATING INDICATOR
ENTER 1 IF LOWER RANGE PERCENTILE IS CONSIDERED BEST
(i.e. 0 TO 50)
ENTER 5 IF UPPER RANGE PERCENTILE IS CONSIDERED BEST
(i.e. 51 TO 99)

	DEFAULT INDICATORS
ASSET ANALYSIS	
TOTAL EARNING ASSETS	5
TOTAL LOANS TO AVG ASSETS	1
COMMERCIAL AND INDUSTRIAL LOANS	1
1 - 4 FAMILY RESIDENTIAL LOANS	1
LOANS TO INDIVIDUALS	1
LOAN GROWTH	1
LOSS RESERVE TO TOTAL LOANS	5
NET LOSSES TO TOTAL LOANS	1
RECOV TO PRIOR PERIOD LOSS	5
EARN COVERAGE OF NET LOSSES (X)	5
LOSS RESERVE X NET LOSSES	5
EARNINGS ANALYSIS	
NET INCOME TO AVG ASSETS	5
NET INCOME TO AVG EQUITY	5
EARNING ASSET YIELD	5
NET INTEREST MARGIN	5
LOAN YIELD	5
INV SECURITY YIELD (TE)	5
RATE: TOTAL INT BEARING DEP	1
NONINTEREST INC TO ASSETS	5
OVERHEAD TO OPERATING INCOME	1

NET OVERHEAD TO OPR INCOME   1

MARGINAL TAX RATE   1

          LIQUIDITY ANALYSIS

VOLATILE LIABILITIES TO ASSETS   1

TEMPORARY INVEST TO ASSETS   5

VOLATILE LIAB. DEPENDENCE   1

CORE DEPOSIT GROWTH   5
SECURITY APPREC. (DEPREC.)
     TO PRIMARY CAPITAL   5
NET ASSETS REPRICEABLE
     1 YR TO ASSETS   1

NET LOANS TO ASSETS   1

NET LOANS TO DEPOSITS   1

          CAPITAL ANALYSIS

EQUITY CAPITAL TO ASSETS   5

PRIMARY CAPITAL TO ASSETS   5

PRIMARY + SEC CAP TO ASSETS   5

RETAINED EARNINGS TO EQUITY   5

CASH DIVIDENDS TO NET INCOME   1

* * *

D-G DATA ENTRY -- ASSET QUALITY (D), EARNINGS (E), LIQUIDITY (F), AND CAPITAL (G).

Menus D, E, F, and G include data entry for asset quality, earnings, liquidity, and capital. Under each category, several ratios have been randomly selected from the UBPR located in Appendix B. In each section the ratios are listed and defined, using the UBPR User's Guide, available when ordering UBPRs.

The analyst is asked to input three UBPR values for each ratio: (1) the bank ratio value, (2) the peer group ratio value, and, finally, (3) the percentile level of the bank ratio value compared to the peer group. The model calculates the absolute bank/peer group variance in basis points and assigns a percentile rating based on the inputted proportions under Menu B. The UBPR peer group ratio is an adjusted mean value found by averaging the ratio values of all banks, with the exception of extreme values.

The percentile value associated with the bank's ratio refers to where the bank ratio falls compared to the peer group. A value of 90 percent indicates that 10 percent of the peer group banks have values above (below for expense ratios) and 90 percent are below the bank's ratio value. A 50 percentile ratio value should equal the mean of the peer group.

The bank/peer variance is computed by subtracting the peer ratio value from the bank ratio value. A positive sign (no sign) means that the bank ratio value is above the peer value; a negative sign indicates that the bank value is below the peer value. The analyst must then relate "good" or "bad" depending on the type of ratio. See Menu C.

The percentile rating of 1, 2, 3, 4, or 5 is based upon the percentiles inputted under Menu B above and the bank ratio percentile taken from the UBPR (second variable entered). The two values are compared and a rating is assigned. If the ratio percentile ranking is equal to or less than the cumulative basis (Menu B), the appropriate rating is assigned. Move the cursor to the percentile rating cell with the arrow key and study the formula at the top of the screen. The arithmetic average of the percentile ratings is later listed in Menu G, Rating Summary, and is averaged with the average values of Earnings, Liquidity and Capital to determining an overall composite value.

The ratios used in this model are listed and defined below. The list does not include all the ratios in the UBPR, only those selected by the authors.

<u>Asset Analysis</u>: An analysis of loan quality and asset structure.

Total Earning Assets -- average earning assets divided by average total assets.

Total Loans to Average Assets -- total average loans net of unearned income divided by average total assets.

Commercial and Industrial Loans -- a loan mix ratio of average commercial and industrial loans divided by total average gross loans and lease financing receivables.

1-4 Family Residential Loan -- a loan mix ratio of average loans secured by one-to-four-family real estate loans divided by average gross loans and lease financing receivables.

Loans to Individuals -- a loan mix ratio of average personal loans to individuals divided by average gross loans.

Loan Growth -- annualized change in net loans and leases.

Loss Reserve to Total Loans -- ending period allowance or reserve for loan losses divided by total loans and leases.

Net Losses to Total Loans -- gross loan and lease charge-offs, less gross recoveries divided by average total loans and leases.

Recoveries to Prior Period Losses -- gross loan recoveries in current year divided by gross loan charge offs of the preceding year.

Earnings Coverage of Net Losses X -- net operating income before taxes, security gains, extraordinary items, and provision for loan losses divided by net loan and lease losses (net charge offs). X indicates "times". Enter X ratios as whole numbers.

Loss Reserve to Net Losses X -- ending period allowance or reserves for loan losses divided by net loan losses (net charge offs). Measures times (X) coverage.

Earnings Analysis

Return on Assets -- net income divided by average assets.

Return on Equity -- net income divided by average total equity capital (may appear as a capital ratio in UBPR).

Earning Asset Yield -- interest income (TE) as a percent of average earning assets.

Net Interest Margin -- net interest income (TE) divided by average total assets. TE refers to a tax equivalent basis.

Loan Yield -- interest and fees on loans and income on direct lease receivables (TE) divided by average total loans and leases, net of unearned income.

Investment Security Yield (TE) -- total investment security interest divided by total investment securities outstanding (book).

Rate: Interest Bearing Deposits -- total deposit interest divided by total interest-bearing deposits.

Noninterest Income to Assets -- total noninterest revenue divided by average total assets.

Overhead to Operating Income -- personnel, occupancy and other expenses divided by net interest income (TE) plus total noninterest income (total revenue).

Net Overhead to Operating Income -- overhead less noninterest revenue divided by the sum of net interest income (TE) and noninterest income (total revenue).

Marginal Tax Rate -- provision for income taxes plus tax equivalent adjustment on tax exempt securities divided by pre-tax income, including TE adjustment.

Liquidity Analysis

Volatile Liabilities to Assets -- large time deposits and purchased funds divided by average assets.

Temporary Investments to Assets -- sum of interest-bearing due froms, federal funds sold, securities purchased under agreements to resell, trading-account assets and debt securities repriceable in one-year divided by total assets.

Volatile Liability Dependence -- volatile liabilities (above), less temporary investments, divided by sum of net loans, leases and investment securtiies with maturities over one year.

Core Deposit Growth -- annual change in the sum of demand, savings deposits and time deposits less than $100,000.

Security Appreciation (Depreciation) to Primary Capital-- difference between book and market value of investment securities divided by primary capital.

Net Assets Repriceable 1 Year to Assets -- assets less liabilities repriceable in one year divided by average interest bearing assets.

Net Loans to Assets -- average net loans to average total assets.

Net Loans/Deposits -- total loans and leases, net of unearned income to total deposits.

Capital Analysis

Equity Capital to Assets -- total common stock, surplus, undivided profits, capital reserves and perpetual preferred stock divided by total assets.

Primary Capital to Assets -- the sum of common equity, loan and lease loss reserves, permanent and convertible preferred and mandatory convertible debt securities to total assets.

Total Primary and Secondary Capital to Assets -- the sum of primary and secondary capital to total assets. Sometimes called total capital.

Retained Earnings to Total Equity -- net income less dividends divided by total equity. The capital formation rate or internal capital generation rate.

Cash Dividends to Net Income -- the payout ratio of cash dividends to net income.

Menu G provides a rating summary for each of the four ratio categories and a final composite rating for the bank. The summary rating of each ratio category is simply the arithmetic average (mean) of each of the ratio ratings. The analyst is able to review the relatively strong/weak ratio areas of the bank, followed by the overall rating, again an average of the asset, earnings, liquidity, and capital areas.

P   -   PRINT REPORT

Entering P prints your report which includes the name of your bank indicator settings, peer group percentile ratings, all ratio values and ratings, and a summary review.

S   -   SAVE TO DISKETTE (REPLACES CURRENT FILE CONTENTS)

MODEL K
Data Input Sheet
Bank Performance Analysis

ASSET ANALYSIS	BANK RATIO	PEER RATIO	PERCENTILE PCT
TOTAL EARNING ASSETS			
TOTAL LOANS TO AVG ASSETS			
COMMERCIAL & INDUSTRIAL LOANS			
1-4 FAMILY RESIDENTIAL LOAN			
LOANS TO INDIVIDUALS			
LOAN GROWTH			
LOSS RESERVE TO TOTAL LOANS			
NET LOSSES TO TOTAL LOANS			
RECOV TO PRIOR PERIOD LOSS			
EARN COVERAGE NET LOSSES X			
LOSS RESERVE TO NET LOSSES X			

EARNINGS ANALYSIS	BANK	PEER	PCT
NET INCOME TO AVG. ASSETS			
NET INCOME TO AVG. EQUITY			
EARNING ASSETS YIELD			
NET INTEREST MARGIN			
LOAN YIELD			
INV. SECURITY YIELD (TE)			
RATE: T. INT. BEARING DEP.			
NONINTEREST INC TO ASSETS			
OVERHEAD TO OPERATING INCOME			
NET OVERHEAD TO OPR INCOME			
MARGINAL TAX RATE			

LIQUIDITY ANALYSIS	BANK	PEER	PCT
VOLATILE LIAB. TO ASSETS			
TEMPORARY INVEST TO ASSETS			
VOLATILE LIAB. DEPENDENCE			
CORE DEPOSIT GROWTH			
SECURITY APPREC. (DEPREC.) TO PRIMARY CAPITAL			
NET ASSETS REPRICEABLE 1 YR TO ASSETS			
NET LOANS TO ASSETS			
NET LOANS TO DEPOSITS			

CAPITAL ANALYSIS	BANK	PEER	PCT
EQUITY CAPITAL TO ASSETS	_____	_____	_____
PRIMARY CAPITAL TO ASSETS	_____	_____	_____
T. PRIM & SEC CAP/ASSETS	_____	_____	_____
RETAINED EARNINGS TO EQUITY	_____	_____	_____
CASH DIV/NET INCOME	_____	_____	_____

SAMPLE PROBLEMS/ASSIGNMENTS

1. First Bank is a $115 million (assets) midwestern bank in a small suburban community. The 1987 UBPR data have been entered as your default data on diskette B. The peers of First Bank are nonmetropolitan banks with $100-300 million in assets and three or more banking offices. The peer group is estimated to have ratings similar to those entered under Menu B. Print the Bank Performance Analysis and analyze the ratios in each area. Identify the "red flags" or "outlier" ratios (extreme values compared to those of peers) and develop two or three possible economic or decision explanations for the variation. Remember: different does not always mean wrong or bad. Write up your analysis of this bank and be prepared to discuss your findings in class.

2. Two years ago the ROA of First Bank was .92 percent compared to .66 percent in 1987. Input the 1985 First Bank data into your model (leave the ratings proportion, Menu B, and indicators, Menu C, as is) and note (1) the relative position of First Bank compared to its peers in 1985 and (2) the major changes and possible factors affecting earnings between 1985 and 1987. Remember: the program default data are the 1987 data. Use another diskette (make a copy) or print the 1987 report before inputting the 1985 data.

Data Input Sheet
First Bank, 1985

ASSET ANALYSIS	BANK RATIO	PEER RATIO	PERCENTILE PCT
TOTAL EARNING ASSETS	90.46	90.70	41
TOTAL LOANS TO AVG. ASSETS	59.84	52.11	75
COMMERCIAL & INDUSTRIAL LOANS	17.98	20.95	44
1-4 FAMILY RESIDENTIAL LOAN	22.24	24.13	47
LOANS TO INDIVIDUALS	38.22	23.99	87
LOAN GROWTH	24.71	12.85	84
LOSS RESERVE TO TOTAL LOANS	.82	1.02	26
NET LOSSES TO TOTAL LOANS	.23	.61	30
RECOV TO PRIOR PERIOD LOSS	25.43	27.36	57
EARN COVERAGE/NET LOSSES X	9.10	9.97	60
LOSS RESERVE TO NET LOSSES X	4.13	3.18	69

EARNINGS ANALYSIS	BANK	PEER	PCT
NET INCOME TO AVG. ASSETS	0.92	1.00	42
NET INCOME TO AVG. EQUITY	11.42	12.20	39
EARNING ASSETS YIELD	12.64	12.51	59
NET INTEREST MARGIN	5.02	4.95	59
LOAN YIELD	13.60	13.09	73
INV. SECURITY YIELD (TE)	11.16	11.70	73
RATE: INT BEAR DEPOSITS	9.10	9.03	55
NONINTEREST INC TO T. ASSETS	1.10	.61	92
OVERHEAD TO OPERATING INCOME	69.85	57.74	85
NET OVERHEAD TO OPR INCOME	50.52	45.88	70
MARGINAL TAX RATE	39.72	45.19	11

LIQUIDITY ANALYSIS	BANK	PEER	PCT
VOLATILE LIAB. TO ASSETS	14.99	9.37	81
TEMPORARY INVEST TO ASSETS	12.00	17.68	25
VOLATILE LIAB. DEPENDENCE	3.77	-12.55	85
CORE DEPOSIT GROWTH	15.10	7.14	87
SECURITY APPREC. (DEPREC.) TO PRIMARY CAPITAL	-11.49	-3.64	17
NET ASSETS REPRICEABLE 1 YR TO ASSETS	-9.59	-6.96	40
NET LOANS TO ASSETS	63.97	52.17	87
NET LOANS TO DEPOSITS	73.64	58.55	90

CAPITAL ANALYSIS	BANK	PEER	PCT
EQUITY CAPITAL TO ASSETS	7.76	7.98	49
PRIMARY CAPITAL TO ASSETS	8.50	8.65	51
T. PRIM & SEC CAP/ASSETS	8.50	8.74	49
RETAINED EARNINGS TO EQUITY	8.65	6.87	57
CASH DIV/NET INCOME	24.26	37.06	32

CHAPTER 14

Model L
Loan Loss Reserve Analysis

INTRODUCTION AND CONCEPTS

This model illustrates a procedure for determining the adequacy of the loan loss reserve associated with a loan portfolio. Investors, analysts, and regulators are always concerned about the "sufficiency" or "adequacy" of the loan loss reserve, and today, more than ever, they are concerned with the procedures, timeliness, and consistency of the loan review and "reserve determination" process. In larger banks, timeliness and consistency depend upon effective software and adequate training, especially if the loan review is delegated to the loan officer. There is no doubt that this area is one of the subjective "soft spots" in an earnings analysis of a credit institution. Increasing or decreasing the provision for loan loss expense has had a tremendous impact on bank net earnings in the last few years. The external analyst is concerned with a consistent loan review process; bank managers are interested in being consistent and maintaining credibility with the investing public and regulators. In the following paragraphs, the conceptual framework of the loan loss reserve is discussed, followed by a description of the model and how it can best be used to understand this important aspect of credit management and bank financial accounting.

The "reserving" process, in contrast to the "when realized" method, evolved with financial accounting from "cash basis" to "accrual basis" accounting. A cash basis recognition of a loan loss at the time of the charge-off involved a debit to bad debt expense and a write-off or reduction in (credit) the loan portfolio. The loan portfolio, of which some loans will probably default, generates interest income in all periods, good and bad economically. Charge-offs, however, are more likely to occur in recessions or troubled times. Earnings tend to be overstated in good times and understated in bad ones. Earnings fluctuate considerably, something a credit institution with depositors does not like to report. Defenders of cash basis, loan loss accounting argue that there are good times and bad times and that the earnings will reflect the change in value of the assets. It is assumed that the charge-offs policy of the institution is consistent over the business cycle, which was possibly an illusion in a troubled year.

The accrual process attempts to match reported accounting income with true economic income or changes in shareholders' wealth: income when earned, expenses when incurred. In the loan loss reserve process, credit losses are allocated (matched) to the revenue-generating periods of the loan portfolio -- in both good times and bad. The driving force behind the reserve method is the adequacy or sufficiency of the loan loss reserve. In any balance sheet (at any point in time), the credit portfolio is adjusted (reduced) by the amount of expected loan losses, called the reserve for loan losses, allowance for credit losses and many other names. The asset adjustment, of course, flows through the income statement, with a noncash provision for loan loss expense (debit) and a credit to the reserve for loan losses.

The amount of the periodic provision expense is dependent upon the changes needed in the loan loss reserve (expected future losses). As the size of the loan portfolio grows, as economic conditions change and/or as actual write-offs are made, management must constantly review the sufficiency of the loan loss reserve and make adjustments (provision for loan loss) as needed. The net loans (gross loans less reserve for loan losses) should reflect the amount of collectable principal at any point in time. When a loan is charged off, based on a preset policy, the loan is removed (credited) from the portfolio and the reserve for loan losses is "charged" (debited). If write-offs are sudden and/or significant, the reserve may need to be replenished with an additional amount of expense provision in the period. Note: the reserve is not a cash account. It represents a write-down (valuation adjustment) of the loan portfolio based on the current assessment of management. On the other side of the balance sheet, equity is written down (expensed) through the noncash provision for loan losses in the income statement.

Bank managers and credit officers are the best judges of the collectability of loans outstanding. A consistent, periodic review of the loan portfolio and fine tuning of the loan loss reserve are necessary to prevent large, surprise adjustments (provision) to earnings. The current and expected economic conditions, past experience, peer bank experience, pending charge-offs, expected recoveries, past-due and nonperforming (nonaccrual) loans and other factors should be reviewed and analyzed on a consistent, timely basis.

In each period, the reserve for loan losses in a period of time is affected by the following variables:

* * *

RESERVE FOR LOAN LOSSES, BEGINNING OF PERIOD

+   PROVISION FOR LOAN LOSSES

=   RESERVE AVAILABLE FOR LOSSES

−   NET LOAN CHARGE-OFFS

      −   LOANS CHARGED OFF

      +   LOAN RECOVERIES

=   RESERVE FOR LOAN LOSSES, END OF PERIOD

* * *

Additions to the loan loss reserve contra-asset account in any period are made with a debit to the expense provision and a credit to the reserve, leaving a reserve available for losses. Net loan charge-offs, loan charge-offs less recoveries for the period, are deducted, leaving the end-of-period reserve balance. While charge-offs represent a reduction (debit) to the loan loss reserve and loan portfolio (credit), recovered cash or assets (collateral) (debit) increase the loan loss reserve (credit). When a loan is charged off (credited), accrued uncollected interest revenue (current-period portion) is deducted (debited) from interest revenue. Any prior-period (year-end) accrued but uncollected interest is charged off (debit to the reserve account), similar to the principal amount of the loan.

The purpose of this model and of the text which follows is to provide a tutorial on how this very subjective loan loss reserve process can be approached in a variety of ways. The end product, a sufficient level of loan loss reserves, is a number. The PC combined with LOTUS 1-2-3 is an effective number-crunching tool. This model, in this academic context, provides a means to teach concepts. An operational model for managers and bank examiners may be more detailed, but the authors feel that the loan loss reserve analysis should be more than one-dimensional. A multidimensional review of the loan portfolio, including historic loss trends, peer bank loss levels, and bank reserve policy levels, should be incorporated into this very difficult, subjective analysis. Discussion of the model, screens and assumptions follows.

* * *

Table 1
ACCOUNTING FOR LOAN LOSSES

CASH BASIS:

       INCOME PERIOD CONSIDERATION: LOAN LOSS EXPENSE (DR)
                                             WHEN LOAN IS CHARGED OFF

       LOAN CHARGE OFF: LOAN LOSS EXPENSE (DR)
                        LOANS (CR)

ACCRUAL BASIS:

       INCOME PERIOD CONSIDERATION: PROVISION FOR LOAN LOSS
                                           (EXPENSE) (DR)
                                         RESERVE FOR LOAN LOSSES
                                       (CR)

       LOAN CHARGE OFF: RESERVE FOR LOAN LOSSES (DR)
                        LOAN (CR)

* * *

APPLICATIONS

This model provides an organizational framework in which to study a variety of methods used today to determine an adequate loan loss reserve for any credit portfolio.   The model is designed as a tutorial, but its multidimensional approach could easily be expanded into a full operational model. An effective reserve analysis should include (1) a thorough review of the collectability of the loan portfolio, tempered by an overview of the national, regional and economic climates; (2) an analysis of historic loan loss activity; (3) a review of management's policy level of loss reserves/loans (minimum); and (4) peer group experience.

MENU AND SCREENS

The menu for Model L is listed below, followed by a specific description, definitions and sample screens of the various menus.

* * *

```
A    -    TUTORIAL
B    -    SET REPORT DATE AND MINIMUM DETAILED LOAN
          LEVEL
C    -    SET CURRENT PERFORMANCE MEASUREMENT METHOD
D    -    ENTER PROJECTED CHARGE-OFFS
E    -    ENTER PROJECTED RECOVERIES
F    -    ENTER DETAILED LARGE-RISK LINES
G    -    ENTER GENERAL LOAN DATA
H    -    REVIEW SUMMARY
P    -    PRINT REPORT
S    -    SAVE TO DISKETTE (REPLACES CURRENT FILE
          CONTENTS)
Q    -    QUIT PROGRAM
```

* * *

A   -   TUTORIAL

The tutorial provides a brief overview of the model, including sample screens. Review the tutorial, and then review the rest of the menu and the textbook. No data may be entered in the tutorial.

B   -   SET REPORT DATE AND MINIMUM DETAILED LOAN LEVEL

Two necessary variables are imputted from this menu. First, the report date is entered by depressing the "F2" edit key, backspacing (erasing the default date), and entering the new date in the sequence day, month, and year. Later, under Menu F, list the names and amounts of loans which are now judged to be significantly more risky than others and the amount of probable loss that might occur. Here one is able to set a minimum level of loan amount at risk. Any amounts in excess of the amount inputted here will be included in total loans at risk. Loan risk amounts below the minimum, while listed for reporting and analyses, are not included in the total loans at risk. Here one is able to set a dollar level of "significance" in the model.

* * *

DEPRESS "F2" KEY TO EDIT TO DESIRED REPORT DATE: 30-Jun-87
                    ENTER AS (YEAR,MONTH,DAY)

MINIMUM BALANCE TO BE USED IN DETAILED RISK LINES: 25,000

* * *

C   -   SET CURRENT PERFORMANCE MEASUREMENT METHOD

In this model, one aspect of the analysis of the loan loss reserve involves a peer group comparison, or a comparison of the bank with the experience of banks of similar size. In this menu section, one is able to choose one of two ratios which is later used as part of the loan loss reserve analysis. The choice involves selecting a current level ratio that best estimates the level of future loan losses. Two ratios from the Uniform Bank Performance Report, representing different approaches, are available. Which ratio makes a better peer group comparison and is a better predictor of future loan losses? Are future loan losses best estimated by a measure of the recent past level of nonperforming loans (past due, etc.) or by the recent actual net charge-offs? The first involves an identification and analysis of current troubled loans; the second establishes a level of expected net losses based on recent loss experience. Below is the first screen of Menu C, from which one must select either the nonperforming loan ratio (NP) or net charge-offs ratio (CO).

* * *

CURRENT PERFORMANCE ADJUSTMENT
DETERMINING LOAN RESERVE ADEQUACY SHOULD INCLUDE AN ADJUSTMENT FOR CURRENT ECONOMIC CONDITIONS IN THE INSTITUTIONS MARKET AREA AND GENERAL ECONOMIC CONDITIONS. THESE MAY AFFECT FUTURE CHARGES TO THE RESERVE BALANCE. TWO ALTERNATIVES ARE PROVIDED IN THE PROGRAM. REVIEW THESE ALTERNATIVES AND SELECT THE METHOD THAT BEST MEETS THE REQUIRED OBJECTIVES. DETERMINE WHICH BEST MEASURES CONDITIONS SUCH AS UNEMPLOYMENT LEVELS, POOR BUSINESS CONDITIONS, INDUSTRY WEAKNESSES AND OTHER SIMILAR ECONOMIC INDICATORS.

N - NONPERFORMING LOANS MEASURES THE LAST REGULATORY REPORTING PERIOD OF PAST DUE, NONACCRUAL AND RENEGOTIATED LOANS AS COMPARED TO PEER GROUP DATA.

C - NET CHARGE-OFFS TO AVERAGE TOTAL LOANS MEASURES THE LAST REGULATORY REPORTING PERIOD OF NET CHARGE-OFFS AS COMPARED TO PEER GROUP DATA.

ENTER LETTERS FOR METHOD.

* * *

Nonperforming Loans to Average Total Loans Option. This ratio assumes that the level of loan loss reserves needed for the future can best be assessed by a review of current troubled loans.

The analyst is asked to input all past due, nonaccrual and renegotiated loan amounts, classified, in this case, by general type of loan. One could further differentiate by term or maturity, geographic location/industry, etc. Past due loans represent contract amounts that are currently not paid as agreed: from 1 day late on an interest and/or principal payment up to the point of nonaccrual status, either 90 days or less as defined by management. Nonaccrual status loans represent contract amounts with past due interest exceeding a specific time period. Regulators generally require that a loan with interest receivable greater than 90 days be removed from the normal interest accrual and be placed on a "cash," when received, income basis. Management policy may specify less than the 90 days noted above. The timely removal of late-payment loans from the accrual system leaves a level of revenue accrual that closely matches the cash revenue received. Repayment of past due interest will provide the basis for returning (reinstating) the loan to the accrual system.

Renegotiated loans represent contract totals whose terms have been altered in the past in favor of the customer. Lowering the rate below market rates, extending the term beyond the original maturity, and other adjustments constitute renegotiated loans. In the screen below, enter the amounts that relate to the specific categories.

* * *

PAST DUE, NONACCRUAL, AND RENEGOTIATED LOANS

COMMERCIAL	800,000
REAL ESTATE	1,500,000
CONSUMER	250,000
CREDIT CARD	75,000
TOTAL	2,625,000

NONPERFORMING LOAN REFERENCE LEVEL: 2.250%
NONPERFORMING LOAN/TOTAL LOANS: 2.625%
A SOURCE FOR DETERMINING THE REFERENCE LEVEL COULD BE THE UNIFORM BANK PERFORMANCE REPORTS PROVIDED BY REGULATORY AGENCIES.

* * *

The total past due, nonaccrual and renegotiated loans, also called nonperforming loans, are then totaled, Below the total one is able to input a peer group reference ratio, used later in the model. One aspect of the loan review is comparing the bank's ratios with those of other similar banks, perhaps from the Uniform Bank Performance Report (UBPR). The UBPR is a summary ratio analysis of prior call report information prepared by the specific regulator for the senior management of every bank. In the above case, the reference group average of nonperforming loans/total gross loans less unearned income of 2.25% is less than the bank's ratio of $2.625 million in nonperforming loans to a total of 2.625%. On a $100 million loan portfolio the bank would have approximately 2.625% - 2.25% = .375% x $100 million = $375,000 more in nonperforming loans than the peer average. One may wish to enter a goal level or a competitor bank level of nonperforming loans/total loans for comparison purposes.

     Net Losses to Average Total Loans Option. One may select an alternative peer group comparison for inclusion in the comprehensive loan loss reserve analysis (printed report). Instead of using the nonperforming loans/total ratio, one may wish to use the recent net loan charge-offs ratio. In the screen below, the peer group net losses/total from the latest UBPR is .73% compared to the recent bank level of 1.74%. The model will later consider this higher "experience" as a variable in determining the adequate level of current reserves for future charge-offs. If the experience of the bank has been higher than average, it may well need higher levels of loan loss reserves/total loans than its peers.

                              * * *

CURRENT PERFORMANCE - NET LOSSES TO AVERAGE TOTAL LOANS OPTION

        NET LOSSES (NET CHARGE-OFFS) TO AVERAGE LOANS DATA
     ENTER AS DECIMALS (e.g. .72% as . 0072)

NET LOSSES TO AVERAGE TOTAL LOANS REFERENCE LEVEL: 0.72%

   NET LOSSES TO AVERAGE TOTAL LOANS ACTUAL LEVEL: 1.74%

     A SOURCE FOR DETERMINING THE REFERENCE LEVEL COULD BE THE UNIFORM BANK PERFORMANCE REPORTS PROVIDED BY REGULATORY AGENCIES.

                            * * *

D   -   ENTER PROJECTED CHARGE-OFFS

     The projected or pending charge-offs are listed under Menu D. An important aspect of determining the adequacy of the loan loss reserve involves a review of the current loan portfolio, especially loans that may soon be charged off. In an operational program, the loans may be classified by geographic region, industry, size, or any other meaningful classification.

* * *

PENDING CHARGE-OFFS

		LOSS	BALANCE
1	ABC CORPORATION	100,000	100,000
2			
3			
4			
5			
6			
7			
8			
9			
10			
	TOTAL	100,000	100,000

* * *

One has the opportunity to list the name of the borrower, the loan balance outstanding and the expected loss. The estimated loss balance may include accrued interest income and may be either higher than the loan principal balance or lower if collateral is involved. If the bank is holding title (securities or autos) or has a specific mortgage (real estate) or lien on specific assets (inventories or accounts receivable), one must estimate the minimum value, net of expenses, to be recovered and deduct it from the loan balance to determine the expected loss. When a loan is charged off, the reserve for loan loss is reduced (debited) and the loan is removed (credited) from the portfolio.

E - ENTER PROJECTED RECOVERIES

Once a loan is charged off, the legal recovery processes continue. In this section pending recoveries of loans previously charged off are listed, along with recovery estimates.

* * *

PENDING RECOVERIES

1	ABC CORPORATION	10,000
2		
3		
4		
5		
6		
7		
8		
9		
10		
	TOTAL	10,000

* * *

Expected recoveries will increase the loan loss reserve, with an increase in cash or specific assets (debit) and a credit to the reserve for loan losses.

F - ENTER DETAILED LARGE-RISK LINES

The loan review should identify loans that originally had or now have above-average risk. Both the loan balance and the amount at risk should be identified. Unsecured loans, such as those of Last Try Corporation below, or weakly collateralized loans, such as those of No-Luck Company, are listed in this section. Changing economic conditions, such as a decline in commodity prices (agricultural or oil), may impact specific industries and customers at various times. A later review may find these loans as pending or actual charge-offs if conditions get worse. If economic conditions improve, these loans may be removed from the higher-risk category and may again become part of the general loan portfolio.

* * *

DETAILED RISK LINES (UNSECURED RISK IN PROBLEM
LOANS OR LINES CONTAINING RISK ABOVE THE ESTABLISHED
MINIMUM DETAILED LEVEL):   25,000

	ACCOUNT NAME	RISK AMOUNT	LOAN BALANCE
1	NO-LUCK COMPANY	150,000	400,000
2	JOHN Q. CUSTOMER	30,000	50,000
3	LAST TRY CORPORATION	300,000	300,000
4			
5			
6			
7			
8			
9			
10			
	TOTAL	480,000	750,000

* * *

In the sample screen above, the bank has identified three customers with loans totaling $750,000 that are now in the high-risk category, all above the $25,000 minimum amount set under Menu B. Currently the bank has a loss exposure (unsecured or undercollateralized) of $470,000.

G - ENTER GENERAL LOAN DATA

Several important variables are inputted under this menu. A sample screen is presented below, followed by a review of the inputs. Each of the variables below has been assigned a number and is discussed.

* * *

DATA ENTRY

```
1   CURRENT YEAR (SET FIRST TIME USED FOR YEAR ONLY):        1987
2                   BANK MINIMUM RESERVE/LOANS (%):          1.00%

3   CURRENT BALANCES FOR THE FOLLOWING:   TOTAL LOANS   100,000,000

4                               BANKERS ACCEPTANCES      2,500,000
                            FEDERAL FUNDS SOLD-TERM       2,500,000

5               VALUATION RESERVE FOR LOAN LOSSES         1,000,000
6   PROPOSED ADDITIONS (PROVISIONS FOR LOAN LOSSES):         70,000

7   EXPERIENCE PERCENTAGES OF NET CHARGE-OFFS TO TOTAL LOANS:
                                         1986              0.30%
                                         1985              0.40%
                                         1984              0.50%
                                         1983              0.45%
                                         1982              0.40%
```

* * *

1. Current Year -- used in the model to establish the 5 previous years below under item 7.

2. Bank Minimum Reserve/Loans (%) -- enter the minimally acceptable proportion of gross loans that management feels should be a minimum reserve level. This is a general, nonspecific method for determining the amount of loan loss reserve. The authors call the figure a minimum for later comparison of reserve levels determined by another process.

3. Current Loan Balances -- enter the total gross loans net of unearned income at the time of the loan loss reserve analysis. This figure represents the total principal outstanding.

4. Enter the amount of nonreservable loans or the highest-quality loans such as banker's acceptances issued by money center and large regional banks, and federal funds sold, the balances loaned to other banks. This adjustment reduces total loans in item 3 to "loan principal outstanding at risk."

5. Valuation Reserve for Loan Losses -- the current amount of the bank's loan loss reserve. This amount will later be compared to the needs determined in a variety of ways.

6. Proposed Additions to the reserve or the amount of the expected or proposed expense provision for loan losses. The first iteration may be based on a targeted reserve level or

historic expense provisions, or may be left blank to see what total the model later recommends. The analyst should return to this input position for adjustments or inputting after a needs assessment has been made. Note: the adequate loan loss reserve level is the goal of this model; the provision for loan loss adjustments is made to bring the reserve to the desired level.

7. Experience Percentages of Net Charge-Offs to Total Loans for the last 5 years, quarters or periods. The dates are established by the first line inputted above. The actual charge-offs/total gross loans are then inputted. These historical data, if extrapolated into the future, are another way to define expected net losses, desired loan loss reserve levels, and the provision expense needed in the period. These actual write-off data are used later in the printed report to compute a minimum average, an expected charge-off amount, an input in determining the amount of loss reserves needed, or the calculated loss exposure of the bank.

H   -   REVIEW SUMMARY

A brief summary review of the expected reserve levels compared to that needed is provided in the screen below.

* * *

ADEQUACY EVALUATION

COMPARISON OF PROJECTED RESERVE BALANCE	980,000
TO	
CALCULATED BANK MINIMUM RESERVE BALANCE (POLICY)	950,000
EXCESS (DEFICIENCY) TO POLICY	30,000
COMPARISON OF PROJECTED RESERVE BALANCE	980,000
TO	
CALCULATED EXPOSURE: NONPERFORMING LOAN OPTION (N)	930,351
EXCESS (DEFICIENCY)	49,649
COMPARISON OF PROJECTED RESERVE BALANCE	980,000
TO	
CALCULATED EXPOSURE: NET CHARGE-OFFS OPTION (C)	1,412,870
EXCESS (DEFICIENCY)	(432,870)

DEPRESS "ENTER" TO RETURN TO MENU.

* * *

The first adequacy evaluation compares the estimated actual (projected) reserve balance at the end of the period with the minimum amount established by a policy of 1% of loans. The proposed expected loan loss reserve of $980,000 is calculated by estimating the factors affecting the reserve in the coming period. (See details in the report that follows.) The preliminary summary indicates that the expected actual loan loss reserve balance of $980,000 will exceed the minimum 1% ($950,000) by $30,000. In addition, the projected reserve balance of $980,000 exceeds the calculated loss exposure of $930,351, using the nonperforming loan (N option in Menu C) and derived from a study of large, detailed risk loans, pending charge-offs and historical experience. When using the Net Charge-Off option of Menu C, the amount of risk exposure is calculated as $1,412,870, which exceeds the estimated reserve balance of $980,000. (See details in the report that follows.)

The preliminary summary indicates that the projected loan loss reserve exceeds the loss exposure by a small amount, indicating an adequate level of loan loss reserve at this time, if using the 1% policy or the nonperforming loan method for determining the minimum loan loss reserve balance. If one feels that historic net charge-off levels and recent net charge-off experience relative to peers are important predictors of future loan losses, then the projected reserve balance of $980,000 is less than the loan loss exposure of $1,412,870. If the projected reserve balance is inadequate (deficit), a larger provision for loan loss expense will be needed.

P   -   PRINT REPORT

The final report condenses all variables discussed in the various menus into a three-page report, which includes a single page of analysis and two pages of supporting tables. Generally, the report (1) computes a minimum policy level of loan loss reserve; (2) calculates and sums the level of loan loss reserve needed by the bank from a variety of inputs; (3) computes the expected (proposed) loan loss reserve; and (4) compares the loan loss reserve level proposed to that needed and to the minimum policy level. The comparison indicates whether the reserve is inadequate, is just right, or is excessive. Changes in the proposed reserve is made by a variation in the monthly expense provision for loan losses.

Specifically, the report is dated for later reference, followed by calculation of the minimum reserve balance established by management policy, in this case 1% of total loans subject to a reserve of $95 million. Money market loans were deducted from total loans to determine a total loans at risk. (See Menu G.) Based on a general management policy, the level of the loan loss reserve should be $950,000 (1% of $95 million).

* * *

```
        ** MINIMUM BALANCE CALCULATION **          30-Nov-87

TOTAL LOANS SUBJECT TO RESERVE                      95,000,000
BANK MINIMUM RESERVE/LOANS (%)                            1.00%
                                                   _____
MINIMUM ALLOWABLE RESERVE                              950,000
```

* * *

The next part of the report calculates an estimate of the total reserve needed by the bank or the expected loss exposure of the bank. This will be the sum of (1) the amount of identifiable above-risk loans, (2) an amount of loan loss reserve needed, based on the average experience (either the nonperforming loans ratio or the net charge-offs option in Menu C) over the last 5 years, and (3) an adjustment for either above- or below-average nonperforming loans or net charge-offs compared to the peer group of the bank.

* * *

```
     BALANCE ADEQUACY EVALUATION: NONCURRENT LOAN OPTION
TOTAL LOANS SUBJECT TO RESERVE                       95,000,000

DETAILED RISK LINES (UNSECURED RISK  IN  PROBLEM  LOANS  OR LINES
CONTAINING  RISK  ABOVE  THE  AVERAGE  EXPERIENCE LEVEL), PENDING
CHARGE-OFFS AND CURRENT PERFORMANCE RISK ADJUSTMENT:
                                    RISK AMOUNT     LOAN BALANCES
DETAILED LARGE-RISK LOANS             480,000           750,000
PENDING CHARGE-OFFS (NO RISK AMT REQ FOR FUTURE)       100,000
CURRENT PERFORMANCE RISK ADJUSTMENT   64,336
     OPTION SELECTED WAS NONCURRENT LOANS
PREVIOUS 5 YEARS EXPERIENCE PERCENTAGE
OF NET LOSSES TO TOTAL LOANS X REMAINING
LOAN BALANCES:
        1986      0.30%
        1985      0.40%
        1984      0.50%
        1983      0.45%
        1982      0.40%
5-YEAR AVERAGE    0.41%            386,015           94,150,000

TOTAL AVERAGE EXPERIENCE, DETAILED          _____
  RISK AND CURRENT PERFORMANCE ADJUST-
  MENT AND DETAILED RISK (EXPOSURE) 930,351           95,000,000
```

* * *

Balance Adequacy Evaluation: Nonperforming Loan Option.
The Balance (Reserve) Adequacy Evaluation Report is available, using either the noncurrent or nonperforming loan (N) peer group

evaluation option or the net loan charge-off option (C) covered in Menu C. In the right-hand column of the report, outstanding loan balances are evaluated. See the Loan Balance Analysis below and the explanation which follows.

* * *

LOAN BALANCE ANALYSIS

1	$100,000,000	GROSS LOANS OUTSTANDING
2	- 5,000,000	QUALITY MONEY MARKET LOANS
3	95,000,000	LOANS SUBJECT TO RESERVE
4	- 750,000	DETAILED LARGE-RISK LOANS
5	- 100,000	PENDING CHARGE-OFFS
6	$ 94,150,000	LOANS NET OF SPECIFIC CONCERNS

* * *

In the above Loan Balance Analysis, the actual loans outstanding balance (1) has been adjusted by the amount of high-quality loans, (2) for which a loan loss reserve is unnecessary to determine (3) loans ($95 million) at risk that need an estimate of future losses (reserve). Some of the loans have been identified as problems, specifically the detailed large-risk loans (4) of $750,000 and pending charge-offs (5) of $100,000. This leaves a balance of $94,150,000 (16) loans outstanding without specific, current problems. Some of these $94.15 million in loans may have problems in the future and will require an amount of reserve for loan losses. This is discussed in the next paragraph.

The next step is to estimate the amount of future loan losses, which is the reserve for loan losses amount the bank should have. This estimated amount includes:

$480,000 — Detailed amounts of large-risk loans that the bank may charge off (net) in the future.

+ 375,882 — An amount of net charge-offs associated with nonspecific problem loans, identified above as loans, net of specific concerns. The 5-year average net charge offs/loan ratio of 0.41% times the $91.7 million yields an estimated $375,882 in loan loss reserve needed, assuming conservatively that the past is a good indicator of the future.

+ 64,336 — An added amount of reserve needed based on the bank's 16.7% higher nonperforming loan ratio relative to its peer group times the 5-year net losses average (0.41%) times the 94.15 million of nonspecific loans at risk. ($94,150,000 x 0.41% x 2.625 - 2.25/ 2.25). If the net charge-off ratio was selected for peer comparison in Menu C, the adjustment factor would be based on the percentage variation of the bank's net charge-offs relative to those of the peer group. See the "Balance Adequacy Evaluation: Net Charge-Offs Option" which follows this section.

$930,351   The total estimated loan losses (exposure) based upon specific identification, historical experience, and an adjustment for the extent above or below the experience of the bank's peer group.

The final section of the report compares the actual and estimated loan loss reserve levels of the bank (will have) with the levels thought needed as determined by the various methods described above. The first comparison weighs the estimated loan loss reserve balance at the end of the coming period (will have) against the probable losses or loan loss reserve (calculated exposure) needed. The proposed reserve (1) exceeds the calculated exposure (2) by $49,649 or covers the exposure by 1.05 times (4). Note that the proposed reserve for loan losses assumes a loan loss provision of $70,000. The expense provision is the variable in this analysis that increases when management feels that the loan loss reserve is too low, decreasing when the reserve appears to be more than adequate.

* * *

```
CURRENT RESERVE                                          1,000,000
+ PROPOSED ADDITIONS (PROVISIONS FOR LOAN LOSSES)           70,000
- PENDING CHARGE-OFFS              (B)                     100,000
+ PENDING RECOVERS    (C)                                   10,000
(1) TOTAL PROPOSED RESERVE                                 980,000
(2)  LESS: CALCULATED EXPOSURE                             930,351
(3) PROPOSED RESERVE ABOVE EXPOSURE                         49,649
(4) PROPOSED RESERVE DIVIDED BY EXPOSURE (COVERAGE)           1.05
(5) PROPOSED RESERVE                                       980,000
   LESS: MINIMUM RESERVE (POLICY)                          950,000
   PROPOSED RESERVE ABOVE MINIMUM RESERVE (POLICY)          30,000
(6) CURRENT RESERVE                                      1,000,000
   LESS: CALCULATED EXPOSURE                               930,351
   CURRENT RESERVE ABOVE EXPOSURE                           69,649
   CURRENT RESERVE                                       1,000,000
   LESS: MINIMUM RESERVE (POLICY)                          950,000
   CURRENT RESERVE ABOVE MINIMUM RESERVE (POLICY)           50,000
```

* * *

One may also compare the expected loan loss reserve (based on a $70,000 expense provision) with the 1% of loans minimum policy level of $950,000 (5). In the above case, the proposed reserve of $980,000 exceeds the policy level by $30,000.

Two other comparisons complete the analyses. First, the current loan loss reserve of $1 million (6) is compared to the calculated exposure or the amount of the reservable loans that management feels it will write off or lose in the future. The current reserve exceeds the exposure by 69,649. Second, the current reserve of $1 million is compared to the minimum policy level of $950,000 (1% of reservable loans). Again, the bank's current reserve exceeds the minimum.

The analysis above assumed that the current nonperforming loans ratio, and the ratio relative to that of peer banks, are important determinants of future losses (loss exposure). Bank managers must determine the extent to which the current, proposed or expected loan loss reserve should cover (exceed) (1) the policy level of $950,000, and (2) the level of estimated exposure or expected net losses in the future. The level of reserve that will be needed (future losses) is actually a frequency distribution with a range of loss values. The analyst should not only consider a "most likely" value, but should review "worst case," "recession," and a number of other scenarios. Planning does not tell the manager what will happen. Planning enables the manager to view the dollar impact (future losses) of a range of economic possibilities. The manager, having reviewed the dollar implications of what could happen, must then select a level of loan loss reserve that is economically realistic while meeting the demands of shareholders, large investors and the regulatory authorities. An excessive reserve requires large loan loss expense provisions and lower earnings for shareholders but lower probabilities of surprise adjustments. Pressure for current earnings tends to paint the future with brighter colors, and underreserving may result. Significant underreserving is a "pay me now or pay me later" situation for the shareholders: higher earnings now (low reserve), but possible large adjustments (lower earnings) later. Managers who have taken, and have been rewarded to take, a long-term shareholder perspective will determine and establish loan loss reserve levels conservatively, based on economic reality. Planning models like this one enable managers to consider many assumptions and variables and, hopefully, make better decisions.

Balance Adequacy Evaluation: Net Charge-Offs Option. In this model, one may also use the current net charge-off ratio of the bank to estimate the reservable loan balance and the resulting level of loan loss reserve needed (exposure). If the net charge-offs (C) option was selected in Menu C, the following printed report is provided for the analyst. Using the net charge-offs ratio option changes three numbers (listed as 1-3) that were explained in an earlier section. If the manager feels that net charge-offs, historically (0.41%) and recently (1.74%), are a good predictor of loan losses in the future, the analysis indicates a loss exposure level of $1,412,870 (3), which, upon further analysis, is found to exceed the proposed reserve of

$980,000. To review the formulas, escape from the Macro, depress
the Home key, and move the cursor to the desired cell with the
arrow key. Use the F2 (edit) key if the formula under review is
longer than one line.

* * *

BALANCE ADEQUACY EVALUATION: NET CHARGE-OFFS OPTION
TOTAL LOANS SUBJECT TO RESERVE   95,000,000

DETAILED RISK LINES (UNSECURED RISK IN PROBLEM LOANS OR LINES
CONTAINING RISK ABOVE THE AVERAGE EXPERIENCE LEVEL), PENDING
CHARGE-OFFS AND CURRENT PERFORMANCE RISK ADJUSTMENT:

	RISK AMOUNT	LOAN BALANCES
DETAILED LARGE-RISK LOANS	480,000	750,000
PENDING CHARGE-OFFS (NO RISK AMT REQ FOR FUTURE)	100,000	

CURRENT PERFORMANCE RISK ADJUSTMENT 546,855 - (1)
     OPTION SELECTED WAS NET CHARGE-OFFS
PREVIOUS 5 YEARS EXPERIENCE PERCENTAGE
OF NET LOSSES TO TOTAL LOANS X REMAINING
LOAN BALANCES:
          1986   0.30%
          1985   0.40%
          1984   0.50%
          1983   0.45%
          1982   0.40%
5-YEAR AVERAGE   0.41%   386,015 (2)   94,150,000

TOTAL AVERAGE EXPERIENCE, DETAILED
  RISK & CURRENT PERFORMANCE ADJUST-
  MENT & DETAILED RISK (EXPOSURE   1,412,870 (3)   95,000,000
CURRENT RESERVE   1,000,000
+ PROPOSED ADDITIONS   70,000
- PENDING CHARGE-OFFS   (B)   100,000
+ PENDING RECOVERIES   (C)   10,000

TOTAL PROPOSED RESERVE   980,000
  LESS: CALCULATED EXPOSURE   1,412,870

PROPOSED RESERVE ABOVE EXPOSURE   (432,870)
PROPOSED RESERVE DIVIDED BY EXPOSURE (COVERAGE)   0.69

PROPOSED RESERVE   980,000
  LESS: MINIMUM RESERVE (POLICY)   950,000

PROPOSED RESERVE ABOVE MINIMUM RESERVE (POLICY)   30,000

CURRENT RESERVE   1,000,000
  LESS: CALCULATED EXPOSURE   1,412,870

CURRENT RESERVE ABOVE EXPOSURE   (412,870)

CURRENT RESERVE   1,000,000

LESS: MINIMUM RESERVE (POLICY)	950,000
CURRENT RESERVE ABOVE MINIMUM RESERVE (POLICY)	50,000

* * *

In summary, determination of the adequacy of the loan loss reserve requires a careful analysis and is a combination of several considerations:

1. The current and expected economic climate.

2. A careful review of the existing large loans that have above-average risk or are not performing as agreed.

3. An assessment of the net loan loss history of the bank relative to the conditions of the present.

4. An assessment of the nonperforming loans and net charge-offs of the bank relative to the experience of a specific peer group.

5. An estimate of the loan loss reserve one will have in the future based on estimated charge-offs, recoveries, and a given expense provision compared to what the bank is likely to lose (exposure).

6. An estimate of a minimum policy level of reserves and current reserve levels to estimated exposure.

The objective of this process is to establish and maintain a reserve level necessary to estimate correctly the amount of net loans (principal) that will be collected in the future. The adjustment (provision), of course, flows through the income statement and can, at times, have a varied impact on net earnings. While this process is clouded with subjectivity, bank managers are best able to assess the amount of collectable principal. In order to maintain credibility with analysts and investors, bank managers must establish and consistently maintain a policy related to the loan review process, charge-offs, and minimum reserve levels. An effective, consistent review process will provide over time an adequate loan loss reserve consistent with the economic environment and not dominated by the current earning needs of the bank. The investor/analyst and the financial market will be the ultimate judges of management's decisions and results.

SAMPLE PROBLEMS/ASSIGNMENTS

1. First Bank has a current reserve for loan losses of $1,250,000, and expects $300,000 to be charged off next year and $60,000 in recoveries. What is the amount of next year's expense provision for loan losses needed to establish a year-end reserve for a loan losses/total loan ratio of 1.25%? Total loans are estimated to be $106.8 million at the end of next year.

2. If First Bank's community is suddenly hit by a major industrial plant closing, what steps should the bank take to study the adequacy of its loan loss reserve?

3. Which ratio is a better indicator of future net charge-offs: (1) nonperforming loans/total loans or (2) the recent net charge-off (write-offs minus recoveries)?   Discuss.   Are there other predictor ratios variables that managers might utilize to better predict future loan losses?

CHAPTER 15

Model M

GAP and Net Interest Margin Analysis

INTRODUCTION AND CONCEPTS

Interest rate risk, always present but seldom a concern in a constant interest rate environment, became a major concern to depository institutions in the 1970s and 1980s. A combination of volatile interest rates and mismatched asset and liability cash flows and maturities caused net interest margins (NIM) and net interest income (NII) to vary considerably. The profitability of banks, and especially savings and loans institutions, was severely impaired, and shareholder value declined as cash flows became more volatile and investor capitalization rates increased. Managers now must monitor and influence the extent of interest rate risk assumed. This chapter and model, and the next, entitled "Rate Sensitivity Analysis," use the number-crunching ability of the personal computer and LOTUS 1-2-3 to explain and study interest rate risk.

This chapter reviews the concept of interest rate risk and illustrates the impact of varying levels of risk on bank profitability. The GAP concept is introduced, followed by an opportunity to (1) input various GAP and net interest margin levels, (2) estimate future interest rate changes, and (3) observe estimated changes in the NIM and NII. The model enables the student to observe the impact of interest rate risk. Through the use of varied inputs, the analyst is able to identify high or low interest rate risk situations in depository institutions. The next chapter reviews tools and techniques used to measure, control or hedge interest rate risk.

With the goal of maximizing the long-run value (present value) of shareholders' investment, bank managers make investment and financing decisions, attempting to maximize cash flows (earnings) within risk levels tolerable to investors. There are several decision areas which affect the risk/return or variability/level of profit flow:

1. Management of the net interest income difference between interest-bearing assets and liabilities, often

178

called spread management. Managers attempt to maximize the level of NII or NIM (NII divided by total average or earning assets) while minimizing the risk or variability of NII over time.

2. Management of loans and investments -- an attempt to maximize investment yields with a reasonable credit risk or default risk assumption.

3. Management of overhead -- an attempt to provide optimum production facilities and staffing for long-term profitability within tolerable risk limits.

4. Management of capital funds -- an attempt to provide the optimal level of equity/assets compatible with the benefits of financial leverage and the presence of financial risk.

5. Management of taxes -- an attempt to minimize the present value of tax obligations. Tax management entails a multiyear framework.

All of the above add up to an attempt to maximize and stabilize returns, in both dollars and percentage terms, for investors. This demands both profit production and risk monitoring and containment. Interest rate risk primarily affects the level and variability of NII (or revenue). Awareness of the factors that impact the level and variability of NII is the first step in risk monitoring and control. A planning or analysis (historical) model must include the variables that are most likely to affect NII. Several of these variables are discussed below.

Two of the major variables affecting the level of NII are (1) the classic spread, the difference between asset yields and liability costs, and (2) the volume or amount of assets and liabilities. The variability of NII is related to (1) changes in interest rates over time; (2) the repricing opportunities of assets and liabilities over time; and (3) the varied repricing pattern between interest-bearing assets and liabilities over time. Repricing occurs either at maturity, at repricing points in the contract such as a variable rate loan, or with the receipt of cash flows related to the asset or liability when the funds are either reinvested or reborrowed. Assets and liabilities, and their associated cash flows, seldom have exactly the same repricing pattern. So, as interest rates vary, asset repricing may lead or lag liability repricing, causing variation in NIM and NII.

One method used to measure the future repricing ability of assets and liabilities involves listing, by future time periods, the amounts of interest-bearing assets and liabilities, or their associated cash flows, that will have a repricing opportunity in the period. This management report, prepared at a specific point in time, is often called a <u>rate sensitivity</u> or <u>repricing schedule</u> and lists, by asset and liability categories, the amounts of funds that may be repriced in future specified periods (see the next chapter for a detailed analysis). One part of the report totals the amounts of assets and liabilities that may be repriced in various future time periods. The total rate-sensitive (or repriceable) (RSA) interest-bearing assets and liabilities (RSL) are then compared. The assets and liabilities that will not likely be repriced in a specified period (fixed rate contract) are considered a fixed rate asset (FRA) or liability (FRL).

The difference between RSA and RSL is called the <u>$ (dollar) GAP</u>. The GAP ratio is RSA divided by RSL. See the screen below. If RSA > RSL, the $GAP is positive (+) and the RSA/RSL ratio is greater than 1.   If RSA < RSL, the $GAP is negative (-) and the GAP ratio is less than 1. If RSA and RSL are equal, or if the cash flow patterns of interest-bearing assets and liabilities in a period of time are the same, the $GAP is zero and the GAP ratio is equal to 1.

* * *

GAP CONCEPTS

$GAP = RATE SENSITIVE ASSETS (RSA) - RATE SENSITIVE LIABILITIES (RSL)

GAP RATIO = RSA/RSL

+ GAP = RSA > RSL (OR) $\dfrac{RSA}{RSL}$ > 1

- GAP = RSA < RSL (OR) $\dfrac{RSA}{RSL}$ < 1

0 GAP = RSA = RSL (OR) $\dfrac{RSA}{RSL}$ = 1

* * *

Both the $GAP and the GAP ratio are relative measures of interest rate risk.   A $GAP represents a mismatch of future repriceable cash flows associated with interest-bearing assets and liabilities. If the $GAP is zero for a future period of time and if interest rates change, RSAs and RSLs will be repriced up or down together. Assuming that a reasonable spread existed before the rate change, and assuming that asset and liability rates change by the same amount, there would be little or no change in NII or NIM in the period. A zero $GAP assumes that RSA cash flows and RSL cash flows are matched during the period studied. If this is the case, interest rate risk is eliminated or is not present in the specified time period. Interest rates may go up or down in the period, and there would be little or no change in NII or the NIM.

If RSA > RSL, a positive $GAP exists. If interest rates change in the defined period, more RSA will be repriced than RSL, and the NIM and NII will change. If interest rates increase in the period, NII and NIM will increase because the $GAP amount of RSA will be repriced upward while financed in the period by an amount of fixed rate, nonrepriceable liabilities. If rates fall, the opposite impact on NII and NIM occurs. Repriceable asset cash flows are priced downward at the declining market rates, while financed by FRL. See the $GAP diagram below.

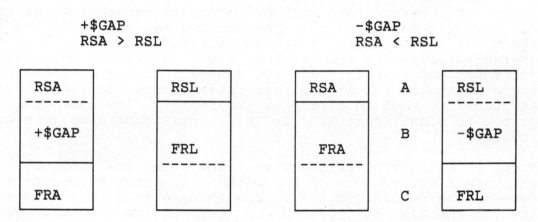

If RSA < RSL, a negative $GAP exists. If interest rates change in the defined future period, more RSL cash flow will be repriced relative to RSA. In the right-hand diagram above, the "A" amount of RSA and RSL will be repriced up or down together, and the NII and NIM associated with the "A" amount will stay about the same. The NIM of the "C" amount will also remain the same because the yields (costs) on the fixed or nonrepriceable amounts of the period will not change. The "B" amount of interest-bearing assets and liabilities represents a repricing mismatch: fixed rate, nonrepriceable assets financed by repriceable liabilities. If interest rates change in the period, the NIM and NII related to amount "B" will change. Hence, interest rate risk is present. If rates fall, the NIM associated with the "B" amount of FRA and RSL will increase. Why? If rates rise, this negatively gapped depository institution will have a decline in the NII and NIM on the "B" amount of interest-bearing assets and liabilities. Liability amounts (costs) are repriced upward in the period, while the yield on the "B" amount of interest-bearing assets does not change.

As noted above, managers would like to maximize NII and NIM within certain limits of variability (interest rate risk). There are three major factors which influence the variability of NII and NIM. They are:

1.   The relative size of the $GAP, or the GAP ratio.

2.   The extent of future changes in interest rates.

3.   The current level of the NIM.

Arithmetically, the relationship may be expressed as follows[1]:

$$\text{Percentage change in NIM} = \frac{\text{average \$GAP}}{\text{earning assets}} \times \frac{\text{change in rates}}{\text{NIM}}$$

The extent of interest rate risk or potential variability of the NIM is directly related to the GAP/earning assets ratio and to the extent of the absolute change in interest rates in a period, and inversely related to the level of NIM. A bank with a high relative $GAP and a relatively low NIM will have a considerable percentage change in NIM if interest rates change in the future. A bank with a high NIM and a relatively low $GAP is less susceptible to significant NIM and NII variations when interest rates change.

From a manager's perspective, how can one control the interest rate risk exposure of the bank? In today's competitive environment, one cannot control future changes in interest rates. The level of the NIM is related to competitive factors, loan pricing and default risk taking, and the cost of funds; and the trends of most major banks have not looked good. The last variable under the influence of management is the $GAP relative to earning assets.

With varying success, management can control or influence the $GAP and relative GAP ratio; however, competition and other market factors may reduce the ability to control the GAP level. Some levels of $GAP or GAP ratios may be within tolerable risk-taking limits as prescribed in policy statements. With decreased NIM, loan problems, restructuring pressures, etc., some reasonable, intentional gapping may be necessary to produce competitive returns to shareholders. Extreme, aggressive gapping may also be viewed by analysts and investors as "betting the

---

[1] Joseph E. Sinkey, Jr., _Commercial Bank Financial Management_ (New York: Macmillan Publishing Co., 1986), p. 310.

bank," and may be rewarded with higher capitalization rates and lower stock prices.

Several techniques, both on and off the balance sheet, may be utilized to control the level of interest rate risk exposure. In the case of an excessively positive $GAP (RSA > RSL), managers may take actions to lengthen the term of some of their RSAs or delay the cash flow (maturity, repricing interval) to be repriced in a specific period. On the other side of the balance sheet, funding assets with short-term federal funds or repos rather than 6-month CDs would increase RSL for the next 30- or 60-day period. Off-balance-sheet activities such as buying financial futures and call options on financial futures and participating in interest rate SWAPS may hedge an undesirable +$GAP position. Refer to various bank management or financial market texts for details.

In the case of an excessive negative $GAP (RSA < RSL), shortening the repricing cycle of interest-bearing assets and lengthening the repricing cycle of selected RSL in a specific period may reduce the $GAP to tolerable levels. If balance sheet structuring is not viable from a competitive standpoint, selling financial futures and buying put options on financial futures may be the least costly way to reduce interest rate risk exposure.

Managing interest rate risk in a depository institution also necessitates having a reasonable planning capability and an effective, flexible accounting software system. The next chapter studies one management planning tool used to assess the extent of interest rate risk at any point in time. Estimating repriceable amounts of interest-bearing assets and liabilities in future periods in a competitive customer-driven world is, in itself, a risky exercise. After you have reviewed the following model and are satisfied that you understand the concepts presented in this chapter, move on to the next chapter. The better you grasp the concepts of this chapter, the more you will glean from Model N.

MENU AND SCREENS

Model M has the following menus:

A	-	TUTORIAL
B	-	INTEREST RATE RISK CONCEPTS, GAP CONCEPTS AND NIM CHANGE
C	-	INTEREST RATE MOVEMENT EXERCISE
P	-	PRINT REPORT
S	-	SAVE TO DISKETTE (REPLACES CURRENT FILE CONTENTS)
Q	-	QUIT PROGRAM

A   -   TUTORIAL

The tutorial provides a short introduction to the model. Proceed to "B" for a more detailed look at the concepts.

B   -   INTEREST RATE RISK CONCEPTS, GAP CONCEPTS, AND NIM CHANGE

This section has six screens which summarize the major concepts discussed in the last section. Review these screens after reading the first section of the chapter. If your understanding is still shaky, return to the beginning of this chapter or to your primary textbook or other textbooks for more detailed reading and analysis of the concepts.

C   -   INTEREST RATE MOVEMENT EXERCISE

In this four-screen exercise, the analyst may study the impact of interest rate changes on the NIM at various GAP levels. The purpose of the exercise is to reinforce several important concepts studied earlier: that interest rate risk, measured by the potential variability of the NIM, is directly related to the relative size of the $GAP and the extent of future changes in interest rates, and inversely related to the current level of NIM.

The first screen provides the ability to enter sufficent data to calculate later the NIM and $GAP to earning assets ratio. See the sample screen below. You can enter the interest revenue rate level, often called the gross earning asset yield, found by dividing total interest revenue by the total interest-earning assets. The interest expense rate, found by dividing total interest expense by total earning assets, is the next item entered. The difference between the two rates, calculated later, is the NIM, or the NII divided by total interest-earning assets.

* * *

GAP, AVERAGE EARNING ASSETS, AND INTEREST RATES INPUT
ENTER PERCENTAGES AS DECIMAL (e.g., .10 = 10%)

ENTER BEGINNING INTEREST REVENUE RATE LEVEL:		15.00%
ENTER BEGINNING INTEREST EXPENSE RATE LEVEL:		10.00%
ENTER BASIS POINT CHANGE EXPECTED:		200

GAP IN $'S (ENTER NEG. -)	EARNING ASSETS (FILL ALL PERIODS	$ GAP IN %
($50,000,000)	$1,000,000,000	-5.00%
INTEREST REVENUE RATE PROJECTIONS	INTEREST EXPENSE RATE PROJECTIONS	
17.00%	12.00%	

* * *

The next item entered is the expected change in interest rates (annualized), entered in basis points. There are 100 basis points in 1%. In the sample screen, interest rates are expected to change by 2% or 200 basis points.

The average $GAP and total average earning assets are entered next. If the $GAP is negative, place a negative sign before the number. If the field is too small for your number, round the numbers. After entering, the GAP to earning assets ratio is calculated and is displayed at the right.

The forecasted level of the gross asset yield (interest revenue rate) and the interest expense rate are calculated and displayed at the bottom of the screen. The RSAs and their associated cash flows in a specific period are expected to be repriced at 17%, while RSL will be repriced to the higher 12%.

On the next screen, the percentage change in NIM is calculated using the variables inputted in the first screen. If interest rates increase by 2% and if the bank has a negative 5% GAP and a current NIM of 5%, the bank's NIM will decline by 2% to 4.90%.

* * *

COMPUTE CHANGE IN NIM

		AVERAGE $ GAP		CHANGE IN RATES
% CHANGE IN NIM	=	-------------	x	-------------
		EARNING ASSETS		NIM

STEP 1	(50,000,000)	x	2.00%
	-------------		-------------
	1,000,000,000		5.00%

STEP 2	-5.00%	x	40.00%

STEP 3	-2.00%	=	% CHANGE IN NIM

* * *

The next screen compares the NIM impact of a change in interest rates on both a zero GAP situation and that inputted above. The beginning NIM is first calculated, followed by estimates of the NIM with a zero GAP and, in this case, a negative 5% GAP. With a zero GAP ratio, RSA = RSL, variations in interest rates do not impact NIM. With a negative GAP, RSA < RSL, an increase in interest rates of 2% will cause a 2% decline in NIM. The NIM will decline by 10 basis points to 4.90%.

* * *

NET INTEREST MARGIN MOVEMENT

```
    BEGINNING INTEREST REVENUE RATE:        15.00%
    BEGINNING INTEREST EXPENSE RATE:        10.00%
      BEGINNING NET INTEREST MARGIN:         5.00%
GAP:  ZERO
    PROJECTED INTEREST REVENUE RATE:        17.00%
    PROJECTED INTEREST EXPENSE RATE:        12.00%
      PROJECTED NET INTEREST MARGIN:         5.00%
GAP:  -5.00%
    PROJECTED INTEREST REVENUE RATE:        17.00%
    PROJECTED INTEREST EXPENSE RATE:        12.00%
-2.00%         x         5.00%              -0.10%
      PROJECTED NET INTEREST MARGIN:         4.90%
```

** NOTE **   OBSERVE THE NET INTEREST MARGIN MOVEMENT UNDER DIFFERENT GAP SCENARIOS.

* * *

Note three items about the above discussion. First, this exercise assumes that one is able to match RSA and RSL cash flows in a period -- a very difficult exercise in practice. Second, the analyst has estimated RSA and RSL repricing flows for future time periods in the Rate Sensitivity Analysis report. This is a plan, an estimate. What occurs as time proceeds may vary due to competition, other management or customer decisions, etc. The third point refers to our rather loose definition of RSA and RSL. Most GAP management discussions focus on matching maturities, but a 1-year fixed rate installment loan, interest and principal paid monthly, financed by a 1-year CD, interest and principal paid at maturity, have identical maturities but differing cash flow patterns. One must match cash flow and/or repricing patterns of assets and liabilities, not just maturities. Hence, we use the term cash flows in our discussion. Matching the cash flows or duration of assets and liabilities is conceptually sound but operationally very difficult; hence maturity matching, which eliminates considerable interest rate risk, will continue to be the focal point. Now that regulatory influences on deposit contracts have been curtailed, deposit contracts of the future may be designed with terms and repricing abilities similar to those of assets, or vice versa, in order to influence the true cash flow $GAP.

The last screen underscores the earnings impact of interest rate risk. With an interest earning asset level averaging $1 billion, a 10 basis point decline in NIM will reduce NII by $1 million. With a zero GAP, changes in market interest rates, assuming that both asset and liability rates change by the same amount, do not change the NIM or NII. The real concern with interest rate risk is the impact on NII and net earnings. This screen visualizes the earnings impact of interest rate risk under certain conditions. This is an important consideration when assessing the level of risk to assume and is an important financial planning tool.

* * *

NET INTEREST INCOME CHANGE
(ANNUALIZED)
EARNING ASSET LEVEL: 1,000,000,000

GAP = ZERO
NIM =   5.00%

NET INTEREST INCOME: 50,000,000
(NIM x EARNING ASSET LEVEL)

GAP =   -5.00%
NIM =   4.90%

NET INTEREST INCOME: 49,000,000
(NIM x EARNING ASSET LEVEL)

   -0.10%   x   1,000,000,000   (1,000,000)
(NIM CHANGE % x EARNING ASSET LEVEL = NET INTEREST INCOME CHANGE)

* * *

Once you have read through the textbook and, in general, understand the screens, return to the first screen of this section and begin testing various ideas. Change one variable at a time and see the impact on NIM and NII. When moving to another variable, restore the original amount in the prior variable before changing the next one. Work several scenarios until you have established the relationships. Memorize the short equation on screen 2, if necessary.

The purpose of this model and the exercises above is to give the student analyst an understanding of how interest rate risk affects financial institutions. Interest rate risk, as measured by the potential variability of the NIM or NII, has had a significant impact upon most banks, savings and loan institutions, savings banks, and credit unions over the last 20 years. The primary, and most manageable, variable affecting the level of risk assumed is the $GAP or GAP ratio. As noted in the above exercise, the future change in interest rates and the current level of NIM also affect the level of risk (potential variation in NIM), but these variables are either beyond the control of management or are influenced by other management actions. Controlling the level of interest rate risk begins with holding the GAP within tolerable limits. If other factors, such as competition, prevent internal GAP control, managers can use financial futures, options on financial futures, rate SWAPS, and other off-balance-sheet methods to hedge or offset an undesirable GAP position.

P   -   PRINT REPORT

S   -   SAVE TO DISKETTE (REPLACES CURRENT FILE CONTENTS)

SAMPLE PROBLEMS/ASSIGNMENTS

1. Write a definition of interest rate risk. What do we use as a measure of interest rate risk in depository financial institutions? What other risks do these institutions and their shareholders assume?

2. What is the relationship (direct or inverse) between (a) the size of the GAP ratio; (b) expected changes in interest rates; and (c) the level of NIM on the changes in NIM? What is the relationship between positive/negative GAP situations, changes in interest rates, and changes in NIM?

3.   First Bank is in the following situation:

BEGINNING INTEREST REVENUE RATE LEVEL: 9.00%
BEGINNING INTEREST EXPENSE RATE LEVEL: 6.50%
        BASIS POINT CHANGE EXPECTED: 100

GAP IN $'S	EARNING ASSETS
$10,000,000	$100,000,000

Before entering the variables in Menu C, calculate:

a)   NIM.

b)   Current level of net interest income.

c)   GAP ratio.

d)   Expected directional change in NIM.

e)   Expected percentage change in NIM.

f)   Expected level of NIM.

g)   Expected change in NII.

(Try to determine the answers with a calculator; then input the
variables in Menu C and compare the answers with your
calculation.   If you cannot prove a particular answer, move the
cursor to the answer cell on the screen and observe the formula
at the top of the screen.)

4. First Bank has a rather low NIM of 2.50%. How would interest rate risk affect the bank if its NIM were 3.50%?

5. If First Bank had a ($10 million) $GAP, what is the potential impact of a 1% increase in interest rates?

CHAPTER 16

Model N
Rate Sensitivity Analysis

Special Instructions: This rather large model is different from other models in that the program calculates each time when returning to the menu or printing the lengthy report. This will cause a delay, as evidenced by the "wait" indicator.

INTRODUCTION AND CONCEPTS

This chapter continues the analysis of interest rate risk which began in the last chapter. In that chapter interest rate risk and GAP concepts were developed. Through use of Model M one was able to see the impact of interest rate changes upon the net interest income (NII) and net interest margin. If you have not reviewed interest rate risk or GAP concepts, a study of the previous chapter is necessary before proceeding with this chapter.

This chapter reviews and analyzes a management financial planning tool, called a rate sensitivity or repricing opportunity report. Forecasting $GAPs or GAP ratios and the repriceable yields and costs of funds for future periods of time has become an important part of the bank financial planning. Knowing or estimating the extent of interest rate risk ($GAP) for future periods is the first step toward changing, hedging, or controling the level of risk assumed by the bank. Not every bank can or desires to eliminate interest rate risk, but a rate sensitivity analysis provides a reasonable estimate of the risk to be assumed in future periods. If the risk levels forecasted ($GAP or GAP ratio) is beyond acceptable policy levels, internal balance sheet, or asset-liability management contingency plans can be exercised to reduce the undesirable GAP level for a future period. If internal balance sheet management options are not available, or are not cost justified, the off-balance sheet hedging plan may be used. The emphasis here is anticipating, or planning, what may occur. The bank cannot control future interest rate movements, but its managers can, to some reasonable extent, be aware of their future interest rate risk exposure, and make conscious decisions about what to do about it.

192

This model is designed to be used as an instructional tool, not as an operational model.   Specific bank variations in accounts, time frames and summaries are needed for an operational model.   This model does display the power of the PC and spreadsheet programs, as well as the added information about ledger balances and software that is now needed to efficiently analyze interest rate risk.

When analyzing the past or future (planning) level and variability of net interest revenue, the time dimension becomes a major focus.   If interest rates change over time, how will that affect net interest revenue, given our current interest assets and liabilities?   The time period layout of the rate sensitivity analysis model is related to the dollar implications of the need to know.   Months and quarters of a year are used in this model. Weekly, daily or less may be cost justified in large depository institutions or those that are involved in aggressive gapping strategies.

Within each time period, the dollar level and the revenue/cost yield of interest assets and liabilities that will be repriced in that time period are entered into the model in the appropriate accounts.   What is desired is the total repriceable, rate sensitive assets (RSA) relative to the repriceable, rate sensitive liabilities (RSL) in a time period. The repriceable assets (RSA) minus the RSL equals the dollar GAP, or the amount of funds in the time period vulnerable to interest rate risk if rates change. If RSA – RSL is positive (positive $ GAP), the net interest margin associated with the positive GAP amount will increase (decrease) if interest rates increase (decrease). Why? The $ GAP assets will be repriced upward or downward, while the liability cost will remain constant in the defined time period. If rates can go up, they can go down as well. If RSA – RSL is negative (negative $ GAP), the net interest margin associated with the – $GAP amount will decrease (increase) if rates increase (decrease). During this period the asset yield on the – $GAP amount will be constant, while the cost of funds varies up or down.

The GAP is often measured in dollars, in ratio form, such as RSA/RSL, or the GAP/earning or total assets ratio. The larger the $GAP and the $GAP relative to earning or total assets, the greater the change in the net interest margin should rates change in the defined time period.   Watch for these GAP amounts and ratios as you study the model. See Model M. Keep analyzing in your mind how and why net interest margins and net interest revenue would change if interest rates were to move up or down.

One final concept should be mentioned before the model is discussed. Most interest rate risk analyses focus on balances and GAP analysis. If the concern is related to possible changes in NIM or NI revenue if interest rates change, then a study of the repriceable rates in a period as well as balances is necessary. Focusing on balances alone may promote a decision to close a GAP position while also closing (reducing) the net interest margin. Rates (yields) and balances together affect net interest revenue levels and changes. Thus they should both be a part of the planning models used to make asset and liability decisions.

APPLICATION

This model can be applied to a sophisticated case analysis or simulation game situation, or can be used with minimal inputs to explain and learn the basic concepts related to managing interest rate risk. Use the default data situation for an analysis or create your own situation. Instructors may use this model in a computer lab setting to "tell" and quickly "show" the usefulness of a planning model. The model is useful (cases or problems) to set up a situation and let the students make recommendations to reduce or change the GAP.

MENU AND SCREENS

Model N includes the following menus:

A   -   TUTORIAL

B   -   DATA INPUT

C   -   CURRENT HORIZON

D   -   SIX-MONTH HORIZON

E   -   CUMULATIVE - TWELVE MONTHS

F   -   SET REPORT DATE AND TOTAL ASSETS

G   -   VIEW GRAPH (REQUIRES GRAPHIC ABILITY.)

P   -   PRINT REPORT

S   -   SAVE TO DISKETTE (REPLACES CURRENT FILE)

Q   -   QUIT PROGRAM

THE PROGRAM CALCULATES EACH TIME WHEN RETURNING TO MENU OR PRINTING REPORTS.

A   -   TUTORIAL

The tutorial provides a brief review of the program.

B   -   DATA INPUT

Please note: this   section does   not have   automatic cursor movement.   Use   arrow   keys,   PGUP,   PGDN,   or Tab keys to move cursor.

This model focuses on monthly repricing of interest-bearing assets and   liabilities.   Several standardized and typical asset and liability accounts   have   been   pre-selected   for   the model. They   are   listed   below.   If   the user has accounts not listed below, select a listed   category   and   combine   the   inputs   on a consistent basis.

* * *

DATA ENTRY OF AMOUNTS AND RATES	DAILY/WEEKLY		Oct-87
AMOUNTS IN THOUSANDS	AMOUNT	RATE	AMOUNT
DESCRIPTION			
SENSITIVE ASSETS			
COMMERCIAL LOANS	83	12.25%	240
REAL ESTATE LNS-FIXED RATE	0	0.00%	11
REAL ESTATE LNS-VAR RATE	0	0.00%	300
INSTALLMENT LOANS	1,220	14.40%	15
U.S. TREASURY SECURITIES	0	0.00%	1,000
U.S. GOVERNMENT AGENCIES	0	0.00%	0
MUNICIPAL OBLIGATIONS	0	0.00%	5
OTHER SECURITIES	0	0.00%	0
FEDERAL FUNDS SOLD	1,500	9.75%	0
BANKERS ACCEPTANCES	0	0.00%	0

DEPRESS PGDN KEY FOR SENSITIVE LIABILITIES

* * *

DATA ENTRY OF AMOUNTS AND RATES **AMOUNTS IN THOUSANDS** DESCRIPTION	DAILY/WEEKLY AMOUNT	RATE	Oct-87 AMOUNT
SENSITIVE ASSETS			
SENSITIVE LIABILITIES			
MONEY MARKET DEPOSIT ACCOUNTS	3,000	8.00%	0
NOW ACCOUNTS	2,575	7.00%	0
C/D'S - $100,000 OR MORE	0	0.00%	2,500
C/D'S - 91 DAY MONEY MARKET	0	0.00%	250
C/D'S - 182 DAY MONEY MARKET	0	0.00%	450
C/D'S - 18 MONTHS	0	0.00%	55
C/D'S - 30 MONTHS	0	0.00%	100
REPURCHASE AGREEMENTS	1,500	8.25%	0
FEDERAL FUNDS PURCHASED	0	0.00%	0

DEPRESS ALT AND M KEYS WHEN DATA ENTRY IS FINISHED TO RETURN TO MENU. THERE WILL BE A PAUSE WHILE THE PROGRAM CALCULATES YOUR DATA.

* * *

The amounts represent dollar amounts of repriceable assets and liabilities during the period. Repriceable amounts include maturities, principal repayments, or a repricing ability with contracts with variable rates. Under commercial loans above $83,000 are repriceable on a daily or weekly basis; an amount of $240,000 in October, 1987. Loans and other contracts tied to prime and other market-based rates are entered in the daily/weekly column. Note that the plan above began September 30, 1987. The date is entered in menu F as is the total average assets. The rate entry (in decimal) represents the weighted average yield related to the repriceable amount entered for the period. Use the arrow keys to move to the right, and the PGDN key to move down to the liability section. Depressing the Home key will return the cursor to the Commercial Loan/Daily cell.

C   -   CURRENT HORIZON

Once the amounts and rates are entered one may view the individual and total RSA and RSL and summaries for both the first six-month period (Menu C) and the second six-month period (Menu D). The summary screen lists the total RSA and RSL for each period. The $GAP equals RSA - RSL. The GAP ratio of RSA divided by RSL and the $GAP/total average assets are also displayed for each period. In the example screen below, a negative GAP of 427 exists for the daily/weekly period. Consistently, the GAP ratio is less than one and the GAP/T. Assets is a negative percentage. More importantly, a sudden upturn in market interest rates would increase more RSL than RSA, reducing net interest revenue. The larger the $GAP, absolutely and relative to total assets, the greater the variation in the net interest income and margin.

* * *

CURRENT HORIZON - BY PERIOD DESCRIPTION	DAILY/WEEKLY	Oct-87	Nov-87
SENSITIVE ASSETS	2,803	1,571	4,727
SENSITIVE LIABILITIES	7,075	3,355	1,455
GAP	(4,272)	(1,784)	3,272
RATIO (RSA/RSL)	0.40	0.47	3.25
GAP/TOTAL AVERAGE ASSETS CURRENT YTD	-3.41%	-1.42%	2.61%
SENSITIVE ASSETS (RATES)	11.85%	11.50%	11.04%
SENSITIVE LIABILITIES (RATES)	7.69%	10.10%	9.87%
NET INTEREST	4.16%	1.40%	1.17%

* * *

Dollar and relative GAP data are important in assessing interest rate risk, but a rate analysis of repriceable balances is also important. A decision perhaps to reduce a dollar GAP (asset or liability change) must include an analysis of the impact on the NIM. Sacrificing NIM to change a GAP position should be a conscious decision rather than unknown.

Often a repriceable asset/liability combination may have a rather high or low net interest margin, which, after that month passes, would lower (if high) or increase (if low) the cumulative net interest margin. Tracking future repriceable rates (NIM) is an important aspect of managing the net interest margin and net interest revenue. Thus, rate analysis is included in this model.

The cumulative totals at 90 days and 180 days are also presented under Menu C. The daily/weekly data items, and all period amounts out to 90 and 180 days, would be a part of the cumulative totals. In another way, the 90-day cumulative total lists RSAs and RSLs, and the corresponding rates and costs, which are repriceable out to the next 90 and 180 days.

D - SIX-MONTH HORIZON

This is an extension of Menu C. It includes period data and summaries, and cumulative totals for the second six months, including 270-day and 365-day summaries.

E   -   CUMULATIVE - TWELVE MONTHS

This report enables the analyst to view cumulative totals at any monthly period end out to one year.   The daily/weekly balances have been combined with the first month, October, 1987, balances to determine a cumulative total.   Each month the cumulative total is determined by adding the current period data to the previous cumulative total.   The extent of the $GAP, the GAP ratio and $GAP per average assets is also displayed in a summary screen. The GAP impact of past or pending asset and liability decisions, or pending or past decisions to alter the GAP, may be analyzed in this section.   The corresponding cumulative rate and net interest margin effect are also available for analysis. Most normal loan/financing decisions have a spread or NIM impact analysis, but the rate effects of GAP management past and pending decisions should also be analyzed.   Closing a GAP at a reduced or negative NIM, and the resultant impact on net interest revenue, should be reviewed at the same time that the benefits of a reduced GAP are considered.

F   -   SET REPORT DATE AND TOTAL ASSETS

When changing report data, the report date and average total assets must be entered.   Note the special edit procedure used when entering the report date. See the screen below.

* * *

EDIT THIS FIELD TO REFLECT THE CURRENT MONTH DESIRED IN THE REPORT.   THIS IS ACCOMPLISHED BY DEPRESSING "F2" FUNCTION KEY AND USING THE BACKSPACE TO ERASE IMPROPER DATA AND REENTER THE DESIRED DATA.
THIS FIELD IS ENTERED AS @DATE(YEAR,MONTH,DAY):   Sep-87
                                        (i.e., @DATE (87,9,30)
ENTER AVERAGE TOTAL ASSETS FOR BANK BELOW. REPORT WILL   PRINT AS YEAR-TO-DATE AVERAGE ASSETS.

125,420 (IN THOUSANDS)

(IF **** APPEARS IN REPORT COLUMNS, MAXIMUM
DOLLAR SIZE HAS BEEN EXCEEDED FOR THE FIELD)

* * *

G   -   VIEW GRAPH

The GAP ratio GAP/average assets and net interest margin, cumulative basis, are plotted for the twelve month period. GAP management efforts to reduce the GAP, and the impact on NIM, are provided on the same screen.   In the attached plot of default data, the negative GAP declines in the twelve-month period as high negatives in the early periods are offset by positive GAP

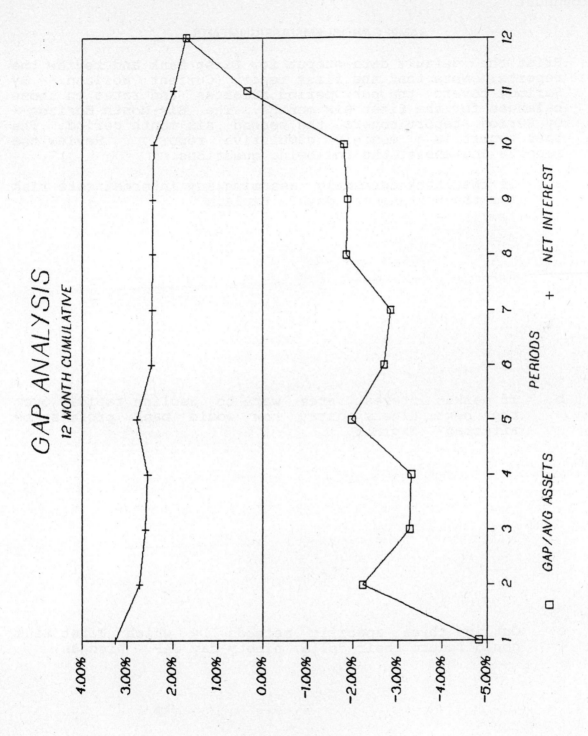

GAP ANALYSIS
12 MONTH CUMULATIVE

alignments in the later months. The NIM, however, is projected to decline, incrementally by months, reducing the cumulative NIM throughout.

SAMPLE PROBLEMS/ASSIGNMENTS

1. Print the default data output for First Bank and review the reports. Note that the first report (Current Horizon -- By Period) covers the per period balances and rates on those balances for the first six months. The Six-Month Horizon-- By Period report covers the second six-month period. The last report is a monthly cumulative report. Review the reports and answer the following questions.

    a. Is the bank currently assuming any interest rate risk for the next ninety days? Explain.

    b. If market interest rates were to decline rapidly over the next ninety days, how would bank profits be affected? Explain.

    c. Outline three specific methods by which First Bank could reduce their dollar ninety-day GAP. Discuss.

d.   If interest rates were to continue their decline throughout the 360 day period, what is the likely impact on net interest revenue?

e.   Study the forecasted changes in the net interest margins associated with repriceable RSA and RSL over the next 360 days.   First Bank has taken steps to reduce the GAP in the later months.   How has their decision affected the net interest margin?   View the graph if your computer has graphic capability. Analyze.

CHAPTER 17

Model O
Pro Forma Financial Statements

INTRODUCTION AND CONCEPTS

Financial planning has always been 75% manual number crunching and 25% analysis. Spreadsheet programs like LOTUS 1-2-3 have placed financial planning analyses in the 75% position and, thank goodness, have reduced manual number crunching to 25%. In the classroom, we can now do financial planning rather than just talk about it. This model permits one to plan using financial statements, project bank income and future balance sheets, and later input the actual data and study the variance.

Financial planning considers the financial implications of business decisions and economic events. One may consider the cash implications of a series of assumptions (cash budget) or the income and financial condition (assets and financing) impact of various economic activities and decisions. A plan in an uncertain world does not necessarily indicate what will happen; it provides insight into the financial implications of a wide range and combination of future economic events. Planning prepares one for what does occur, as well as providing goals and targets of effective business performance.

Financial planning with electronic spreadsheets provides an opportunity to change assumptions and to immediately see the results. Every time a new variable is entered, the entire spreadsheet recalculates. The spreadsheet plan may be constructed in a variety of ways, limited only by the imagination of the analyst. This model is but one way to arrange a planning spreadsheet. While this planning model may be useful in many assignments, it is also designed as an example of what can be constructed.

Construction of a planning model begins with the manager in mind. Start with the needs of the user and work backward. Do not start with the data available but with the data the manager needs. The accounting and operating data base (software package) of the business may constrain the development of an effective

202

plan. Conversion of data may be necessary. If daily and monthly figures are available but weekly figures are desired and useful, convert. Initially, don't let data base standard reports determine data needs. Let the decision maker (manager) determine the critical planning variables, time period, etc. Later, one may have to resort to the data available, but start your plan independently of such data and avoid the attitude that "this is how we have always done it!"

The quality of the data included in the plan is a critical variable contributing to plan effectiveness. Planning data are often based upon assumptions such as movements in interest rates, loan demand, and competitors' reaction to decisions. The ability to correlate numbers with economic events and decisions is the essence of effective planning. Historical review and experience seem to be major factors in planning effectiveness. Consistent, regular plan/actual comparisons and analyses are an important part of the planning process and contribute to more effective planning in the periods to come.

APPLICATIONS

Model O provides an opportunity to input up to five periods of plan and actual data in the form of a bank income statement and balance sheet. The model is extremely useful and should be an integral part of bank simulation games. Plan data submitted at data input time, followed by a plan/actual comparison and analysis, enables simulation teams to establish goals and policies and to follow through with consistent decision making. Student teams are able to relate forecasted economic events and decisions, and the resulting impact on their bank's income and financial condition.

This model is an important part of many case analyses. Cases generally focus on specific policy and decision areas. Requesting an impact forecast of policy and decisions reveals the thoroughness of the plan and knowledge of economic relationships. If loan rates are to be increased, what will be the impact on loan volume and total loan interest revenue? Assigning a pro forma statement requires a focus on demand elasticity and the financial "fallout" of specific decisions. This is an integral part of the development of the finance student.

The pro forma balance sheet is constructed so as to calculate totals and "balance" the balance sheet with either federal funds sold (assets greater than liabilities and capital) or federal funds purchased (assets less than liabilities and capital). This permits a "funds needed" plan to evolve from specific forecasted ledger balances. One may assume average or specific point balances in the forecast. Pro forma income projections are easier if balance sheet items, such as loans, are estimated as averages. Average rate times average volume equals interest income.

The ledger accounts used in the model may be used for a bank of any size. However, it is likely that not all simulations, cases, and situations will exactly match the ledger accounts listed in this model. Additional ledger balances may be included in the "other" category or reassigned to a zero balance (unused) line.

MENU AND SCREENS

The menu for Model O is listed below.

* * *

```
A    -    TUTORIAL
B    -    SPECIAL MENU TO CLEAR PREVIOUS DATA
C    -    SET PERIOD DATES TO BE ENTERED
D    -    SET TAX RATE SCHEDULE
E    -    BALANCE SHEET DATA ENTRY
F    -    INCOME STATEMENT DATA ENTRY
P    -    PRINT MENU
S    -    SAVE WORKFILE  TO DISKETTE (REPLACES CURRENT FILE
          CONTENTS)
Q    -    QUIT PROGRAM
```

* * *

(Note: Because of the size of this model, the program is set to calculate when returning to the menu. This will cause a temporary delay, as evidenced by the "wait" indicator in the upper-right-hand portion of the screen.)

A   -   TUTORIAL

The tutorial provides a general summary of the model and several key explanations. Be sure to read it carefully.

B   -   CLEAR PREVIOUS DATA

A special submenu is available so that all previous data entered in the cells may be erased. It is especially helpful to begin with a clean spreadsheet, but be mindful that all prior data in the specific financial statement will be erased. The Workfile Clear Menu screen is listed below.

* * *

WORKFILE CLEAR MENU

THROUGH THIS SELECTION ALL PREVIOUS DATA FROM THE SELECTED FILES WILL BE CLEARED.   BE SURE THE ENTRY IS THAT DESIRED BEFORE ENTERING A SELECTION.

         A - CLEARS ALL BALANCE SHEET FIELDS

         B - CLEARS ALL INCOME STATEMENT FIELDS

         C - RETURN TO MODEL MENU

** CAUTION ** BE SURE SELECTION IS PROPER BEFORE DEPRESSING SELECTION KEY.

* * *

One may select one of the three options above: clear all balance sheet fields (A), clear all income statement fields (B), or return to the model menu.

C   -   SET PERIOD DATES

    Enter the first period date in years or any other numerical value. The model will then add one whole integer to identify each of the next four periods.

D   -   SET TAX RATE SCHEDULE

    Enter the appropriate tax rate for the bank studied. The rate structure, listed below, relates to the brackets under the 1981 tax law, but it is easily adapted to the brackets of the 1986 tax law. One may also enter a constant average rate in each bracket. Projected taxable income will be taxed at the rates entered on this screen.   Municipal and state bond interest revenue is excluded from the tax computation.

* * *

TAX SCHEDULE

TAXABLE INCOME	TAX RATE
0 TO 25,000.00	15.00%
25,000.01 TO 50,000.00	15.00%
50,000.01 TO 75,000.00	25.00%
75,000.01 TO 100,000.00	34.00%
100,000.01 OR MORE	34.00%

PROGRAM WILL CONSIDER ALL "STATE AND POLITICAL SUBDIVISION" INTEREST AND FEES AS NONTAXABLE INCOME. SET TAX RATE SCHEDULE ABOVE TO REFLECT RATES DESIRED FOR CALCULATION OF "APPLICABLE TAX" REFLECTED IN BOTH ACTUAL AND PLAN INCOME STATEMENTS.

A TAX ADJUSTMENT LINE IS PROVIDED TO ADJUST CALCULATED TAXES FOR OTHER ITEMS THAT MAY AFFECT YOUR TAX FIGURES SUCH AS INVESTMENT TAX CREDIT, NOL CARRY-BACKS AND CARRY-FORWARDS, AND OTHER SPECIAL TAX ADJUSTMENTS.
DEPRESS "ENTER" KEY TO CONTINUE

* * *

E and F - FINANCIAL DATA ENTRY - BALANCE SHEET AND INCOME STATEMENT

All plan and actual financial data are entered using Menu E or Menu F. Having selected either the balance sheet or the income statement, you may begin data entry. Before entering data, note the special instructions at the top of the screen:

* * *

REMOVE "NUM-LOCK" IF ACTIVATED FOLLOWED BY "HOME" KEY TO RETURN TO TOP OF STATEMENT. CURSOR THEN MAY BE MOVED TO RIGHT FOR PLAN DATA OR TAB TO RIGHT FOR ADDITIONAL YEARS. FIVE YEARS ARE PROVIDED. DEPRESS "CTRL" & "BREAK" FOLLOWED BY "ALT" & "M" TO RETURN TO PROGRAM MENU. DEPRESSING "ALT" & "B" RESTARTS PROGRAM AT THIS SCREEN. DEPRESSING "ALT" & "A" RESTARTS AUTO-MATIC CURSOR MOVEMENT DOWN IF ERROR BREAKS OPERATION.

PRO FORMA BALANCE SHEET STATEMENTS

ASSETS	1987 PLAN	1987 ACTUAL	PERIOD VARIANCE
CURRENCY & COIN	0	0	0.00%
DUE FROM BANKS-DEMAND	0	0	0.00%
DUE FROM BANKS-INTEREST BEARING	0	0	0.00%
TOTAL CASH & DUE FROM BANKS	0	0	0.00%
U.S. TREASURY SECURITIES	0	0	0.00%
U.S. GOVERNMENT AGENCIES	0	0	0.00%

STATE/MUNICIPAL SECURITIES	0	0	0.00%
OTHER SECURITIES	0	0	0.00%
TOTAL INVESTMENTS	0	0	0.00%

* * *

One can use the "num-lock" and numeric key entry with a Macro command, moving the cursor down the screen. If you must move up the screen to input a number, remove the "num-lock" and use the arrow key to move up to position. Press the "num-lock" key again and enter. If the automatic cursor movement is broken, depress "Control" and "Break" followed by "Alt" and "A" to resume automatic cursor movement. If you wish, use the "Data Entry Forms" (make copies) at the end of the chapter to prepare your data for entry. If data must be reclassified to fit the ledger accounts of the model, relabeling can be entered on the Data Entry Form. Prove your reclassification later by comparing the last calculated total, such as total assets or net income.

Balance Sheet. Enter the plan, estimated or forecasted data first. The program will balance the differences between projected assets and projected liabilities/equity with either the federal funds sold (asset) or purchased (liability) ledger account. If you are forecasting a balance sheet related to a bank simulation game, evaluate the forecasted economy, study the trends, estimate the rather fixed data items such as cash items, etc., and then spend time preparing the loan and deposit forecast. Later, after receiving your simulation output, enter the actual data and study the variances. Variances are percentage overages or underages (negative signs). Absolute dollar variations are important, but percentage changes (using the plan as a base) are more significant. (Note: If quarterly data are compared, annualize for consistency.) What caused the variation? The analyst should not be satisfied with just reviewing the variations. Always answer the question "Why did the variation occur?"

The ledger accounts utilized in the pro forma balance sheets are listed below. A maximum of 11 digits (10 billion) and three commas may be entered to record on the screen. Round where appropriate. Refer to Model Q for definitions. The accounts with an asterisk to the left are calculated (totaled) by the model and are not entered data items. Use the totals to prove the accuracy of your input. At the end of the balance sheet, the following notes and instructions are provided:

* * *

** NOTE ** FEDERAL FUNDS SOLD/PURCHASED ENTRIES ARE CALCULATED BY THE MODEL TO BALANCE THE STATEMENT.

END OF STATEMENT - DEPRESS "NUM-LOCK" FOLLOWED BY "HOME" KEY TO RETURN TO TOP OF STATEMENT. CURSOR THEN MAY BE MOVED TO RIGHT

FOR PLAN DATA OR TAB TO RIGHT FOR ADDITIONAL YEARS.   FIVE YEARS
ARE PROVIDED.   DEPRESS "CTRL" AND "BREAK" FOLLOWED BY "ALT" AND
"M" TO RETURN TO PROGRAM MENU.

* * *

One is reminded that the federal funds ledger accounts serve
to balance the pro forma (projected) balance sheet. Directions
for entering data for the next period are also included.

* * *

ASSETS
CURRENCY AND COIN
DUE FROM BANKS-DEMAND
DUE FROM BANKS-INTEREST BEARING
*   TOTAL CASH AND DUE FROM BANKS

U.S. TREASURY SECURITIES
U.S. GOVERNMENT AGENCIES
STATE/MUNICIPAL SECURITIES
OTHER SECURITIES
*   TOTAL INVESTMENTS

*   FED FUNDS SOLD AND SEC PURCHASED
          U/A TO RESELL (MODEL CALC)

COMMERCIAL LOANS
CONSUMER LOANS
REAL ESTATE LOANS
BANKERS ACCEPTANCES
*   TOTAL LOANS
LESS: UNEARNED INCOME
          VALUATION RESERVE FOR LOAN LOSSES
*   NET LOANS

PREMISES AND FIXED ASSETS
OTHER ASSETS
*   TOTAL ASSETS

LIABILITIES
DEPOSITS-DOMESTIC
 NON-INTEREST-BEARING
 INTEREST-BEARING
*   TOTAL DEPOSITS-DOMESTIC
DEPOSITS-FOREIGN
 NON-INTEREST-BEARING
 INTEREST-BEARING
*   TOTAL DEPOSITS-FOREIGN
*   TOTAL DEPOSITS

*   FED FUNDS PURCHASED AND SEC SOLD U/A
          TO REPURCHASE (MODEL CALC)

```
          OTHER LIABILITIES
*             TOTAL LIABILITIES

              EQUITY CAPITAL
          PERPETUAL PREFERRED STOCK
          COMMON STOCK
          SURPLUS
            UNDIVIDED PROFITS (PRIOR PER)
            LESS: CASH DIVIDENDS PAID
*           CURRENT PERIOD NET EARNINGS
*            TOTAL UNDIVIDED PROFITS
*             TOTAL EQUITY CAPITAL
*              TOTAL LIABILITIES AND
                  EQUITY CAPITAL
```

* * *

The ledger accounts for the pro forma (plan) and actual income statements are listed below.   If the accounts do not exactly coincide with your income statement layout, use the "other" accounts or an unused account, with a note of reassignment in your working papers.   As in the balance sheet, the accounts with asterisks to the left are program calculated balances. Other taxes may be entered in the tax adjustment account.

* * *

```
          INTEREST INCOME
              INT AND FEES ON LOANS AND LEASES
              INT ON DUE FROM BANKS
              INT ON FUNDS SOLD
              U.S. TREASURY SECURITIES
              U.S. GOVERNMENT AGENCIES
              STATE/MUNICIPAL SECURITIES
              OTHER SECURITIES
*             TOTAL INTEREST REVENUE

          INTEREST EXPENSE
              INT ON DEPOSITS
              INT ON FUNDS PURCHASED
              INT ON BORROWED FUNDS
              OTHER INTEREST EXPENSE
*             TOTAL INTEREST EXPENSES

*   NET INTEREST REVENUE BEFORE
        PROVISION FOR LOAN LOSSES

        PROVISION FOR LOAN LOSSES

*   NET INTEREST REVENUE AFTER
        PROVISION FOR LOAN LOSSES
```

```
                    OTHER INCOME
                          TRUST INCOME
                          SERVICE CHARGE ON DEPOSITS
                          TRADING ACCOUNT PROFITS
                          OTHER NONINTEREST INCOME
                          SECURITIES GAINS (LOSSES)
                    *           TOTAL OTHER INCOME

                    OTHER EXPENSE
                          SALARIES AND WAGES
                          PENSION AND EMPLOYEE BENEFITS
                          OCCUPANCY EXPENSE - NET
                          OTHER NONINTEREST EXPENSE
                    *           TOTAL OTHER EXPENSE

                    *           INCOME BEFORE INCOME TAXES

                    *           APPLICABLE INCOME TAXES
                          TAX ADJUSTMENTS
                    *           NET INCOME
```

* * *

Model O may be used for applications and analyses other than pro forma (plan) and actual analyses. One may input two actual balance sheets/income statements and study the percentage variance. Percentage change reveals a relative change compared to actual dollar changes. Be sure to annualize the percentage changes mentally if the time between statements is less than or greater than 1 year. A 5% change in an expense item in a month is $(1.05)^{12} - 1 = 79.5\%$ annualized. A 20% increase in earnings over 5 years, on the other hand, is a $(1.20)^{.2} - 1 = 3.7\%$ rate of change per year.

P   -   PRINT/SAVE MENU

Model O has a separate submenu associated with the print and save options. The menu screen is listed below.

* * *

PRINT AND SAVE MENU

ENTER LETTERS FOR DESIRED FUNCTION:
                              (DEPRESS "ENTER" KEY)

```
          B  -  PRINT BALANCE SHEET
          I  -  PRINT INCOME STATEMENT
          M  -  EXIT TO PRO FORMA MODEL MENU
```

PROGRAM WILL ALWAYS CALCULATE WHEN RETURNING TO THIS MENU.

* * *

One can choose to print the balance sheet (B) or the income statement (I), or return to the menu (M). If both statements are to be printed, a print instruction is needed for each.

PROBLEMS/ASSIGNMENTS

1. (Pro forma) The recent balance sheet of First Muncie Bank are included below. First Muncie estimates that the following assets and liabilities will grow at the indicated rates next year:

U.S. Treasury securities	10%
State/political subdivision securities	(10%)
Commercial loans	25%
Consumer loans	20%
Premises	10%
Domestic Deposits:	
Non-interest-bearing	(5%)
Interest-bearing	7%
Other liabilities	10%

Net income is expected to be 15 and dividends 7. Common stock and surplus will increase by 2 each.

a) What added amount of funds must be financed by First Muncie (note changes in the federal funds accounts)? Unchanged accounts are assumed to be the same next year.

b) What will happen to the capital/asset ratio if the accounts change as planned? What causes the change in the ratio?

c) Should First Muncie fund its growth with federal funds purchased? Discuss.

FIRST MUNCIE BANK	Actual	Plan	Variance
ASSETS			
CURRENCY & COIN	50		
DUE FROM BANKS-DEMAND	100		
DUE FROM BANKS-INTEREST BEARING	0		
TOTAL CASH AND DUE FROM BANKS	150		
U.S. TREASURY SECURITIES	200		
U.S. GOVERNMENT AGENCIES	0		
STATE/MUNICIPAL SECURITIES	150		
OTHER SECURITIES	0		
TOTAL INVESTMENTS	350		
FED FUNDS SOLD AND SEC PURCHASED			
U/A TO RESELL (MODEL CALC)	0		
COMMERCIAL LOANS	700		
CONSUMER LOANS	300		
REAL ESTATE LOANS	200		
BANKERS ACCEPTANCES	0		
TOTAL LOANS	1,200		
LESS: UNEARNED INCOME	20		
VALUATION RESERVE FOR			
LOAN LOSSES	25		
NET LOANS	1,155		
PREMISES AND FIXED ASSETS	55		
OTHER ASSETS	20		
TOTAL ASSETS	1,730		
LIABILITIES			
DEPOSITS-DOMESTIC			
NON-INTEREST-BEARING	500		
INTEREST-BEARING	750		
TOTAL DEPOSITS-DOMESTIC	1,250		
DEPOSITS-FOREIGN			
NON-INTEREST-BEARING	0		
INTEREST-BEARING	0		
TOTAL DEPOSITS-FOREIGN	0		
TOTAL DEPOSITS	1,250		
FED FUNDS PURCHASED AND SEC SOLD U/A			
TO REPURCHASE (MODEL CALC)	182		
OTHER LIABILITIES	35		
TOTAL LIABILITIES	1,467		
EQUITY CAPITAL			
PERPETUAL PREFERRED STOCK	0		
COMMON STOCK	25		
SURPLUS	35		
UNDIVIDED PROFITS (PRIOR PER)	200		
LESS: CASH DIVIDENDS PAID	30		
CURRENT PERIOD NET EARNINGS	33		
TOTAL UNDIVIDED PROFITS	203		
TOTAL EQUITY CAPITAL	263		
TOTAL LIABILITIES AND			
EQUITY CAPITAL	1,730		

2.   Historical Analysis. The balance sheet and income statement
     of First Akron Bank for the last 2 years are listed below.
     What has happened (decisions, economic events) in the last 2
     years? Write your evaluation below, linking the variances
     with economic/decision variables.

	1986	1987	Variance
ASSETS			
CURRENCY & COIN	50	50	0.00%
DUE FROM BANKS-DEMAND	100	122	22.00%
DUE FROM BANKS-INTEREST-BEARING	0	0	0.00%
TOTAL CASH & DUE FROM BANKS	150	172	-14.67%
U.S. TREASURY SECURITIES	200	200	0.00%
U.S. GOVERNMENT AGENCIES	0	0	0.00%
STATE/MUNICIPAL SECURITIES	150	150	0.00%
OTHER SECURITIES	0	0	0.00%
TOTAL INVESTMENTS	350	350	0.00%
FED FUNDS SOLD AND SEC PURCHASED			
U/A TO RESELL (MODEL CALC)	0	0	0.00%
COMMERCIAL LOANS	700	850	21.43%
CONSUMER LOANS	300	350	16.67%
REAL ESTATE LOANS	200	210	5.00%
BANKERS ACCEPTANCES	0	0	0.00%
TOTAL LOANS	1,200	1,410	17.50%
LESS: UNEARNED INCOME	20	24	20.00%
VALUATION RESERVE FOR			
LOAN LOSSES	25	27	8.00%
NET LOANS	1,155	1,359	17.66%
PREMISES AND FIXED ASSETS	55	60	9.09%
OTHER ASSETS	20	22	10.00%
TOTAL ASSETS	1,730	1,963	13.47%
LIABILITIES			
DEPOSITS-DOMESTIC			
NON-INTEREST-BEARING	500	650	30.00%
INTEREST-BEARING	750	800	6.67%
TOTAL DEPOSITS-DOMESTIC	1,250	1,450	16.00%
DEPOSITS-FOREIGN			
NON-INTEREST-BEARING	0	0	0.00%
INTEREST-BEARING	0	0	0.00%
TOTAL DEPOSITS-FOREIGN	0	0	0.00%
TOTAL DEPOSITS	1,250	1,450	16.00%
FED FUNDS PURCHASED AND SEC SOLD U/A			
TO REPURCHASE (MODEL CALC)	182	225	23.62%
OTHER LIABILITIES	35	33	-5.71%
TOTAL LIABILITIES	1,467	1,708	16.43%
EQUITY CAPITAL			
PERPETUAL PREFERRED STOCK	0	0	0.00%
COMMON STOCK	25	25	0.00%
SURPLUS	35	35	0.00%
UNDIVIDED PROFITS (PRIOR PER)	200	200	0.00%
LESS: CASH DIVIDENDS PAID	30	30	0.00%

CURRENT PERIOD NET EARNINGS	33	25	-24.58%
TOTAL UNDIVIDED PROFITS	203	195	-3.97%
TOTAL EQUITY CAPITAL	263	255	-3.06%
TOTAL LIABILITIES AND			
EQUITY CAPITAL	1,730	1,963	13.47%

	1986	1987	Variance
INTEREST INCOME			
INT & FEES ON LOANS & LEASES	90	98	8.89%
INT ON DUE FROM BANKS	0	0	0.00%
INT ON FUNDS SOLD	0	0	0.00%
U.S. TREASURY SECURITIES	40	43	7.50%
U.S. GOV'T AGENCIES	0	0	0.00%
STATE/MUNICIPAL SECURITIES	20	23	15.00%
OTHER SECURITIES	0	0	0.00%
TOTAL INTEREST REVENUE	150	164	9.33%
INTEREST EXPENSE			
INT ON DEPOSITS	50	55	10.00%
INT ON FUNDS PURCHASED	16	19	18.75%
INT ON BORROWED FUNDS	0	0	0.00%
OTHER INTEREST EXPENSE	12	14	16.67%
TOTAL INTEREST EXPENSES	78	88	12.82%
NET INTEREST REVENUE BEFORE			
PROVISION FOR LOAN LOSSES	72	76	5.56%
PROVISION FOR LOAN LOSSES	9	12	33.33%
NET INTEREST REVENUE AFTER			
PROVISION FOR LOAN LOSSES	63	64	1.59%
OTHER INCOME			
TRUST INCOME	4	3	-25.00%
SERVICE CHARGE ON DEPOSITS	10	8	-20.00%
TRADING ACCOUNT PROFITS	0	0	0.00%
OTHER NONINTEREST INCOME	2	2	0.00%
SECURITIES GAINS (LOSSES)	2	0	-100.00%
TOTAL OTHER INCOME	18	13	-27.78%
OTHER EXPENSE			
SALARIES AND WAGES	36	40	11.11%
PENSION AND EMPLOYEE BENEFITS	4	5	25.00%
OCCUPANCY EXPENSE - NET	12	14	16.67%
OTHER NONINTEREST EXPENSE	3	5	66.67%
TOTAL OTHER EXPENSE	55	64	16.36%
INCOME BEFORE INCOME TAXES	26	13	-50.00%
APPLICABLE INCOME TAXES	1	(2)	-266.67%
TAX ADJUSTMENTS	0	0	0.00%
NET INCOME	25	25	-42.23%

Pro Forma Financial Statements
DATA ENTRY FORM

	Date	Plan	Actual

ASSETS
CURRENCY AND COIN _____ _____
DUE FROM BANKS-DEMAND _____ _____
DUE FROM BANKS-INTEREST-BEARING _____ _____
    TOTAL CASH & DUE FROM BANKS _____ _____

U.S. TREASURY SECURITIES _____ _____
U.S. GOVERNMENT AGENCIES _____ _____
STATE/MUNICIPAL SECURITIES _____ _____
OTHER SECURITIES _____ _____
    TOTAL INVESTMENTS _____ _____

FED FUNDS SOLD AND SEC PURCHASED _____ _____
    U/A TO RESELL (MODEL CALC)

COMMERCIAL LOANS _____ _____
CONSUMER LOANS _____ _____
REAL ESTATE LOANS _____ _____
BANKERS ACCEPTANCES _____ _____
    TOTAL LOANS _____ _____
LESS: UNEARNED INCOME _____ _____
     VALUATION RESERVE FOR _____ _____
       LOAN LOSSES
     NET LOANS _____ _____

PREMISES AND FIXED ASSETS _____ _____
OTHER ASSETS _____ _____
    TOTAL ASSETS _____ _____

    LIABILITIES
DEPOSITS-DOMESTIC
 NON-INTEREST-BEARING _____ _____
 INTEREST-BEARING _____ _____
    TOTAL DEPOSITS-DOMESTIC _____ _____
DEPOSITS-FOREIGN
 NON-INTEREST-BEARING _____ _____
 INTEREST-BEARING _____ _____
    TOTAL DEPOSITS-FOREIGN _____ _____
      TOTAL DEPOSITS _____ _____

FED FUNDS PURCHASED AND SEC SOLD U/A _____ _____
  TO REPURCHASE (MODEL CALC)
OTHER LIABILITIES _____ _____
    TOTAL LIABILITIES _____ _____

    EQUITY CAPITAL
PERPETUAL PREFERRED STOCK _____ _____
COMMON STOCK _____ _____

SURPLUS
  UNDIVIDED PROFITS (PRIOR PER) _____ _____
  LESS: CASH DIVIDENDS PAID _____ _____
  CURRENT PERIOD NET EARNINGS _____ _____
   TOTAL UNDIVIDED PROFITS _____ _____
    TOTAL EQUITY CAPITAL _____ _____
     TOTAL LIABILITIES AND
      EQUITY CAPITAL _____ _____

	Date	Plan	Actual
INTEREST INCOME			
INT & FEES ON LOANS & LEASES			
INT ON DUE FROM BANKS		_____	_____
INT ON FUNDS SOLD		_____	_____
U.S. TREASURY SECURITIES		_____	_____
U.S. GOV'T AGENCIES		_____	_____
STATE/MUNICIPAL SECURITIES		_____	_____
OTHER SECURITIES		_____	_____
TOTAL INTEREST REVENUE		_____	_____

INTEREST EXPENSE
    INT ON DEPOSITS _____ _____
    INT ON FUNDS PURCHASED _____ _____
    INT ON BORROWED FUNDS _____ _____
    OTHER INTEREST EXPENSE _____ _____
     TOTAL INTEREST EXPENSES _____ _____

NET INTEREST REVENUE BEFORE
  PROVISION FOR LOAN LOSSES _____ _____

  PROVISION FOR LOAN LOSSES _____ _____

NET INTEREST REVENUE AFTER
  PROVISION FOR LOAN LOSSES _____ _____

OTHER INCOME
    TRUST INCOME _____ _____
    SERVICE CHARGE ON DEPOSITS _____ _____
    TRADING ACCOUNT PROFITS _____ _____
    OTHER NONINTEREST INCOME _____ _____
    SECURITIES GAINS (LOSSES) _____ _____
      TOTAL OTHER INCOME _____ _____

OTHER EXPENSE
    SALARIES & WAGES _____ _____
    PENSION & EMPLOYEE BENEFITS _____ _____
    OCCUPANCY EXPENSE - NET _____ _____
    OTHER NONINTEREST EXPENSE _____ _____
     TOTAL OTHER EXPENSE _____ _____

     INCOME BEFORE INCOME TAXES _____ _____

APPLICABLE INCOME TAXES

TAX ADJUSTMENTS

NET INCOME

CHAPTER 18

Model P
Capital Planning

INTRODUCTION AND CONCEPTS

The adequacy of equity capital in any business is of concern to all the publics of the business: its customers, suppliers, creditors, shareholders, employees, and, in the case of businesses affected by the public interest, governmental regulators. The adequacy of capital in depository financial institutions is a matter of extreme interest, concern, and continued discussion. From the perspective of the bank manager, equity capital must be sufficient to satisfy the most demanding of the "publics" listed above. This capital planning model provides a study of several variables which affect the level of equity capital. Capital sufficiency occurs when the level of capital is above the minimum set by the most demanding public. Sufficiency may vary with economic conditions and business expectations; thus, bank managers must establish a minimum capital level sufficient to suit their publics in the most difficult economic periods. Equity capital serves a number of economic functions within a business:

1. Equity, new shares sold or earnings retained, is a source of funds.

2. Equity serves as a base to attract debt funds to finance assets. In a bank, $1 of equity may support from $15 to $20 of debt (deposits).

3. Equity serves to absorb losses incurred on investments, on loans and in other operations.

4. Finally, and especially for banks, equity capital is an important ingredient for maintaining confidence in the bank and in banks in general. Capital is adequate if it is sufficient to finance growth in a competitive environment, sufficient to absorb losses which occur even with reasonable risk taking, and sufficient to convince customers and investors that the bank will open tomorrow.

There are several variables which affect the <u>level</u> of bank capital, all of which are considered together in this model:

1. The growth rate of assets.

2. The rate of return on assets (net income).

3. The estimated profitability improvement in the future.

4. The dividend policy of the bank.

5. The estimated capital (common stock) to be sold in the future.

6. The minimum capital/asset ratio established by the bank.

This model enables the bank analyst to interrelate the above variables in a financial plan covering up to a fifteen-year period. By utilizing "what if" sensitivity analysis, one can note the impact of changes in one or more variables on the future capital level of the bank. While developed with banks in mind, this model may be adapted to any business.

<u>Important Concept</u>: The level of external equity capital that must be raised in the future is:

1. Directly related to:
   a. The growth rate of the assets.
   b. The riskiness of the assets.
   c. The minimum capital/asset ratio established by management.
   d. The proportion of earnings paid out in cash dividends (payout ratio).

2. Inversely related to:
   a. The profitability of the business (return on assets).
   b. The improvement in profitability in the planning period.

The equity capital needs of the bank (financing decision) is closely related to the asset investment decision (type and rate of growth) and the dividend decision. This model combines these three major financial decisions in a simple, but functional planning exercise.

APPLICATIONS

This model will (1) enhance the understanding of long-range business planning and the variables affecting the equity needs of a business and (2) serve as a useful tool for any long range planning assignments. One is able to estimate the future equity capital needs of a worst case, likely case, or most optimistic situation that may develop.

MENU AND SCREENS

Model P includes the following menus:

A   -   TUTORIAL
B   -   CAPITAL PLANNING MODEL
C   -   VIEW DETAIL YEARS OF PLANNING MODEL
G   -   VIEW GRAPH PRESENTATION (GRAPHIC ABILITY REQUIRED)
P   -   PRINT REPORT
S   -   SAVE FILE TO DISKETTE (REPLACES CURRENT FILE
          CONTENTS)
Q   -   QUIT PROGRAM

A   -   TUTORIAL

The tutorial program offers a brief description of the program and an opportunity to view the screens used in the model. No data may be entered in the tutorial section.

B   -   CAPITAL PLANNING MODEL

Planning data may be entered under Menu B. The default data input screen appears below, along with a description and instructions.
                                   * * *

     NOTE: ENTER PERCENTAGES AS DECIMAL (i.e. 5% as .05).
             FIFTEEN YEAR PERIOD - ASSUMPTIONS

ASSET GROWTH RATE   10.00%

RETURN ON ASSETS   0.90%

ANNUAL IMPROVEMENT IN ROA   2.00%
   ENTER DIVIDENDS BELOW BY PERCENTAGE *OR* DOLLAR AMOUNT
DIVIDEND PAYOUT   30.00% $0
   (IF USING DOLLARS ABOVE, PERCENTAGES MUST BE ZERO)
FIRST PLAN YEAR   1987

TOTAL ASSETS (BEGINNING OF 1ST YEAR) $100,000,000

TOTAL CAPITAL (BEGINNING OF 1ST YEAR) $8,000,000

MINIMUM CAPITAL/ASSET RATIO   7.75%
**NOTE CAPITAL DEFICIENCY YEAR

                         * * *

Asset Growth Rate (%) -- annual growth rate of year-end assets. May be assumed to be average assets. Enter all percentages as a decimal (i.e., 5 percent as .05 and .60 percent as .006).

Return on Assets (%) -- the ratio of net income to year-end or (average) assets.

Annual Improvement -- offers the opportunity to assume
in ROA (%) increased profitability at a constant rate of improvement. If the improvement is 5 percent, an ROA of .60 percent this year will be .60 percent (1.05) or .63 percent next year.

Dividend Payout (%) -- either the proportion of dividends/net
or ($) income or a constant dollar dividend level may be entered. Do not enter both, or the payout ratio will override.

First Plan Year -- enter the first year of your plan. This sets the timetable identification for future years.

Total Assets ($) -- (beginning of first year): this establishes the present asset position of your bank. You may input up to $99 billion. Above this number round to $000.

Total Capital ($) -- (beginning of first year): this establishes the starting total equity position.

Minimum Capital/ -- this establishes the minimally
Asset Ratio acceptable level of total equity capital relative to total assets and the minimum dollar level of capital for future periods. The minimum capital/asset ratio is determined by management after an appraisal of asset risk, deposit mix, and business and economic conditions.

Capital Deficiency -- the program calculates and displays the
Year year in the future if and when the actual capital/asset ratio is less than the minimum set above.

At the bottom of the screen, one may select one of three options:

1.   Capital Issues -- Advances the user to the screen where the yearly amounts of capital deficiency (sufficiency) are listed, along with the option of selecting up to five years and amounts of new common stock sale.

2.   Change Above Data Assumptions -- Returns the cursor to the top of the screen so that specific planning variables can be changed.

3.   Menu -- Returns to the program menu.

C   -   VIEW DETAIL YEARS OF PLANNING MODEL

Menu C allows the user to scroll through each of the fifteen planning years and study the asset growth, capital reconciliation and other variables. A sample screen appears below, followed by a discussion of each item.

	1987	1988	1989
TOTAL ASSETS	$110,000,000	$121,000,000	$133,100,000
PREVIOUS CAPITAL	$8,000,000	$8,693,000	$9,470,546
+ NET PROFIT	$990,000	$1,110,780	$1,246,295
+ NEW CAPITAL	$0	$0	$0
- DIVIDENDS	$297,000	$333,234	$373,889
TOTAL CAPITAL	$8,693,000	$9,470,546	$10,342,953
CAPITAL/ASSETS	7.90%	7.83%	7.77%
MIN CAP LEVEL	$8,525,000	$9,377,500	$10,315,250
MIN CAP/ASSETS	7.75%	7.75%	7.75%
SURPLUS (DEFICIT)	$168,000	$93,046	$27,703
RETURN ON ASSETS	0.90%	0.92%	0.94%

DEPRESS ENTER KEY TO CONTINUE THROUGH PROGRAM

Each of the above is described below:

Total Assets   --   Ending or average assets for the plan year

Previous Capital -- Starting or previous year-end capital

+ Net Profits   --   ROA, listed below, times T. Assets (above)

+ New Capital   --   Added capital sales (see Screen 3)

- Dividends   --   The net income times the payout ratio or the dollar level established in Screen 1

Total Capital   --   The total year-end equity capital level

Capital/Assets --   The ratio of ending capital (above) to total assets

Min Cap Level   --   The minimum dollar capital level computed by multiplying the minimum capital/assets ratio by total assets

Min Cap/Assets --   The minimum capital/assets ratio inputted in the capital planning model.

Surplus (Deficit)--   The difference between total capital and the minimum capital level. A surplus means that the planned total capital level exceeds the minimum capital level. A capital (deficit) in the planning year means that expected total capital will fall below the minimum capital level established by the minimum capital/assets ratio.

Return on Assets -- Was inputted in the plan in the capital planning model. Includes improvement factor of previous x (1 + improvement rate)

    At the end of the screens detailing the fifteen planning years, a combination summary and capital issues screen appears for review and analysis.

```
NOTE:   LIMIT OF ONE ISSUE PER YEAR      ACTUAL CAPITAL PROJECTED
        IS PERMITTED IN THIS PROGRAM    COMPARED TO MINIMUM CAPITAL
                                          YEAR      DOLLAR VARIANCE
            NEW CAPITAL ISSUES PLANNED    1987           $168,000
            (MAXIMUM OF FIVE ISSUES)      1988          $93,046
                 YEAR       AMOUNT        1989          $27,703
                                          1990         ($24,982)
1ST ISSUE   _____       1991         ($61,401)
                                          1992         ($77,300)
2ND ISSUE                                 1993         ($67,679)
                                          1994         ($26,680)
3RD ISSUE                                 1995          $52,547
                                          1996         $177,988
4TH ISSUE                                 1997         $358,935
                                          1998         $606,182
5TH ISSUE                                 1999         $932,238
                                          2000       $1,351,583
                                          2001       $1,880,950
```

At the right of the screen is a list of the planning years and
the estimated capital surplus (deficits) for each year. Deficit
capital means that the planned capital for the year falls below
the minimum capital level established by the minimum
capital/asset ratio. The cursor option on this screen permits
(A) capital issues, (B) assumptions screen (Menu B) or (C) return
to program menu. If (A) capital issues is selected, one may
select up to five years to issue (sell common stock) and enter
the amount of new common equity. In the example above, the
planner may wish to issue capital in 1990 (perhaps $100,000) to
remove the capital deficiency in 1990-1994. Of course the
capital deficiency may be removed by slower asset growth, higher
ROA's, greater improvement in ROA, lower dividends, or a lower
minimum capital/assets ratio. As soon as a new capital issue is
inputted, the capital surplus (deficit) amounts are adjusted at
the right of the screen. If you wish to remove the capital
previously issued, scroll to the bottom of the screen (enter
key), return to (A) capital issues, and enter zeros in years and
amounts.

G   -   VIEW GRAPH PRESENTATION (GRAPHIC ABILITY REQUIRED)

    If the computer is equipped with graphics, Menu G displays a
plot of the actual and minimum required capital for the fifteen-
year planning period. The minimum capital/assets ratio is fixed
and appears as a horizontal line, while the "actual" takes a
variety of shapes depending upon the inputs to the capital plan.
The bank objective is to generate an actual ratio at or above the
minimum level. See next page.

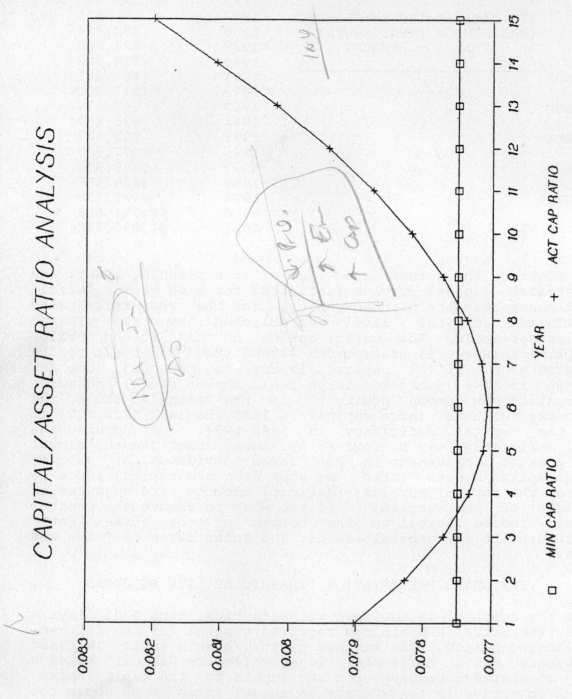

CAPITAL/ASSET RATIO ANALYSIS

P   -   PRINT REPORT

The menu P option prints a report of the last capital plan inputted.

S   -   SAVE FILE TO DISKETTE (REPLACES CURRENT FILE CONTENTS)

SAMPLE PROBLEMS/ASSIGNMENTS

The J & J Bank is a bank with $100 million in total assets located in a rapidly growing sunbelt community. Loan and deposit growth has been about 15 percent for the last three years, and J & J's equity capital/asset position has undergone some strain, hitting 7 percent recently. Profitability, because of higher overhead and competition, has not been able to keep the capital position growing with assets. Management would like to maintain a capital/ratio above 6.5 percent. The bank has maintained a payout ratio of 40 percent over the last several years. This policy has satisfied shareholders because net income and dividends have been growing. Last year J & J earned an ROA of .8 percent and expects to maintain this level of profitability in the years to come. Total assets are expected to grow at a rate of around 10 percent per year.

Prepare a capital plan for J & J and answer the following questions.

1. Based on the above assumptions, will added capital be needed in the next five years? How much?

2. What is the relationship (direct or inverse) between the amount of capital needed and the following variables? Change one of the variables and note the impact on the actual level of capital relative to the minimum.

	Item	Related to Capital Needs
a.	Asset growth	D
b.	ROA level	I
c.	Payout ratio	
d.	Minimum capital ratio	
e.	Actual capital level	
f.	Annual improvement in ROA	D

3.   If raising external equity is not available to J & J, what asset growth rate (assume risk level constant) can J & J maintain and still meet their minimum capital levels? (Hint: Change the asset growth rate until the capital deficiency is eliminated.)

4.   What level of ROA would enable J & J to meet their minimum capital and dividend goals (payout)?

5.   Can J & J meet their growth (assets) and minimum capital goals by altering their dividend policy?

6.   What ROA improvement would be needed to adequately capitalize the bank over the next five years?

CHAPTER 19

Model Q
Bank Financial Statement Review

INTRODUCTION

This model provides an opportunity to test the recognition of various general ledger accounts from bank financial statements. A list of ledger line items is presented for your identification as an asset, contra-asset, liability, capital account, revenue, or expense. The purpose of the exercise is (1) to recognize the ledger components of bank financial statements and associate the items with a financial statement; (2) to associate the ledger items with specific bank investments, services, and activities; and (3) to relate balance sheet accounts to corresponding income statement accounts. The materials which follow present an explanation of each of the financial statement accounts and their relationship to bank services and activities. Students are encouraged to look over this material before taking the Account Recognition Quiz on the computer.

HOW TO USE THE MODEL

If you are not familiar with bank financial statements, or if it's been a while since you have worked with this material, first look over the Financial Statement Review section which follows. The proper way to identify a line item with a financial statement is to associate the ledger item with a specific service, activity, or event.

Once you have covered the Financial Statement Review, return to the computer model, review the tutorial menu (A), and take the Account Recognition Quiz (B). When the quiz has been completed, review your answers (C) and look over the balance sheet (D) and income statement (E) to reinforce and analyze your decisions made during the quiz. If there is a need for further explanations, return to this manual and look up the troublesome items in the Financial Statement Review.

229

FINANCIAL STATEMENT REVIEW

In this section, the more common line items of the bank balance sheet and income statement are (1) defined in terms of a bank service or activity, (2) identified as a debit or credit balance item; and (3) related to a corresponding balance sheet or income statement account, such as loans (balance sheet) are associated with interest income in the income statement. Remember, the balance sheet is a point in time while the income statement aggregates or sums revenue/expense in a period of time.

Asset Accounts

Account	Debit/Credit	Brief Definition	Income Statement Association
Currency and Coins	Debit	Vault cash	
Due from Banks	Debit	Deposit balances in other banks	Interest income of time deposits
Federal Funds Sold	Debit	Short-term loans to other banks	Interest Income
U.S. Treasury Securities	Debit	Debt obligations of the U.S. Treasury	Interest Income
U.S. Government Agencies	Debit	Debt securities of agencies	Interest Income
Municipal and State Securities	Debit	Securities issued by cities and states	Interest Income
Other Securities	Debit	May include corporate bonds, etc.	Interest Income
Commercial Loans	Debit	Gross business loan contracts outstanding	Interest Income

Consumer Loans	Debit	Total gross loans outstanding to consumers	Interest Income
Real Estate Loans	Debit	Gross loans secured by real estate	Interest Income
Unearned Income	Credit	A contra-asset representing the amount of unearned income in the gross loan amounts	Interest income (Cr); unearned income (Dr) in each period
Valuation Reserve for Loan Losses	Credit	A contra-asset representing the expected amount of future loan losses	Provision for loan loss (Dr); valuation reserve (Cr)
Net Loans	Debit	The amount of loan principal the bank expects to collect	
Bank Premises	Debit	Bank-owned real estate and buildings	Occupancy expense; (depreciation expense)
Leasehold Improvements	Debit	Permanent capital additions to leased facilities	Occupancy expense (amortized expense)
Customers' Liability for Acceptances	Debit	Obligations of customers for banker's acceptances outstanding	

Furniture and Equipment	Debit	F & E owned by the bank	Occupancy expense (maintenance and amortization expense)
Accrued Income Receivable	Debit	Income earned, not received	Previous period income
Other Assets	Debit	Total not significant to be noted alone (see list at end of section)	Income (receivable) or expense (amortized)

Liability Accounts

Non-Interest Bearing Deposits- Domestic	Credit	Generally demand deposits	Service charge income; other expense
Interest- Bearing Deposits- Domestic	Credit	Savings or CD accounts of U.S. origin	Interest expense
Non-Interest Bearing Deposits- Foreign	Credit	Owned by international businesses or persons	Service charge income or other expense
Interest Bearing Deposits- Foreign	Credit	Savings or CDs of internationals	Interest Expense
Bankers Acceptances Outstanding	Credit	Customer trade bills of exchange guaranteed by bank	Fee income
Federal Funds Purchased	Credit	Short-term loans from other banks	Interest Expense

Securities Sold u/a to Repurchase	Credit	Repo agreement	Interest Expense
Accrued Interest Payable	Credit	Interest expense incurred, not paid	Previous period expense
Other Liabilities	Credit	Obligations owed, not classified elsewhere (see list at end of section)	

Capital Accounts

Common Stock	Credit	Par or stated value times shares outstanding
Surplus	Credit	Paid in capital above par
Undivided Profits	Credit	Prior earnings retained

Income Statement Accounts

Account	Revenue (R)/ Expense (E)	Debit/ Credit	Description	Balance Sheet Association
Interest and Fees: Loans	R	Credit	Loan interest income earned in period	Loans

Interest: Time Balances in Banks	R	Credit	Interest earned on balances in other banks (due from)	Due from banks
Interest Income: Securities	R	Credit	Interest earned on Treasury, agency, state, municipal and other securities	Securities owned
Interest: Federal Funds Sold	R	Credit	Income from funds loaned to other banks	Federal funds sold
Interest: CDs	E	Debit	Interest expense on CDs (time deposits)	Interest-bearing deposits
Interest: Other Deposits	E	Debit	Interest expense on savings and transaction accounts	Interest-bearing deposits
Interest: Federal Funds Purchased	E	Debit	Interest expense of short-term funds borrowed from other banks	Federal funds purchased
Interest: Sec Sold u/a to Repurchase	E	Debit	Interest expense of repo funds purchased	Securities sold u/a to repurchase

Provision for Loan Losses	E	Debit	Noncash expense sufficient to bring loan loss valuation reserve to adequate level	ProvLL Dr Reserve Valuation: Cr
Trust Dept Income	R	Credit	Net earnings from trust operations	
Service Charges: Deposits	R	Credit	Non-interest revenue from deposit accounts	Deposit accounts
Other Service Charges and Fees	R	Credit	Non-interest revenue such as loan origina-tion fees, service fees and late fees	
Other Income	R	Credit	Other revenue (see list below)	
Security Gains (Losses)	R	Cr/(Dr)	Sale of investment securities	Invest-ment securi-ties
Salaries and Employee Benefits	E	Debit	Employee expenses	

Net Occupancy Expense of Bank Premises	E	Debit	Occupancy expense less rental income	Bank premises
Furniture and Equipment Expense	E	Debit	Deprecia- tion, mainte- nance expenses, etc.	Furniture and equipment
Other Expenses	E	Debit	Other expenses not yet listed (see list below)	
Applicable Income Taxes	E	Debit	Total tax expense (book)	
Net Income		Credit	Period additions to capital	

The individual accounts listed under the "other" categories are deemed to be less significant than other "stand-alone" ledger items. Typical examples of other accounts are presented below.

Other Assets:

Account	Description
Investments in subsidiaries that have not been consolidated	Stock investment of bank
Other real estate owned by the bank	Repossessed real estate
Prepaid expenses	Expenses paid, not yet incurred: insurance, FDIC premiums, etc.
Suspense accounts	Unrecorded debits at the end of the day, interbranch clearings

Cash surrender value: life insurance	Cash value of bank-owned life insurance policies on key officers
Inventories	Stationery, supplies
Construction in progress	Cost to date

Other Liabilities Account	Description
Accrued payrolls	Expense incurred, not paid
Accrued taxes - current	Expense incurred, not paid
Deferred income taxes	Expense incurred, deferred to later
Undistributed payroll deductions	Employee tax and FICA not yet paid
Cash dividends declared, not paid	Account appearing between record date and payment date

Other Income (Revenue)

Safe deposit rentals	Safe deposit boxes
Commissions earned	Sale of U.S. savings bonds, etc.
Premiums: credit life insurance	Sale of credit life to loan customers

Other Expenses

Accounting, auditing and legal fees

Freight

Postage

Data processing

Courier service

FDIC assessment	Deposit insurance premiums

Business development

Advertising

Credit reports purchased

Loan collection expenses

Travel expenses

Dues, memberships, subscriptions

Security expense

Charitable contributions

Training and development

Director's fees

N.S.F. and forgery losses

Bank differences (shortages)

MENU AND SCREENS

The program menu is listed on two screens and is discussed below.

```
A   -   TUTORIAL
B   -   ACCOUNT RECOGNITION QUIZ (RESTARTS QUIZ)
C   -   REVIEW CORRECT ANSWERS: INDIVIDUAL ACCOUNTS
D   -   VIEW SAMPLE BALANCE SHEET
E   -   VIEW SAMPLE INCOME STATEMENT
P   -   PRINT REPORT
S   -   SAVE TO DISKETTE (REPLACES CURRENT FILE CONTENTS)
Q   -   QUIT PROGRAM
```


A   -   TUTORIAL

A two-screen introduction describes the purpose of the model and general instructions.

B   -   ACCOUNT RECOGNITION QUIZ

The ledger accounts of the balance sheet and income statement have been scrambled and are displayed four at a time. The user has the option of choosing one of the following to match the account with the appropriate section of the financial statement:

```
1 = Assets           4 = Capital
2 = Contra Assets    5 = Revenue
3 = Liabilities      6 = Expense
```

Proceed through the list of accounts, first determining if the account is associated with balance sheet or income statement and then pinpointing the specific sub-area of the financial statement such as revenue or expense. The program will return you to the program menu when all accounts have been reviewed.

C   -   REVIEW CORRECT ANSWERS: INDIVIDUAL ACCOUNTS

This section again lists the ledger accounts but also presents the user's answers, the correct answer and whether the answer was right (1) or wrong (0). As the account answers are reviewed, try to analyze the wrong answers and the answers that were guessed correctly. Why did you make your selection? Why is the answer what it is? You may refer to Menus D and E to view the account in the financial statement or return to the Financial Statement Review at the beginning of this chapter.

D   -   VIEW SAMPLE BALANCE SHEET

All the balance sheet accounts used in the Account Recognition Quiz are presented in a balance sheet format. As you review this presentation, think of the purpose of the individual account and try to define the services, investments, and activity associated with it. In Program I, Bank Ratio Analysis, these accounts are related to each other to measure liquidity, performance, asset quality, etc. Understanding the ledger accounts is an important prerequisite to financial statement analysis.

E   -   VIEW SAMPLE INCOME STATEMENT

The income statement ledger accounts are presented, using a common multi-step display format. Interest revenues less interest expenses is the first step in the presentation. Net interest income is similar to a gross profit figure in a manufacturing firm. The level and stability of net interest income (before other income and other non-interest expense) are important determinants of the level and stability of net income. Thus, a net interest income line item is created. Total noninterest income is becoming more and more important to bank profitability and the content of the total non-interest expense level is becoming critical, thus explaining this totaling figure as we make our way down the income statement.

P   -   PRINT EXERCISE AND SUMMARY

The print/save option permits you to print a hard copy of
the ledger accounts, your answers from the Account Recognition
Quiz and a summary table listing the number of correct answers
and whether your answer was right (1) or wrong (0).

S   -   SAVE TO DISKETTE (REPLACES CURRENT FILE CONTENTS)

Appendix **A**

Uniform Bank Performance Report[a]

[a] Includes pages selected from Federal Reserve Banks, _Functional Cost Analysis, National Average Report, 1987_.

1987

FRB - FUNCTIONAL COST ANALYSIS

ANALYSIS OF ASSET YIELDS AND COST OF MONEY

		129 BANKS DEPOSITS UP TO $50M		247 BANKS DEPOSITS $50M- $200M		58 BANKS DEPOSITS OVER $200M	
ASSET YIELDS							
		PERCENT OF FUNCTIONAL VOLUME					
	INVESTMENTS						
1	GROSS YIELD	1,450,007	8.81 %	4,446,755	8.91 %	16,849,630	8.93 %
2	LESS: EXPENSE	42,031	.26	96,335	.19	321,421	.17
3	NET YIELD	1,407,976	8.56 %	4,332,417	8.72 %	16,528,209	8.76 %
	REAL ESTATE MORTGAGE LOANS						
4	GROSS YIELD	794,879	10.77 %	2,750,995	10.66 %	9,493,489	10.59 %
5	LESS: EXPENSE	109,573	1.48	320,034	1.24	1,105,010	1.23
6	: LOAN LOSSES	37,978	.51	83,036	.32	136,218	.15
7	NET YIELD	647,328	8.77 %	2,347,926	9.10 %	8,252,261	9.21 %
	INSTALMENT LOANS						
8	GROSS YIELD	506,774	12.78 %	1,668,945	12.09 %	10,432,596	11.57 %
9	LESS: EXPENSE	158,224	3.99	451,782	3.27	2,439,370	2.71
10	: LOAN LOSSES	32,244	.81	105,364	.76	368,278	.41
11	NET YIELD	316,306	7.98 %	1,111,800	8.06 %	7,624,949	8.46 %
	CREDIT CARD (CARD BANKS ONLY)						
12	GROSS YIELD	215,393	12.21 %	481,211	25.90 %	2,936,728	23.34 %
13	LESS: EXPENSE	120,318	6.82	295,356	15.90	1,360,445	10.81
14	: LOAN LOSSES	70,791	4.01	28,375	1.53	197,812	1.57
15	NET YIELD	24,284	1.38 %	157,481	8.48 %	1,378,471	10.95 %
	COMMERCIAL AND OTHER LOANS						
16	GROSS YIELD	880,273	10.29 %	2,858,678	10.00 %	16,182,754	9.52 %
17	LESS: EXPENSE	207,755	2.43	565,636	1.98	2,429,400	1.43
18	: LOAN LOSSES	138,708	1.62	334,681	1.17	948,643	.56
19	NET YIELD	533,810	6.24 %	1,958,361	6.85 %	12,804,711	7.53 %
	INTERNATIONAL						
20	GROSS YIELD	******	****** %	******	****** %	******	****** %
21	LESS: EXPENSE	******	******	******	******	******	******
22	: LOAN LOSSES	******	******	******	******	******	******
23	NET YIELD	******	****** %	******	****** %	******	****** %
COST OF MONEY							
		PERCENT OF AVAILABLE FUNDS					
24	INTEREST EXPENSE	1,822,029	4.84 %	6,056,805	4.95 %	27,232,478	4.78 %
25	OPERATING EXPENSE	723,893	1.99	2,056,563	1.67	10,417,930	1.71
26	LESS: SERVICE AND HANDLING CHARGES	210,926	.60	513,721	.43	2,491,980	.42
27	COST OF MONEY	2,334,996	6.23 %	7,599,647	6.20 %	35,158,428	6.07 %
		PERCENT OF FUNCTIONAL VOLUME					
	DEMAND DEPOSITS						
28	INTEREST EXPENSE	258,493	2.54 %	783,116	2.43 %	3,025,256	1.92 %
29	OPERATING EXPENSE	422,498	4.15	1,262,210	3.92	6,671,741	4.23
30	LESS: SERVICE AND HANDLING CHARGES	192,974	1.89	479,325	1.49	2,215,954	1.41
31	COST OF DEMAND DEPOSITS	488,016	4.79 %	1,566,002	4.86 %	7,481,043	4.75 %
	TIME DEPOSITS						
32	INTEREST EXPENSE	1,298,927	6.14 %	4,349,565	6.30 %	18,538,168	6.12 %
33	OPERATING EXPENSE	182,643	.86	536,440	.78	2,718,430	.90
34	LESS: SERVICE AND HANDLING CHARGES	7,104	.03	18,916	.03	146,840	.05
35	COST OF TIME DEPOSITS	1,474,466	6.97 %	4,867,088	7.05 %	21,109,758	6.97 %
	NON-DEPOSIT FUNDS						
36	INTEREST EXPENSE	270,812	4.34 %	931,064	4.23 %	5,669,054	4.63 %
37	OPERATING EXPENSE	118,752	1.90	257,913	1.17	1,027,759	.84
38	LESS: SERVICE AND HANDLING CHARGES	17,050	.27	22,420	.10	129,186	.11
39	COST OF NON-DEPOSIT FUNDS	372,514	5.96 %	1,166,557	5.30 %	6,567,627	5.37 %

1987

AVERAGE BALANCE SHEET - PERCENT OF AVAILABLE FUNDS

FRB - FUNCTIONAL COST ANALYSIS

		129 BANKS DEPOSITS UP TO $50M		247 BANKS DEPOSITS $50M-$200M		58 BANKS DEPOSITS OVER $200M	
ASSETS							
1	CASH AND DUE FROM BANKS	$ 1,591,596	4.24 %	$ 4,529,075	3.68 %	$ 27,723,138	4.76 %
2	CASH ITEMS IN PROCESS OF COLLECTION	222,513	.59	1,446,354	1.17	12,154,847	2.09
3	U. S. SECURITIES	$ 9,258,216	24.64 %	$ 24,703,233	20.05 %	$ 74,428,599	12.77 %
4	TAX-EXEMPT SECURITIES AND LOANS	3,453,496	9.19	11,791,436	9.57	63,978,028	10.98
5	OTHER INVESTMENTS	1,518,533	4.04	4,895,166	3.97	14,352,353	2.46
6	LIQUIDITY LOANS	2,814,628	7.49	8,952,284	7.27	35,849,576	6.15
7	TRADING ACCOUNT SECURITIES	******	******	490,956	.40	******	******
8	INVESTMENTS, SUBTOTAL	$ 16,453,771	43.79 %	$ 49,905,433	40.51 %	$ 188,730,490	32.38 %
9	REAL ESTATE MORTGAGE LOANS	$ 7,381,718	19.65 %	$ 25,799,216	20.94 %	$ 89,619,034	15.37 %
10	INSTALMENT LOANS	3,965,117	10.55	13,799,751	11.20	90,154,873	15.47
11	CREDIT CARD	1,124,214	2.99	1,639,576	1.33	10,282,833	1.76
12	COMMERCIAL AND OTHER LOANS	8,557,882	22.78	28,591,411	23.21	170,035,435	29.17
13	LOANS, SUBTOTAL	$ 19,342,843	51.48 %	$ 67,445,403	54.75 %	$ 353,456,060	60.64 %
14	INTERNATIONAL	******	******	******	******	******	******
15	PORTFOLIO, SUBTOTAL	$ 35,796,615	95.27 %	$ 117,351,519	95.25 %	$ 543,020,433	93.16 %
16	TOTAL AVAILABLE FUNDS	$ 37,574,499	100.00 %	$ 123,197,358	100.00 %	$ 582,898,401	100.00 %
17	BANK PREMISES	729,844	1.94	2,138,483	1.74	9,000,048	1.54
18	OTHER REAL ESTATE AND OTHER ASSETS	987,229	2.63	2,597,480	2.11	10,450,522	1.79
19	TOTAL ASSETS	$ 39,291,572	104.57 %	$ 127,924,663	103.84 %	$ 602,348,971	103.34 %
LIABILITIES AND CAPITAL							
20	CHECKING ACCOUNTS	$ 9,923,845	26.41 %	$ 31,443,955	25.52 %	$ 153,610,038	26.35 %
21	OFFICIAL CHECKS, MONEY ORDERS, ETC.	234,589	.62	630,782	.51	3,304,173	.57
22	TREASURY TAX AND LOAN ACCOUNT	51,515	.14	173,067	.14	815,259	.14
23	DEMAND DEPOSITS, SUBTOTAL	$ 10,188,256	27.11 %	$ 32,223,078	26.16 %	$ 157,559,309	27.03 %
24	REGULAR SAVINGS (INCL CLUB A/CS)	$ 4,239,899	11.28 %	$ 12,483,530	10.13 %	$ 59,832,573	10.26 %
25	TIME OPEN AND OTHER TIME DEPS.	4,930,628	13.12	20,254,858	16.44	111,434,818	19.12
26	RETIREMENT ACCOUNTS	1,615,169	4.30	5,733,131	4.65	27,530,985	4.72
27	CERTIFICATES OF DEPOSIT UNDER $100,000	11,549,368	30.74	33,016,461	26.80	110,842,295	19.02
28	TIME DEPOSITS, SUBTOTAL	$ 21,143,771	56.27 %	$ 68,988,646	56.00 %	$ 302,927,458	51.97 %
29	DEPOSITS, SUBTOTAL	$ 31,332,027	83.39 %	$ 101,211,723	82.15 %	$ 460,486,767	79.00 %
30	BORROWED AND PURCHASED FUNDS	$ 452,334	1.20 %	$ 1,619,776	1.31 %	$ 13,293,673	2.28 %
31	TIME DEPOSITS $100,000 AND OVER	3,503,762	9.32	10,464,803	8.49	52,742,395	9.05
32	OTHER MARKET INSTRUMENTS	867,172	2.31	4,333,819	3.52	24,302,304	4.17
33	OTHER LIABILITIES	482,320	1.28	1,372,139	1.11	6,702,271	1.15
34	TOTAL LIABILITIES, SUBTOTAL	$ 35,715,557	95.05 %	$ 116,527,286	94.59 %	$ 553,677,567	94.99 %
35	CAPITAL NOTES AND DEBENTURES	******	******	******	******	$ 2,921,516	.50 %
36	PREFERRED STOCK	******	******	******	******	******	******
37	COMMON STOCK	548,494	1.46	1,524,112	1.24	6,359,632	1.09
38	SURPLUS, UNDIVIDED PROFITS AND RESERVES	2,797,896	7.45	9,052,326	7.35	36,969,236	6.34
39	VALUATION RESERVES	344,192	.92	1,030,290	.84	4,917,064	.84
40	TOTAL CAPITAL ACCOUNTS, SUBTOTAL	$ 3,580,325	9.53 %	$ 11,428,054	9.28 %	$ 48,671,404	8.35 %
41	TOTAL LIABILITIES AND CAPITAL	$ 39,291,572	104.57 %	$ 127,924,663	103.84 %	$ 602,348,971	103.34 %
MEMORANDUM							
42	NON-DEPOSIT FUNDS	$ 6,245,782	16.63 %	$ 22,016,311	17.87 %	$ 122,411,634	21.00 %

1987

FRB - FUNCTIONAL COST ANALYSIS

NET EARNINGS SUMMARY

EXPENSE DETAIL

OPERATING EXPENSES

PERCENT OF OPERATING EXPENSE

	129 BANKS DEPOSITS UP TO $50M		247 DEPOSITS BANKS $50M-$200M		58 BANKS DEPOSITS OVER $200M	
1 OFFICER SALARIES	$ 263,745	17.74 %	$ 797,247	18.02 %	$ 3,413,272	16.25 %
2 EMPLOYEE SALARIES	236,004	15.88	819,420	18.52	4,301,978	20.48
3 FRINGE BENEFITS	115,215	7.75	345,519	7.81	1,633,962	7.78
4 SALARIES AND FRINGE, SUBTOTAL	$ 612,285	41.19 %	$ 1,957,990	44.25 %	$ 9,349,211	44.51 %
5 OFF-PREMISE COMPUTER EXPENSE	$ 68,431	4.60 %	$ 203,006	4.59 %	$ 1,273,457	6.06 %
6 FURNITURE AND EQUIPMENT	105,398	7.09	289,433	6.54	1,350,354	6.43
7 PRINTING, STATIONERY AND SUPPLIES	43,535	2.93	117,918	2.66	544,532	2.59
8 POSTAGE, FREIGHT AND DELIVERY	28,895	1.94	84,922	1.92	423,679	2.02
9 PUBLICITY AND ADVERTISING	33,043	2.22	100,396	2.27	515,650	2.46
10 FEES, LEGAL & OTHER (INCL HOLD CO MGMT FEES)	41,925	2.82	117,140	2.65	748,389	3.56
11 TELEPHONE AND TELEGRAPH	15,773	1.06	55,907	1.26	364,497	1.74
12 OCCUPANCY	107,202	7.21	309,012	6.98	1,553,282	7.40
13 EXTERNAL EXAMINATIONS AND AUDITS	22,602	1.52	54,692	1.24	122,220	.58
14 DIRECTOR FEES	27,448	1.85	50,465	1.14	107,917	.51
15 FDIC INSURANCE	29,098	1.96	90,667	2.05	411,506	1.96
16 OTHER INSURANCE, EXCEPT REALTY, LIFE, ETC	24,650	1.66	60,765	1.37	212,625	1.01
17 TRAVEL	10,334	.70	25,691	.58	135,231	.64
18 DUES AND MEMBERSHIPS	7,842	.53	21,053	.48	66,440	.32
19 DONATIONS AND GIFTS	5,175	.35	16,654	.38	58,787	.28
20 BOOKS, PERIOD., INFO. SVCS	3,602	.24	13,596	.31	48,045	.23
21 LOAN LOSSES	194,024	13.05	497,464	11.24	1,615,520	7.69
22 COMPUTER SOFTWARE EXPENSE	15,431	1.04	34,328	.78	162,045	.77
23 ALL OTHER EXPENSES	133,218	8.96	398,332	9.00	2,277,893	10.85
24 TOTAL OPERATING EXPENSE	$ 1,486,329	100.00 %	$ 4,424,752	100.00 %	$ 21,002,824	100.00 %
MEMORANDA						
25 OFF-PREMISE COMPUTER EXPENSE	$ 68,431	4.60 %	$ 203,006	4.59 %	$ 1,273,457	6.06 %
26 COMPUTER SOFTWARE EXPENSE	15,431	1.04	34,328	.78	162,045	.77
27 *ON-PREMISE COMPUTER EXPENSE	90,853	6.11	247,093	5.58	1,481,813	7.06
28 TOTAL EXPENDITURES FOR DATA SERVICES	$ 127,598	8.58 %	$ 374,313	8.46 %	$ 2,336,895	11.13 %

PERCENT OF AVAILABLE FUNDS

INTEREST EXPENSE

29 DEMAND DEPOSIT INTEREST	$ 258,493	.69 %	$ 783,116	.64 %	$ 3,025,256	.52 %
30 TIME DEPOSIT INTEREST	1,298,927	3.44	4,349,565	3.52	18,538,168	3.18
31 NON-DEPOSIT INTEREST	270,812	.72	931,064	.76	5,669,054	.97
32 TOTAL INTEREST EXPENSE	$ 1,822,029	4.85 %	$ 6,056,805	4.92 %	$ 27,232,478	4.67 %

MISCELLANEOUS DATA

33 PERSONNEL / $MILLION A/F	.74	.70	.68
34 NUMBER OF BANKING OFFICES	2.02	4.24	19.00
35 3 YEAR LOAN LOSS AVG / AVAIL FUNDS	.64 %	.47 %	.28 %

* INCLUDED IN SEVERAL OPERATING EXPENSES.

7

1987
FRB - FUNCTIONAL COST ANALYSIS

DEMAND DEPOSIT FUNCTION

		130 BANKS DEPOSITS UP TO $50M		247 BANKS DEPOSITS $50M-$200M		58 BANKS DEPOSITS OVER $200M	
1	WEIGHT-UNITS	3,864,498		10,925,172		50,420,862	
	VOLUME						
2	CASH AND DUE FROM BANKS	1,251,849	12.24 %	3,518,376	10.92 %	21,624,047	13.72 %
3	CASH ITEMS IN PROCESS OF COLLECTION	185,035	1.81	1,335,096	4.14	12,154,847	7.71
4	FUNDS INVESTED IN PORTFOLIO	8,792,594	85.95	27,369,606	84.94	123,780,414	78.56
5	TOTAL DEMAND DEPOSITS	10,229,478	100.00 %	32,223,078	100.00 %	157,559,309	100.00 %
	INCOME						
6	SERVICE AND HANDLING CHARGES	168,724	1.65 %	417,366	1.30 %	1,869,544	1.19 %
7	OTHER INCOME	23,592	.23	58,788	.18	346,410	.22
8	TOTAL INCOME	192,316	1.88 %	476,154	1.48 %	2,215,954	1.41 %
	EXPENSE						
9	OFFICER SALARIES	35,670	.35 %	102,050	.32 %	582,638	.37 %
10	EMPLOYEE SALARIES	117,533	1.15	385,303	1.20	1,941,268	1.23
11	FRINGE BENEFITS	38,395	.38	108,396	.34	554,242	.35
12	SALARIES AND FRINGE, SUBTOTAL	191,598	1.87 %	595,750	1.85 %	3,078,149	1.95 %
13	DATA SERVICES	51,364	.50	146,703	.46	937,961	.60
14	FURNITURE AND EQUIPMENT	34,449	.34	97,512	.30	453,001	.29
15	OCCUPANCY	36,489	.36	110,528	.34	610,451	.39
16	PUBLICITY AND ADVERTISING	8,939	.09	23,843	.07	133,460	.08
17	PRINTING, STATIONERY AND SUPPLIES	18,785	.18	48,613	.15	197,577	.13
18	POSTAGE, FREIGHT AND DELIVERIES	16,567	.16	47,122	.15	218,312	.14
19	OTHER OPERATING EXPENSES	64,064	.63	192,140	.60	1,042,830	.66
20	TOTAL OPERATING EXPENSE	422,256	4.13 %	1,262,210	3.92 %	6,671,741	4.23 %
	EARNINGS						
21	NET EARNINGS BEFORE INTEREST	229,940-	2.25-%	786,056-	2.44-%	4,455,786-	2.83-%
22	INTEREST EXPENSE	257,552	2.52	779,946	2.42	3,025,256	1.92
23	NET EARNINGS	487,492-	4.77-%	1,566,002-	4.86-%	7,481,043-	4.75-%
	MEMORANDA						
24	PORTFOLIO INCOME CREDIT	701,038	6.85	2,259,343	7.01	10,432,533	6.62
25	NET EARNINGS AFTER PORTFOLIO CREDIT	213,546	2.09 %	693,341	2.15 %	2,951,490	1.87 %
	NUMBER OF DEMAND DEPOSIT PERSONNEL						
26	OFFICERS	1.33		3.47		17.67	
27	EMPLOYEES	10.13		31.69		147.25	
28	TOTAL PERSONNEL	11.46		35.16		164.92	
29	MEMO- TELLERS (INCLUDED IN EMPLOYEES)	5.58		16.02		66.80	
30	NUMBER OF BANKING OFFICES	1.99		4.22		19.00	
31	CHECKING EXP RECOVERY FROM SERVICE CHGS	45.54 %		37.72 %		33.21 %	
	COMPOSITION						
32	CHECKING ACCOUNTS	9,969,248	97.46 %	31,443,955	97.58 %	153,610,038	97.49 %
33	TT&L AND OFFICIAL CHECKS	260,230	2.54	779,123	2.42	3,949,271	2.51
34	TOTAL DEMAND DEPOSITS	10,229,478	100.00 %	32,223,078	100.00 %	157,559,309	100.00 %
35	MEMO- INTEREST BEARING CHECKING	5,045,778	49.33 %	15,437,922	47.91 %	62,541,794	39.69 %

1987

8

FRB - FUNCTIONAL COST ANALYSIS

DEMAND DEPOSITS - WEIGHT-UNITS AND ITEM COSTS

	130 BANKS DEPOSITS UP TO $50M		246 BANKS DEPOSITS $50M-$200M		57 BANKS DEPOSITS OVER $200M	
	NUMBER	WEIGHT-UNITS	NUMBER	WEIGHT-UNITS	NUMBER	WEIGHT-UNITS
WEIGHT-UNIT CALCULATION						
1 ON-US DEBITS	673,607	1,221,503	1,896,075	3,431,254	8,205,778	14,852,458
2 DEPOSITS	129,321	481,347	359,344	1,336,152	1,615,275	6,008,824
3 TRANSIT CHECKS DEPOSITED	454,836	454,836	1,635,216	1,635,216	8,297,717	8,297,717
4 ACCOUNT MAINTENANCE	2,854	1,706,812	7,475	4,516,709	31,207	18,850,313
5 CHECKING ACCOUNTS, SUBTOTAL		3,864,498		10,919,331		48,009,311
6 ON-US CHECKS CASHED	44,784	125,843	145,000	407,449	953,953	2,680,607
7 TRANSIT CHECKS CASHED	65,536	249,692	132,197	503,671	685,177	2,610,525
8 OFFICIAL CHECKS ISSUED	10,609	57,925	31,746	173,333	134,191	732,682
9 TT&L DEPOSITS	1,229	4,045	4,244	13,963	20,959	68,955
10 TOTAL WEIGHT-UNITS		4,302,003		12,017,747		54,102,080
11 TOTAL OPERATING EXP	$	422,256	$	1,261,990	$	6,310,965
12 COST PER WEIGHT-UNIT (IN CENTS)		9.82		10.50		11.66

1987 COST PER ITEM IN CENTS

ITEM COSTS			
13 ON-US DEBIT	17.80	19.00	21.11
14 DEPOSIT	36.53	39.05	43.39
15 TRANSIT CHECK DEPOSITED	9.82	10.50	11.66
16 ACCOUNT MAINTENANCE PER MONTH	$ 4.89	$ 5.29	$ 5.87
17 CHECK CASHING	33.41	34.52	37.65
18 OFFICIAL CHECK ISSUED	53.59	57.34	63.69
19 TT&L DEPOSIT	32.29	34.55	38.38

ANALYSIS OF EXPENSE BY ACTIVITY						
20 ON-US DEBITS	$ 119,894	28.39 %	$ 360,318	28.55 %	$1,732,528	27.45 %
21 DEPOSITS	47,246	11.19	140,310	11.12	700,925	11.11
22 TRANSIT CHECKS DEPOSITED	44,644	10.57	171,715	13.61	967,922	15.34
23 ACCOUNT MAINTENANCE	167,529	39.67	474,302	37.58	2,198,874	34.84
24 CHECKING ACCOUNT EXP.. SUBTOT.	$ 379,313	89.83 %	$1,146,645	90.86 %	$5,600,249	88.74 %
25 CHECK CASHING	$ 36,860	8.73 %	$ 95,677	7.58 %	$ 617,206	9.78 %
26 OFFICIAL CHECKS ISSUED	5,686	1.35	18,202	1.44	85,467	1.35
27 TT&L DEPOSITS	397	.09	1,466	.12	8,044	.13
28 NON-CHECKING EXPENSE.SUBTOT.	$ 42,943	10.17 %	$ 115,345	9.14 %	$ 710,717	11.26 %
29 TOTAL OPERATING EXPENSE	$ 422,256	100.00 %	$1,261,990	100.00 %	$6,310,965	100.00 %

1987

FRB - FUNCTIONAL COST ANALYSIS

DEMAND DEPOSITS - CHECKING ACCOUNT ANALYSIS

	130 BANKS DEPOSITS UP TO $50M		247 BANKS DEPOSITS $50M-$200M		58 BANKS DEPOSITS OVER $200M	
VOLUME AND ACTIVITY						
1 TOTAL CHECKING ACCOUNTS	$ 9,969,248		31,443,955		153,610,038	
2 NUMBER OF ACCOUNTS	2,854		7,474		32,853	
3 AVERAGE SIZE OF ACCOUNT	$ 3,493		$ 4,207		$ 4,676	
4 ON-US DEBITS PER ACCOUNT PER MONTH	19.67		21.15		22.00	
5 DEPOSITS PER ACCOUNT PER MONTH	3.78		4.01		4.28	
6 TRANSIT CHECKS PER ACCOUNT PER MONTH	13.28		18.27		21.79	
INCOME						
7 SERVICE AND HANDLING CHARGES	$ 167,065	1.68 %	$ 414,891	1.32 %	$ 1,858,683	1.21 %
EXPENSE						
8 ON-US DEBITS	118,258	1.19	357,810	1.14	1,776,889	1.16
9 DEPOSITS	47,874	.48	138,827	.44	715,665	.47
10 TRANSIT CHECKS	41,858	.42	167,520	.53	949,232	.62
11 ACCOUNT MAINTENANCE	167,598	1.68	484,364	1.54	2,296,099	1.49
12 TOTAL OPERATING EXPENSE	$ 375,589	3.77 %	$ 1,148,521	3.65 %	$ 5,737,885	3.74 %
EARNINGS						
13 NET EARNINGS BEFORE INTEREST	208,525-	2.09-%	733,630-	2.33-%	3,879,201-	2.53-%
14 INTEREST EXPENSE	257,552	2.58	779,946	2.48	3,025,256	1.97
15 NET EARNINGS	466,077-	4.68-%	1,513,576-	4.81-%	6,904,458-	4.49-%
MEMORANDA						
16 PORTFOLIO INCOME CREDIT	682,871	6.85 %	2,202,458	7.00 %	10,145,822	6.60 %
17 NET EARNINGS AFTER PORTFOLIO	$ 216,794	2.17 %	$ 688,882	2.19 %	$ 3,241,365	2.11 %

EARNINGS PER ACCOUNT PER MONTH

	130 BANKS DEPOSITS UP TO $50M	247 BANKS DEPOSITS $50M-$200M	58 BANKS DEPOSITS OVER $200M
INCOME			
18 SERVICE AND HANDLING CHARGES	$ 4.88	$ 4.63	$ 4.71
EXPENSE			
19 ON-US DEBITS	3.45	3.99	4.51
20 DEPOSITS	1.40	1.55	1.82
21 TRANSIT CHECKS	1.22	1.87	2.41
22 ACCOUNT MAINTENANCE	4.89	5.40	5.82
23 TOTAL OPERATING EXPENSE	$ 10.97	$ 12.81	$ 14.55
EARNINGS			
24 NET EARNINGS BEFORE INTEREST	6.09-	8.18-	9.84-
25 INTEREST EXPENSE	7.52	8.70	7.67
26 NET EARNINGS	13.61-	16.88-	17.51-
MEMORANDA			
27 PORTFOLIO INCOME CREDIT	19.94	24.56	25.74
28 NET EARNINGS AFTER PORTFOLIO	$ 6.33	$ 7.68	$ 8.22

1987

FRB - FUNCTIONAL COST ANALYSIS

DEMAND DEPOSITS - REGULAR CHECKING ACCOUNT ANALYSIS

	130 BANKS DEPOSITS UP TO $50M		246 BANKS DEPOSITS $50M-$200M		58 BANKS DEPOSITS OVER $200M	
1 REGULAR CHECKING WEIGHT-UNITS	3,143,154		8,455,082		38,724,431	
ACCOUNT DATA						
2 NUMBER OF ACCOUNTS	2,240		5,411		23,219	
3 AVERAGE SIZE OF ACCOUNT	2,179		2,898		3,867	
4 COST PER WEIGHT-UNIT (CENTS)	9.73		10.53		11.30	
VOLUME						
5 CASH AND DUE FROM BANKS AND CIPC	749,057	15.35 %	2,520,316	16.07 %	19,924,182	22.19 %
6 FUNDS INVESTED IN PORTFOLIO	4,131,983	84.65	13,161,166	83.93	69,866,395	77.81
7 TOTAL REGULAR CHECKING VOLUME	4,881,039	100.00 %	15,681,482	100.00 %	89,790,577	100.00 %
INCOME						
8 SERVICE AND HANDLING CHARGES	152,343	3.12 %	356,108	2.27 %	1,508,001	1.68 %
EXPENSE						
9 ON-US DEBITS	97,847	2.00	278,983	1.78	1,358,963	1.51
10 DEPOSITS	38,610	.79	107,773	.69	536,669	.60
11 TRANSIT CHECKS	35,042	.72	149,663	.95	858,130	.96
12 ACCOUNT MAINTENANCE	134,370	2.75	353,731	2.26	1,620,664	1.80
13 TOTAL OPERATING EXPENSE	305,868	6.27 %	890,151	5.68 %	4,374,427	4.87 %
EARNINGS						
14 NET EARNINGS	153,525-	3.15-%	534,043-	3.41-%	2,866,426-	3.19-%
MEMORANDA						
15 PORTFOLIO INCOME CREDIT	325,240	6.66	1,082,429	6.90	5,887,472	6.56
16 NET EARNINGS AFTER PORTFOLIO CREDIT	171,715	3.52 %	548,386	3.50 %	3,021,046	3.36 %

EARNINGS PER ACCOUNT PER MONTH

	130 BANKS DEPOSITS UP TO $50M	246 BANKS DEPOSITS $50M-$200M	58 BANKS DEPOSITS OVER $200M
INCOME			
17 SERVICE AND HANDLING CHARGES	5.67	5.48	5.41
EXPENSE			
18 ON-US DEBITS	3.64	4.30	4.88
19 DEPOSITS	1.44	1.66	1.93
20 TRANSIT CHECKS	1.30	2.30	3.08
21 ACCOUNT MAINTENANCE	5.00	5.45	5.82
22 TOTAL EXPENSE	11.38	13.71	15.70
EARNINGS			
23 NET EARNINGS	5.71-	8.22-	10.29-
MEMORANDA			
24 PORTFOLIO INCOME CREDIT	12.10	16.67	21.13
25 NET EARNINGS AFTER PORTFOLIO CREDIT	6.39	8.45	10.84

ACTIVITY PER ACCOUNT PER MONTH

	130 BANKS DEPOSITS UP TO $50M		246 BANKS DEPOSITS $50M-$200M		58 BANKS DEPOSITS OVER $200M	
ACTIVITY						
26 ON-US DEBITS	554,042	20.61	1,473,347	22.69	6,675,029	23.96
27 DEPOSITS	104,115	3.87	278,401	4.29	1,272,177	4.57
28 TRANSIT CHECKS	389,794	14.50	1,465,267	22.57	7,803,497	28.01

1987

DEMAND DEPOSITS - SPECIAL CHECKING ACCOUNT ANALYSIS

FRB - FUNCTIONAL COST ANALYSIS

12

	13 BANKS DEPOSITS UP TO $50M		66 BANKS DEPOSITS $50M - $200M		11 BANKS DEPOSITS OVER $200M	
1 SPECIAL CHECKING WEIGHT-UNITS						
ACCOUNT DATA						
2 NUMBER OF ACCOUNTS	694		1,499		10,042	
3 AVERAGE SIZE OF ACCOUNT	$	611	$	969	$	671
4 COST PER WEIGHT-UNIT (CENTS)		9.93		10.30		12.50
VOLUME						
5 CASH AND DUE FROM BANKS AND CIPC	$ 52,345	12.34 %	$ 194,410	13.39 %	$ 1,551,589	23.03 %
6 FUNDS INVESTED IN PORTFOLIO	371,966	87.66	1,257,797	86.61	5,185,201	76.97
7 TOTAL SPECIAL CHECKING VOLUME	$ 424,310	100.00 %	$ 1,452,207	100.00 %	$ 6,736,790	100.00 %
INCOME						
8 SERVICE AND HANDLING CHARGES	$ 33,528	7.90 %	$ 84,330	5.81 %	$ 712,472	10.58 %
EXPENSE						
9 ON-US DEBITS	$ 26,663	6.28 %	$ 56,499	3.89 %	$ 467,080	6.93 %
10 DEPOSITS	12,529	2.95	21,198	1.46	189,525	2.81
11 TRANSIT CHECKS	2,504	.59	5,328	.37	43,869	.65
12 ACCOUNT MAINTENANCE	19,857	4.68	88,971	6.13	726,946	10.79
13 TOTAL OPERATING EXPENSE	$ 61,553	14.51 %	$ 171,996	11.84 %	$ 1,427,421	21.19 %
EARNINGS						
14 NET EARNINGS	$ 28,025-	6.60-%	$ 87,666-	6.04-%	$ 714,949-	10.61-%
MEMORANDA						
15 PORTFOLIO INCOME CREDIT	$ 30,169	7.11	102,481	7.06	442,094	6.56
16 NET EARNINGS AFTER PORTFOLIO	$ 2,144	.51 %	14,815	1.02 %	272,855-	4.05-%

EARNINGS PER ACCOUNT PER MONTH

	13 BANKS DEPOSITS UP TO $50M	66 BANKS DEPOSITS $50M - $200M	11 BANKS DEPOSITS OVER $200M
INCOME			
17 SERVICE AND HANDLING CHARGES	$ 4.02	$ 4.69	$ 5.91
EXPENSE			
18 ON-US DEBITS	$ 3.20	$ 3.14	$ 3.88
19 DEPOSITS	1.50	1.18	1.57
20 TRANSIT CHECKS	.30	.30	.36
21 ACCOUNT MAINTENANCE	2.38	4.95	6.03
22 TOTAL EXPENSE	$ 7.39	$ 9.56	$ 11.85
EARNINGS			
23 NET EARNINGS	$ 3.36-	$ 4.87-	$ 5.93-
MEMORANDA			
24 PORTFOLIO INCOME CREDIT	3.62	5.70	3.67
25 NET EARNINGS AFTER PORTFOLIO CREDIT	$ .26	$ .82	2.26-

ACTIVITY PER ACCOUNT PER MONTH

	13 BANKS DEPOSITS UP TO $50M		66 BANKS DEPOSITS $50M - $200M		11 BANKS DEPOSITS OVER $200M	
ACTIVITY						
26 ON-US DEBITS	142,107	17.05	304,684	16.94	2,039,333	16.92
27 DEPOSITS	30,215	3.63	55,673	3.10	414,504	3.44
28 TRANSIT CHECKS	24,158	2.90	51,796	2.88	346,687	2.88

1987

FRB - FUNCTIONAL COST ANALYSIS   DEMAND DEPOSITS - INTEREST BEARING CHECKING ACCOUNT ANALYSIS

	127 BANKS DEPOSITS UP TO $50M		245 BANKS DEPOSITS $50M-$200M		57 BANKS DEPOSITS OVER $200M	
ACCOUNT DATA						
1 INTEREST BEARING CHECKING WEIGHT-UNITS	674,218		2,054,143		9,580,722	
2 NUMBER OF ACCOUNTS	557		1,671		7,740	
3 AVERAGE SIZE OF ACCOUNT	$ 9,260		$ 9,165		$ 8,028	
4 COST PER WEIGHT-UNIT (CENTS)	9.64		10.50		10.96	
VOLUME						
5 CASH AND DUE FROM BANKS AND CIPC	657,515	12.74 %	2,169,693	14.17 %	12,837,769	20.66 %
6 FUNDS INVESTED IN PORTFOLIO	4,501,817	87.26	13,142,677	85.83	49,303,613	79.34
7 TOTAL INTEREST BEARING VOLUME	5,159,332	100.00	15,312,370	100.00	62,141,383	100.00
INCOME						
8 SERVICE AND HANDLING CHARGES	11,499	.22 %	36,730	.24 %	219,340	.35 %
EXPENSE						
9 ON-US DEBITS	18,118	.35 %	64,604	.42 %	321,448	.52 %
10 DEPOSITS	8,189	.16	25,689	.17	137,406	.22
11 TRANSIT CHECKS	6,721	.13	17,077	.11	84,234	.14
12 ACCOUNT MAINTENANCE	31,940	.62	108,329	.71	507,186	.82
13 TOTAL OPERATING EXPENSE	64,969	1.26	215,698	1.41	1,050,274	1.69
EARNINGS						
14 NET EARNINGS BEFORE INTEREST	53,469-	1.04- %	178,968-	1.17- %	830,934-	1.34-%
15 INTEREST EXPENSE	261,347	5.07	773,183	5.05	2,994,419	4.82
16 NET EARNINGS	314,816-	6.10-	952,151-	6.22-	3,825,353-	6.16-%
MEMORANDA						
17 PORTFOLIO INCOME CREDIT	363,145	7.04	1,090,511	7.12	4,192,348	6.75
18 NET EARNINGS AFTER PORTFOLIO CREDIT	48,329	.94 %	138,360	.90 %	366,996	.59 %

EARNINGS PER ACCOUNT PER MONTH

	127 BANKS DEPOSITS UP TO $50M	245 BANKS DEPOSITS $50M-$200M	57 BANKS DEPOSITS OVER $200M
INCOME			
19 SERVICE AND HANDLING CHARGES	1.72	1.83	$ 2.36
EXPENSE			
20 ON-US DEBITS	2.71	3.22	3.46
21 DEPOSITS	1.22	1.28	1.48
22 TRANSIT CHECKS	1.01	.85	.91
23 ACCOUNT MAINTENANCE	4.78	5.40	5.46
24 TOTAL EXPENSE	9.72	10.76	$ 11.31
EARNINGS			
25 NET EARNINGS BEFORE INTEREST	8.00-	8.93-	$ 8.95-
26 INTEREST EXPENSE	39.09	38.56	32.24
27 NET EARNINGS	47.09-	47.49-	$ 41.19-
MEMORANDA			
28 PORTFOLIO INCOME CREDIT	54.31	54.39	45.14
29 NET EARNINGS AFTER PORTFOLIO CREDIT	7.23	6.90	$ 3.95

ACTIVITY PER ACCOUNT PER MONTH

ACTIVITY			
30 ON-US DEBITS	107,654 16.10	346,509 17.28	1,625,142 17.50
31 DEPOSITS	22,685 3.39	67,058 3.34	339,052 3.65
32 TRANSIT CHECKS	64,104 9.59	165,998 8.28	734,360 7.91

1987

FRB - FUNCTIONAL COST ANALYSIS   DEMAND DEPOSITS - COMMERCIAL CHECKING ACCOUNT ANALYSIS   15

	BANKS DEPOSITS UP TO $50M	20 BANKS DEPOSITS $50M-$200M		5 BANKS DEPOSITS OVER $200M	
1 COMMERCIAL CHECKING WEIGHT-UNITS	******	3,867,429		18,428,810	
ACCOUNT DATA					
2 NUMBER OF ACCOUNTS	******	1,115		7,306	
3 AVERAGE SIZE OF ACCOUNT	$ ******	11,327		$ 9,334	
4 COST PER WEIGHT-UNIT (CENTS)	******	10.09		12.50	
VOLUME					
5 CASH AND DUE FROM BANKS AND CIPC	$ ****** %	2,351,491	18.62 %	$ 13,370,320	19.61 %
6 FUNDS INVESTED IN PORTFOLIO	$ ****** %	10,275,443	81.38	$ 54,822,283	80.39 %
7 TOTAL COMMERCIAL CHECKING VOLUME	$ ****** %	12,626,934	100.00 %	$ 68,192,603	100.00 %
INCOME					
8 SERVICE AND HANDLING CHARGES	$ ****** %	114,356	.91 %	$ 1,039,543	1.52 %
EXPENSE					
9 ON-US DEBITS	$ ****** %	124,404	.99 %	$ 784,615	1.15 %
10 DEPOSITS	******	54,117	.43	345,854	.51
11 TRANSIT CHECKS	******	143,641	1.14	621,080	.91
12 ACCOUNT MAINTENANCE	******	68,110	.54	551,490	.81
13 TOTAL OPERATING EXPENSE	$ ****** %	390,272	3.09 %	$ 2,303,039	3.38 %
EARNINGS					
14 NET EARNINGS BEFORE INTEREST	$ ****** %	275,915-	2.19-%	$ 1,263,496-	1.85-%
15 INTEREST EXPENSE	******	******		******	
16 NET EARNINGS	$ ****** %	275,915-	2.19-%	$ 1,263,496-	1.85-%
MEMORANDA					
17 PORTFOLIO INCOME CREDIT	$ ****** %	848,901	6.72 %	$ 4,748,853	6.96
18 NET EARNINGS AFTER PORTFOLIO CREDIT	$ ****** %	572,986	4.54 %	$ 3,485,357	5.11-%

EARNINGS PER ACCOUNT PER MONTH

INCOME					
19 SERVICE AND HANDLING CHARGES	$ ******	$ 8.55		$ 11.86	
EXPENSE					
20 ON-US DEBITS	$ ******	$ 9.30		$ 8.95	
21 DEPOSITS	******	4.05		3.94	
22 TRANSIT CHECKS	******	10.74		7.08	
23 ACCOUNT MAINTENANCE	******	5.09		6.29	
24 TOTAL EXPENSE	$ ******	$ 29.17		$ 26.27	
EARNINGS					
25 NET EARNINGS BEFORE INTEREST	$ ******	$ 20.63-		$ 14.41-	
26 INTEREST EXPENSE	******	******		******	
27 NET EARNINGS	$ ******	$ 20.63-		$ 14.41-	
MEMORANDA					
28 PORTFOLIO INCOME CREDIT	******	63.46		54.16	
29 NET EARNINGS AFTER PORTFOLIO	$ ******	$ 42.83		$ 39.75	

ACTIVITY PER ACCOUNT PER MONTH

ACTIVITY					
30 ON-US DEBITS	******	50.10		40.02	
31 DEPOSITS	******	11.15		8.50	
32 TRANSIT CHECKS	******	106.46		55.52	

1987

FRB - FUNCTIONAL COST ANALYSIS

ANALYSIS OF REGULAR SAVINGS ACCOUNTS

	129 BANKS DEPOSITS UP TO $50M		245 BANKS DEPOSITS $50M-$200M		58 BANKS DEPOSITS OVER $200M	
1 WEIGHT-UNITS	125,545		392,313		1,806,480	
ACCOUNT DATA						
2 NUMBER OF ACCOUNTS	2,157		6,180		25,760	
3 AVERAGE SIZE OF ACCOUNT	$ 1,943		$ 2,020		$ 2,323	
VOLUME						
4 CASH AND DUE FROM BANKS	$ 64,525	1.54 %	$ 153,444	1.23 %	$ 1,043,258	1.74 %
5 FUNDS INVESTED IN PORTFOLIO	4,125,887	98.46 %	12,330,086	98.77 %	58,789,315	98.26 %
6 TOTAL SAVINGS DEPOSITS	$ 4,190,412	100.00 %	$ 12,483,530	100.00 %	$ 59,832,573	100.00 %
7 MEMO: CLUB ACCOUNTS (INCL LN 6)	$ 30,966	.74 %	$ 135,882	1.09 %	$ 535,788	.90 %
INCOME						
8 SERVICE AND HANDLING CHARGES	$ 3,467	.08 %	$ 10,707	.09 %	$ 60,477	.10 %
9 OTHER INCOME	3,716	.09 %	8,346	.07 %	86,363	.14 %
10 TOTAL INCOME	$ 7,182	.17 %	$ 19,053	.15 %	$ 146,840	.25 %
EXPENSE						
11 DEPOSITS	$ 11,905	.28 %	$ 33,447	.27 %	$ 173,745	.29 %
12 WITHDRAWALS	18,479	.44	51,125	.41	290,831	.49
13 ACCOUNTS OPENED	2,863	.07	6,605	.05	36,560	.06
14 ACCOUNTS CLOSED	1,569	.04	3,716	.03	25,452	.04
15 INTEREST POSTINGS	32,412	.77	98,899	.79	537,907	.90
16 ANNUAL ACCOUNT MAINTENANCE	52,528	1.25	135,122	1.08	644,067	1.08
17 TOTAL OPERATING EXPENSE	$ 119,756	2.86 %	$ 328,913	2.63 %	$ 1,708,562	2.86 %
EARNINGS						
18 NET EARNINGS BEFORE INTEREST	$ 112,574-	2.69-%	$ 309,860-	2.48-%	$ 1,561,722-	2.61-%
19 INTEREST EXPENSE	211,830	5.06	649,492	5.20	3,069,709	5.13
20 NET EARNINGS	$ 324,404-	7.74-%	$ 959,352-	7.68-%	$ 4,631,432-	7.74-%
MEMORANDA						
21 PORTFOLIO INCOME CREDIT	$ 343,078	8.19 %	$ 1,037,889	8.31 %	$ 5,002,405	8.36 %
22 NET EARNINGS AFTER PORTFOLIO CREDIT	$ 18,673	.45 %	$ 78,536	.63 %	$ 370,973	.62 %

EARNINGS PER ACCOUNT PER YEAR

	129 BANKS UP TO $50M		245 BANKS $50M-$200M		58 BANKS OVER $200M	
INCOME						
23 TOTAL INCOME	$ 3.33		$ 3.08		$ 5.70	
EXPENSE						
24 DEPOSITS	$ 5.52		$ 5.41		$ 6.74	
25 WITHDRAWALS	8.57		8.27		11.29	
26 ACCOUNTS OPENED	1.33		1.07		1.42	
27 ACCOUNTS CLOSED	.73		.60		.99	
28 INTEREST POSTINGS	15.03		16.00		20.88	
29 ANNUAL ACCOUNT MAINTENANCE	24.35		21.87		25.00	
30 TOTAL OPERATING EXPENSE	$ 55.52		$ 53.23		$ 66.33	
EARNINGS						
31 NET EARNINGS BEFORE INTEREST	$ 52.19-		$ 50.14-		$ 60.63-	
32 INTEREST EXPENSE	98.21		105.10		119.17	
33 NET EARNINGS	$ 150.41-		$ 155.25-		$ 179.79-	
MEMORANDA						
34 PORTFOLIO INCOME CREDIT	$ 159.06		$ 167.96		$ 194.19	
35 NET EARNINGS AFTER PORTFOLIO CREDIT	$ 8.66		$ 12.71		$ 14.40	
ACTIVITY						
36 DEPOSITS	12,340		40,109		178,287	
37 WITHDRAWALS	9,706		30,555		154,843	
38 INTEREST POSTINGS	4		6		7	
39 NO. OF CLUB ACCOUNTS	173		709		2,476	

1987

FRB - FUNCTIONAL COST ANALYSIS ANALYSIS OF CERTIFICATES OF DEPOSIT UNDER $100,000 23

	129 BANKS DEPOSITS UP TO $50M		247 BANKS DEPOSITS $50M- $200M		58 BANKS DEPOSITS OVER $200M	
1 NUMBER OF CERTIFICATES	1,305		3,510		10,482	
2 AVERAGE SIZE	$ 8,798		$ 9,405		$ 10,574	
VOLUME						
3 CASH AND DUE FROM BANKS	$ 147,987	1.29 %	$ 395,678	1.20 %	$ 1,807,442	1.63 %
4 FUNDS INVESTED IN PORTFOLIO	11,332,156	98.71	32,620,783	98.80	109,034,853	98.37
5 TOTAL CERTIFICATES OF DEPOSIT	$ 11,480,142	100.00 %	$ 33,016,461	100.00 %	$ 110,842,295	100.00 %
EXPENSE						
6 ACCOUNTS OPENED	$ 2,301	.02 %	$ 5,913	.02 %	$ 22,613	.02 %
7 ACCOUNTS CLOSED	2,150	.02	5,343	.02	19,350	.02
8 INTEREST PAYMENTS	17,399	.15	48,901	.15	202,558	.18
9 ANNUAL ACCOUNT MAINTENANCE	7,468	.07	19,104	.06	66,356	.06
10 TOTAL OPERATING EXPENSE	29,318	.26	79,261	.24	310,876	.28
EARNINGS						
11 NET EARNINGS BEFORE INTEREST	29,318-	.26-	79,261-	.24-	310,876-	.28-
12 INTEREST EXPENSE	759,014	6.61	2,293,945	6.95	7,751,802	6.99
13 NET EARNINGS	788,332-	6.87-	2,373,205-	7.19-	8,062,678-	7.27-
MEMORANDA						
14 PORTFOLIO INCOME CREDIT	917,741	7.99	2,701,661	8.18	9,144,524	8.25
15 NET EARNINGS AFTER PORTFOLIO CREDIT	$ 129,409	1.13 %	$ 328,455	.99 %	$ 1,081,846	.98 %

1987

FRB - FUNCTIONAL COST ANALYSIS

NON-DEPOSIT FUNDS FUNCTION

		130 BANKS DEPOSITS UP TO $50M		247 BANKS DEPOSITS $50M-$200M		58 BANKS DEPOSITS OVER $200M	
1	NON-DEPOSIT FUNDS	$ 6,282,745		$ 22,016,311		$ 122,411,634	
VOLUME							
2	EQUITY CAPITAL	$ 3,537,083	56.30%	$ 11,345,419	51.53%	$ 47,764,727	39.02%
3	OTHER LIABILITIES	474,091	7.55	1,366,583	6.21	6,702,271	5.48
4	CAPITAL NOTES AND DEBENTURES	26,388	.42	82,634	.38	906,677	.74
5	BORROWED MONEY	65,450	1.04	356,591	1.62	706,273	.58
6	FEDERAL FUNDS PURCHASED	170,731	2.72	830,370	3.77	11,670,595	9.53
7	TIME DEPOSITS $100,000 AND OVER	3,473,235	55.28	10,252,965	46.57	52,742,395	43.09
8	OTHER MARKET INSTRUMENTS	253,481	4.03	2,509,053	11.40	21,369,267	17.46
9	LESS: BANK PREMISES AND OTHER ASSETS	1,717,715	27.34-	4,727,305	21.47-	19,450,570	15.89-
10	NON-DEPOSIT FUNDS (100%)	$ 6,282,745	100.00%	$ 22,016,311	100.00%	$ 122,411,634	100.00%
11	CASH AND DUE FROM BANKS	54,538	.87	147,022	.67	948,454	.77
12	FUNDS INVESTED IN PORTFOLIO	$ 6,228,206	99.13%	$ 21,869,289	99.33%	$ 121,463,181	99.23%
INCOME							
13	TOTAL INCOME	$ 12,253	.20%	$ 18,651	.08%	$ 129,186	.11%
EXPENSE							
14	OFFICER SALARIES	$ 19,015	.30%	$ 38,922	.18%	$ 85,151	.07%
15	EMPLOYEE SALARIES	7,127	.11	14,476	.07	49,641	.04
16	FRINGE BENEFITS	5,816	.09	11,691	.05	28,098	.02
17	SALARIES AND FRINGE, SUBTOTAL	$ 31,958	.51%	$ 65,089	.30%	$ 162,890	.13%
18	DIRECTOR FEES	16,999	.27	30,807	.14	63,898	.05
19	EXAMINATIONS AND AUDITS	13,089	.21	30,283	.14	58,871	.05
20	FEES, LEGAL AND OTHER	4,458	.07	11,259	.05	53,999	.04
21	DONATIONS	4,994	.08	16,115	.07	52,706	.04
22	OTHER OPERATING EXPENSE	47,752	.76	104,360	.47	635,395	.52
23	TOTAL OPERATING EXPENSE	$ 119,250	1.90%	$ 257,913	1.17%	$ 1,027,759	.84%
EARNINGS							
24	NET EARNINGS BEFORE INTEREST	$ 106,997-	1.70-%	$ 239,262-	1.09-%	$ 898,573-	.73-%
25	INTEREST EXPENSE	269,655	4.29	927,295	4.21	5,669,054	4.63
26	NET EARNINGS	$ 376,652-	6.00-%	$ 1,166,557-	5.30-%	$ 6,567,627-	5.37-%
MEMORANDA							
27	PORTFOLIO INCOME CREDIT	489,118	7.79	1,806,807	8.21	10,089,647	8.24
28	NET EARNINGS AFTER PORTFOLIO CREDIT	$ 112,466	1.79%	$ 640,249	2.91%	$ 3,522,020	2.88%
PERSONNEL DATA							
	NUMBER OF NON-DEPOSIT PERSONNEL						
29	OFFICERS		.55		1.00		2.09
30	EMPLOYEES		.58		1.09		3.50
31	TOTAL PERSONNEL		1.12		2.09		5.59
RATES							
	EFFECTIVE INTEREST RATES						
32	CAPITAL NOTES AND DEBENTURES	$ 1,180	4.47%	$ 7,857	9.51%	$ 83,979	9.26%
33	BORROWED MONEY	4,200	6.42	20,851	5.85	49,122	6.96
34	FEDERAL FUNDS PURCHASED	11,224	6.57	61,234	7.37	769,089	6.59
35	TIME DEPOSITS $100,000 AND OVER	238,285	6.86	684,761	6.68	3,473,694	6.59
36	OTHER MARKET INSTRUMENTS	14,766	5.83	152,592	6.08	1,293,169	6.05

1987

FRB - FUNCTIONAL COST ANALYSIS

INVESTMENT FUNCTION

25

	130 BANKS DEPOSITS UP TO $50M		247 BANKS DEPOSITS $50M-$200M		58 BANKS DEPOSITS OVER $200M	
VOLUME						
1 U. S. SECURITIES	$ 9,161,792	56.20	$ 24,503,207	49.10 %	$ 74,428,599	39.44 %
2 TAX-EXEMPT SECURITIES AND LOANS	3,019,177	18.52	11,695,959	23.44	63,978,028	33.90
3 OTHER INVESTMENTS	1,315,456	8.07	4,756,437	9.53	14,352,353	7.60
4 FEDERAL FUNDS SOLD	2,056,201	12.61	6,136,982	12.30	21,685,567	11.49
5 OTHER LIQUIDITY LOANS	739,603	4.54	2,779,057	5.57	14,164,009	7.50
6 TRADING ACCOUNT	10,503	.06	33,791	.07	121,934	.06
7 TOTAL INVESTMENTS	$ 16,302,732	100.00	$ 49,905,433	100.00 %	$ 188,730,490	100.00 %
INCOME						
8 U. S. TREASURY SECURITIES	$ 735,598	8.03 *	$ 1,977,203	8.07 %*	$ 5,958,552	8.01 %*
9 TAX-EXEMPT INCOME (BOOK BASIS)	234,017	7.75 *	861,358	7.36 %*	4,452,871	6.96 %*
10 TAX SAVINGS ON TAX-EXEMPTS	156,019	.96	574,267	1.15	2,968,729	1.57
11 TAX-EXEMPT INCOME (TAXABLE BASIS)	$ 390,036	12.92 *	$ 1,435,625	12.27 %*	$ 7,421,600	11.60 %*
12 OTHER INVESTMENTS	109,951	8.36	374,151	7.87	944,933	6.58
13 FEDERAL FUNDS SOLD	$ 137,550	6.69 *	$ 414,504	6.75 %*	$ 1,469,216	6.78 %*
14 OTHER LIQUIDITY LOANS	$ 54,252	7.34 *	$ 200,479	7.21 %*	$ 996,678	7.04 %*
15 TRADING ACCOUNT	583-	*****	661	******	21,642-	.01-
16 OTHER INCOME	9,191	.06	27,450	.06	80,293	.04
17 TOTAL INCOME (TAXABLE BASIS)	$ 1,435,996	8.81	$ 4,428,752	8.87 %	$ 16,849,630	8.93 %
EXPENSE						
18 OFFICER SALARIES	$ 19,529	.12	$ 37,198	.07 %	$ 100,908	.05 %
19 EMPLOYEE SALARIES	1,750	.01	6,425	.01	36,955	.02
20 FRINGE BENEFITS	4,108	.03	8,867	.02	28,473	.02
21 SALARIES AND FRINGE, SUBTOTAL	$ 25,387	.16	$ 52,489	.11 %	$ 166,336	.09 %
22 DATA SERVICES	1,293	.01	5,593	.01	19,171	.01
23 FEES, LEGAL AND OTHER	1,752	.01	2,821	.01	23,555	.01
24 OTHER OPERATING EXPENSES	13,944	.09	35,433	.07	112,360	.06
25 TOTAL OPERATING EXPENSE	$ 42,375	.26	$ 96,335	.19 %	$ 321,421	.17 %
EARNINGS						
26 NET EARNINGS	$ 1,393,621	8.55	$ 4,332,417	8.68 %	$ 16,528,209	8.76 %
MEMORANDA						
27 COST OF MONEY	$ 998,787	6.13	$ 3,058,752	6.13	$ 11,339,427	6.01
28 NET EARNINGS AFTER COST OF MONEY	$ 394,834	2.42	$ 1,273,665	2.55 %	$ 5,188,782	2.75 %
PERSONNEL DATA						
NUMBER OF INVESTMENT PERSONNEL						
29 OFFICERS		.49		.83		2.46
30 EMPLOYEES		.14		.46		2.36
31 TOTAL PERSONNEL		.63		1.29		4.83
32 SECURITIES GAINS OR LOSSES (NET OF TAX EFFECTS)	$ 33,070	.20	$ 150,195	.30 %	$ 251,193	13 %

* GROSS YIELD

PAGE 25

1987

FRB. - FUNCTIONAL COST ANALYSIS

REAL ESTATE MORTGAGE LOAN FUNCTION

26

		124 BANKS DEPOSITS UP TO $50M		237 BANKS DEPOSITS $50M-$200M		55 BANKS DEPOSITS OVER $200M	
NUMBER OF LOANS							
1	LOANS MADE AND SERVICED	252		714		2,138	
2	LOANS SOLD BUT SERVICED	7		73		422	
3	LOANS SERVICED, SUBTOTAL	259		787		2,560	
4	LOANS PURCHASED NOT SERVICED	2		4		49	
5	TOTAL LOANS	261		791		2,608	
VOLUME							
6	LOANS MADE AND SERVICED	$ 7,325,634	98.64 %	$ 25,559,910	99.07 %	$ 88,120,646	97.61 %
7	LOANS PURCHASED NOT SERVICED	100,631	1.36	239,306	.93	2,155,025	2.39
8	TOTAL REAL ESTATE LOANS	$ 7,426,265	100.00 %	$ 25,799,216	100.00 %	$ 90,275,671	100.00 %
9	MEMO- LOANS SOLD BUT SERVICED	$ 581,835	7.83 %	$ 3,116,243	12.08 %	$ 22,124,062	24.51 %
INCOME							
10	INTEREST - LOANS MADE AND SERVICED	$ 755,849	10.18 %*	$ 2,601,947	10.09 %*	$ 8,771,176	9.72 %*
11	LOANS PURCHASED NOT SERVICED	9,614	.13 %*	23,700	.09 %*	196,195	.22 %*
12	SERVICE FEES, LOANS SOLD BUT SERVICED	2,201	.03 %*	13,186	.05 %*	83,124	.09 %*
13	OTHER INCOME	32,575	.44	134,142	.52	518,876	.57
14	TOTAL INCOME	$ 800,240	10.78 %	$ 2,772,975	10.75 %	$ 9,569,370	10.60 %
EXPENSE							
15	OFFICER SALARIES	$ 33,642	.45 %	$ 96,513	.37 %	$ 322,149	.36 %
16	EMPLOYEE SALARIES	12,652	.17	46,415	.18	174,680	.19
17	FRINGE BENEFITS	9,799	.13	30,075	.12	101,735	.11
18	SALARIES AND FRINGE, SUBTOTAL	56,094	.76 %	173,003	.67 %	598,563	.66 %
19	DATA SERVICES	9,734	.13	20,657	.08	87,737	.10
20	FEES, LEGAL AND OTHER	7,705	.10	18,381	.07	60,438	.07
21	OTHER OPERATING EXPENSES	36,970	.50	110,027	.43	376,359	.42
22	TOTAL OPERATING EXPENSES	$ 110,504	1.49 %	$ 322,067	1.25 %	$ 1,123,097	1.24 %
EARNINGS							
23	NET EARNINGS BEFORE LOSSES	$ 689,736	9.29 %	$ 2,450,908	9.50 %	$ 8,446,274	9.36 %
24	NET LOSSES	20,464	.28	63,923	.25	138,694	.15
25	NET EARNINGS	$ 669,272	9.01 %	$ 2,386,985	9.25 %	$ 8,307,579	9.20 %
MEMORANDA							
26	COST OF MONEY	$ 476,082	6.41 %	$ 1,616,407	6.27 %	$ 5,498,985	6.09 %
27	NET EARNINGS AFTER COST OF MONEY	$ 193,190	2.60 %	$ 770,578	2.99 %	$ 2,808,594	3.11 %
MISCELLANEOUS DATA							
NUMBER OF REAL ESTATE LOAN PERSONNEL							
28	OFFICERS	1.03		2.73		8.34	
29	EMPLOYEES	1.00		3.43		11.67	
30	TOTAL PERSONNEL	2.03		6.17		20.00	
OTHER DATA							
31	NO. OF LOANS MADE	200		268		530	
32	3-YEAR AVERAGE LOAN LOSSES	$ 40,841	.55 %	$ 64,707	.25 %	$ 121,927	.14 %

* GROSS YIELD

1987

FRB - FUNCTIONAL COST ANALYSIS

INSTALMENT LOAN FUNCTION

27

	127 BANKS DEPOSITS UP TO $50M		247 DEPOSITS BANKS $50M-$200M		58 BANKS DEPOSITS OVER $200M	
1 NUMBER OF LOANS OUTSTANDING	977		3,414		19,542	
VOLUME						
2 CONSUMER INSTALMENT LOANS	$3,016,997	76.72 %	$11,240,283	81.45 %	$75,334,839	83.56 %
3 CHECK CREDIT LOANS	50,283	1.28	454,141	3.29	4,013,962	4.45
4 CONSUMER LOANS, SUBTOTAL	$3,067,280	78.00 %	$11,694,424	84.74 %	$79,348,801	88.01 %
5 COMMERCIAL, EQUIPMENT AND OTHER LOANS	839,424	21.35	1,684,268	12.21	6,357,312	7.05
6 FLOOR PLAN	25,647	.65	421,059	3.05	4,448,760	4.93
7 COMMERCIAL LOANS, SUBTOTAL	865,071	22.00 %	2,105,328	15.26 %	10,806,072	11.99 %
8 TOTAL INSTALMENT LOANS	$3,932,350	100.00 %	$13,799,751	100.00 %	$90,154,873	100.00 %
INCOME						
9 CONSUMER INSTALMENT LOANS	$366,047	12.13 %*	$1,309,653	11.65 %*	$8,519,292	11.31 %*
10 CHECK CREDIT LOANS	7,681	15.27 *	57,842	12.74 *	458,379	11.42 *
11 COMMERCIAL, EQUIPMENT AND OTHER LOANS	93,516	11.14 *	181,472	10.77 *	699,118	11.00 *
12 FLOOR PLAN	1,890	7.37	40,882	9.71	402,006	9.04
13 INTEREST AND DISCOUNT, SUBTOTAL	$469,133	11.93 %	$1,589,848	11.52 %	$10,078,795	11.18 %
14 OTHER INCOME	34,113	.87	72,340	.52	353,800	.39
15 TOTAL INCOME	$503,246	12.80 %	$1,662,189	12.05 %	$10,432,596	11.57 %
EXPENSE						
16 OFFICER SALARIES	$44,116	1.12 %	$120,627	.87 %	$523,163	.58 %
17 EMPLOYEE SALARIES	22,155	.56	77,209	.56	498,618	.55
18 FRINGE BENEFITS	14,234	.36	40,310	.29	219,769	.24
19 SALARIES AND FRINGE, SUBTOTAL	$80,504	2.05 %	$238,146	1.73 %	$1,241,550	1.38 %
20 DATA SERVICES	13,289	.34	35,322	.26	211,968	.24
21 FURNITURE AND EQUIPMENT	8,938	.23	22,731	.16	113,558	.13
22 OCCUPANCY	11,834	.30	32,349	.23	190,463	.21
23 PUBLICITY AND ADVERTISING	5,385	.14	16,418	.12	90,383	.10
24 OTHER OPERATING EXPENSES	37,697	.96	106,816	.77	591,448	.66
25 TOTAL OPERATING EXPENSE	$157,648	4.01 %	$451,782	3.27 %	$2,439,370	2.71 %
EARNINGS						
26 NET EARNINGS BEFORE LOSSES	$345,598	8.79 %	$1,210,407	8.77 %	$7,993,226	8.87 %
27 NET LOSSES	31,153	.79	98,607	.71	368,278	.41
28 NET EARNINGS	$314,445	8.00 %	$1,111,800	8.06 %	$7,624,949	8.46 %
MEMORANDA						
29 COST OF MONEY	$245,015	6.23 %	$850,344	6.16 %	$5,462,957	6.06 %
30 NET EARNINGS AFTER COST OF MONEY	$69,430	1.77 %	$261,457	1.89 %	$2,161,992	2.40 %

MISCELLANEOUS DATA

	127 BANKS UP TO $50M	247 BANKS $50M-$200M	58 BANKS OVER $200M
NUMBER OF INSTALMENT LOAN PERSONNEL			
31 OFFICERS	1.44	3.74	15.57
32 EMPLOYEES	1.74	5.78	34.88
33 TOTAL PERSONNEL	3.18	9.52	50.46
34 NUMBER OF TELLERS (INCLUDED IN EMPLOYEES)	.56	1.01	5.22
35 NUMBER OF BANKING OFFICES	1.99	4.22	19.00
36 3-YEAR AVERAGE LOAN LOSSES	$31,967 .81 %*	$86,203 .62 %*	$368,388 .41 %*

* GROSS YIELD

40

1987

FRB - FUNCTIONAL COST ANALYSIS   COMMERCIAL AND OTHER LOAN FUNCTION

		125 BANKS DEPOSITS UP TO $50M		245 BANKS DEPOSITS $50M- $200M		58 BANKS DEPOSITS OVER $200M	
VOLUME							
1	LEASED EQUIPMENT LOANS	$ 27,030	.31 %	$ 264,704	.93 %	$ 3,304,676	1.94 %
2	AGRICULTURAL LOANS	1,292,106	14.95	2,565,695	8.97	2,510,590	1.48
3	CONSTRUCTION LOANS	103,982	1.20	1,344,058	4.70	16,315,189	9.60
4	OTHER COMMERCIAL LOANS	7,221,100	83.54	24,416,954	85.40	147,904,980	86.98
5	TOTAL COMMERCIAL AND OTHER LOAN VOLUME	$ 8,644,218	100.00 %	28,591,411	100.00 %	170,035,435	100.00 %
INCOME							
6	LEASED EQUIPMENT LOANS	$ 3,188	11.79 %	$ 26,621	10.06 %	$ 361,323	10.93 %
7	AGRICULTURAL LOANS	134,284	10.39	261,915	10.21	214,138	8.53
8	CONSTRUCTION LOANS	6,403	6.16	139,298	10.36	1,571,483	9.63
9	OTHER COMMERCIAL LOANS	731,143	10.13	2,360,688	9.67	13,541,491	9.16
10	SUBTOTAL	875,017	10.12 %	2,788,522	9.75 %	15,688,435	9.23 %
11	OTHER INCOME	19,957	.23	64,930	.23	494,319	.29
12	TOTAL INCOME	$ 894,975	10.35 %	$ 2,853,451	9.98 %	$ 16,182,754	9.52 %
EXPENSE							
13	OFFICER SALARIES	$ 68,176	.79 %	$ 203,466	.71 %	$ 792,839	.47 %
14	EMPLOYEE SALARIES	18,366	.21	61,604	.22	330,174	.19
15	FRINGE BENEFITS	17,878	.21	51,683	.18	216,196	.13
16	SALARIES AND FRINGE, SUBTOTAL	$ 104,420	1.21 %	$ 316,753	1.11 %	$ 1,339,209	.79 %
17	DATA SERVICES	12,721	.15	29,403	.10	145,995	.09
18	OCCUPANCY	17,200	.20	42,171	.15	198,022	.12
19	FEES, LEGAL AND OTHER	15,688	.18	34,889	.12	154,386	.09
20	OTHER OPERATING EXPENSES	56,036	.65	143,743	.50	591,788	.35
21	TOTAL OPERATING EXPENSE	$ 206,065	2.38 %	$ 566,960	1.98 %	$ 2,429,400	1.43 %
EARNINGS							
22	NET EARNINGS BEFORE LOSSES	$ 688,910	7.97 %	$ 2,286,491	8.00 %	$ 13,753,354	8.09 %
23	NET LOSSES	130,260	1.51	324,479	1.13	948,643	.56
24	NET EARNINGS	$ 558,650	6.46 %	$ 1,962,013	6.86 %	$ 12,804,711	7.53 %
MEMORANDA							
25	COST OF MONEY	535,979	6.20	1,764,284	6.17	10,237,717	6.02
26	NET EARNINGS AFTER COST OF MONEY	$ 22,671	.26 %	$ 197,729	.69 %	$ 2,566,995	1.51 %

MISCELLANEOUS DATA

		125 BANKS	245 BANKS	58 BANKS
NUMBER OF COMMERCIAL AND OTHER LOAN PERSONNEL				
27	OFFICERS	1.88	5.11	20.60
28	EMPLOYEES	1.39	4.42	21.53
29	TOTAL PERSONNEL	3.27	9.53	42.13
NUMBER OF COMMERCIAL AND OTHER LOANS				
30	LEASED EQUIPMENT LOANS	1	16	188
31	AGRICULTURAL LOANS	70	98	73
32	CONSTRUCTION LOANS	3	15	70
33	OTHER COMMERCIAL LOANS	447	912	3,240
34	TOTAL	520	1,041	3,573
35	NUMBER OF LOANS PER PERSON	159	109	85
36	NUMBER OF BANKING OFFICES	1.98	4.20	19.00
37	3-YEAR AVERAGE LOAN LOSSES	$ 153,757 1.78 %	411,247 1.44 %	951,015 .56 %

* GROSS YIELD

1987

FRB - FUNCTIONAL COST ANALYSIS

TRUST FUNCTION

47

	32 BANKS DEPOSITS UP TO $50M		168 BANKS DEPOSITS $50M-$200M		51 BANKS DEPOSITS OVER $200M	
1 5-YEAR AVERAGE TRUST INCOME	$ 11,089		244,687		1,249,529	
ANALYSIS OF COMMISSIONS AND FEES	**PERCENT OF TOTAL INCOME**					
2 ESTATES	$ 2,006	6.90 %* $	28,122	9.53 %* $	105,419	7.25 %*
3 PERSONAL TRUST	3,848	27.99	128,898	35.07	567,720	36.97
4 EMPLOYEES BENEFITS	112	.77	41,175	9.79	225,548	13.84
5 PERSONAL AGENCIES	324	2.90	41,003	9.26	143,477	8.27
6 CORPORATE TRUSTS	521	5.27	9,193	3.10	96,103	5.15
7 CORPORATE AGENCIES	5	3.12	3,468	1.30	59,042	3.03
8 OTHER TRUSTS	$ 694	6.17 % $	25,847	7.55 % $	99,550	5.87 %
INCOME	**PERCENT OF TOTAL EXPENSE**					
9 TOTAL COMMISSIONS AND FEES	$ 13,479	40.73 %* $	317,339	92.76 % $	1,577,238	103.11 %
10 OTHER INCOME	348	1.05	2,199	.64	21,750	1.42
11 TOTAL INCOME	$ 13,828	41.78 % $	319,538	93.40 % $	1,598,988	104.53 %
EXPENSE						
12 OFFICER SALARIES	$ 12,843	38.80 % $	120,360	35.18 % $	494,948	32.36 %
13 EMPLOYEE SALARIES	4,223	12.76	54,679	15.98	242,192	15.83
14 FRINGE BENEFITS	3,594	10.86	34,784	10.17	151,898	9.93
15 SALARIES AND FRINGE, SUBTOTAL	20,659	62.42 %	209,823	61.33 %	889,039	58.12 %
16 DATA SERVICES	1,210	3.66	22,131	6.47	130,624	8.54
17 FURNITURE AND EQUIPMENT	2,317	7.00	16,432	4.80	74,112	4.84
18 OCCUPANCY	2,321	7.01	26,427	7.72	98,498	6.44
19 PUBLICITY AND ADVERTISING	922	2.79	6,915	2.02	21,787	1.42
20 OTHER OPERATING EXPENSE	5,667	17.12	60,377	17.65	315,623	20.63
21 TOTAL EXPENSE	$ 33,097	100.00 % $	342,104	100.00 % $	1,529,683	100.00 %
EARNINGS						
22 NET EARNINGS	$ 19,269-	58.22-% $	22,566-	6.60-% $	69,304	4.53 %
MISCELLANEOUS DATA						
NUMBER OF TRUST PERSONNEL						
23 OFFICERS	.35		3.18		12.98	
24 EMPLOYEES	.36		3.99		16.09	
25 TOTAL PERSONNEL	.72		7.17		29.07	
MEMORANDA						
26 INCOME PER TRUST DEPT OFFICER	$ 39,332		100,456	$	123,176	$
27 OFFICERS TO TOTAL TRUST PERSONNEL	49.06 %		44.37 %		44.65 %	
TRUST DEPOSITS IN YOUR BANK						
28 NON-INTEREST BEARING DEPOSITS	$ 29,064		233,007	$	964,495	$
29 DEPOSITS BEARING INTEREST	326,295		2,242,235		10,594,805	
30 THEORETICAL EARNINGS ON ABOVE DEPOSITS	$ 5,383		54,995	$	257,502	$
TRUST ASSETS ($000 OMITTED) *	VOLUME	ACCOUNTS	VOLUME	ACCOUNTS	VOLUME	ACCOUNTS
31 ESTATES	191	2	1,915	15	7,106	44
32 PERSONAL TRUSTS	1,014	12	25,124	142	107,990	412
33 EMPLOYEE BENEFITS	385	16	12,743	134	63,339	205
34 AGENCIES	443	2	22,282	68	139,381	204
35 TOTAL TRUST ASSETS	2,166	53	78,554	383	331,686	907

* AVG. FOR BANKS SUBMITTING INCOME AND/OR ASSET ALLOCATIONS.

PAGE   47

1987

FRB - FUNCTIONAL COST ANALYSIS

DATA SERVICES FUNCTION

	65 BANKS DEPOSITS UP TO $50M		145 BANKS DEPOSITS $50M-$200M		36 BANKS DEPOSITS OVER $200M	
1 MONTHLY PRIME SHIFT HARDWARE RENTAL VALUE $	4,269		8,718		25,722	
PERCENT OF TOTAL EXPENSE						
INCOME						
2 TOTAL INCOME $	4,457	3.62 %	40,396	11.82 %	218,219	11.49 %
EXPENSE						
3 OFFICER SALARIES $	16,899	13.72 %	46,092	13.49 %	222,966	11.74 %
4 EMPLOYEE SALARIES	21,232	17.24	71,393	20.90	399,469	21.03
5 FRINGE BENEFITS	9,050	7.35	25,204	7.38	127,816	6.73
6 SALARIES AND FRINGE, SUBTOTAL $	47,181	38.32 %	142,689	41.77 %	750,251	39.49 %
7 PURCHASED SOFTWARE	1,276	1.04	11,415	3.34	91,212	4.80
8 PURCHASED OFF-PREMISE SERVICES	2,365	1.92	6,707	1.96	200,363	10.55
9 FURNITURE AND EQUIPMENT	37,774	30.68	107,409	31.44	443,846	23.36
10 OTHER OPERATING EXPENSE	34,528	28.04	73,413	21.49	414,221	21.80
11 TOTAL EXPENSE $	123,125	100.00 %	341,633	100.00 %	1,899,892	100.00 %
EARNINGS						
12 NET EARNINGS $	118,668-	96.38-%	301,237-	88.18-%	1,681,673-	88.51-%
DISTRIBUTION OF DATA SERVICES EXPENSE						
13 DEMAND DEPOSITS $	49,605	40.29 %	119,339	34.93 %	746,115	39.27 %
14 TIME DEPOSITS	22,488	18.26	60,668	17.76	283,513	14.92
15 NON-DEPOSIT FUNDS	5,746	4.67	12,994	3.80	19,874	1.05
16 INVESTMENTS	892	.72	4,583	1.34	7,428	.39
17 REAL ESTATE MORTGAGE LOANS	12,075	9.81	19,526	5.72	48,790	2.57
18 INSTALMENT LOANS	14,675	11.92	32,901	9.63	159,316	8.39
19 CREDIT CARD	618	.50	1,369	.40	18,403	.97
20 COMMERCIAL AND OTHER LOANS	13,345	10.84	26,898	7.87	120,983	6.37
21 INTERNATIONAL	*****	*****	*****	*****	*****	*****
22 SAFE DEPOSIT	1,483	1.20	2,811	.82	4,051	.21
23 TRUST	88	.07	8,121	2.38	57,922	3.05
24 NON-BANKING DEPARTMENTS	188	.15	1,093	.32	13,984	.74
25 TOTAL INTERNAL DISTRIBUTED EXPENSE $	121,203	98.44 %	290,302	84.97 %	1,480,379	77.92 %
26 CUSTOMER SERVICE EXPENSE $	1,922	1.56 %	51,330	15.03 %	419,513	22.08 %
27 TOTAL EXPENSE $	123,125	100.00 %	341,633	100.00 %	1,899,892	100.00 %
MISCELLANEOUS DATA						
NUMBER OF DATA SERVICES PERSONNEL						
28 OFFICERS	.61		1.31		5.76	
29 EMPLOYEES	1.72		4.79		24.16	
30 TOTAL PERSONNEL	2.33		6.10		29.92	
31 AVERAGE CPU HOURS PER WEEK	45		101		109	

Appendix B

Functional Cost Analysis[a]

[a] Published by the Federal Financial Institutions Examinations Council.

DECEMBER, 1986 UNIFORM BANK PERFORMANCE REPORT

INFORMATION

TABLE OF CONTENTS

INTRODUCTION

THIS UNIFORM BANK PERFORMANCE REPORT COVERS THE OPERATIONS OF YOUR
BANK AND THAT OF A COMPARABLE GROUP OF PEER BANKS. IT IS PROVIDED
FOR YOUR USE AS A MANAGEMENT TOOL BY THE FEDERAL FINANCIAL
INSTITUTIONS EXAMINATION COUNCIL. DETAILED INFORMATION CONCERNING
THIS REPORT IS PROVIDED IN " A USER'S GUIDE FOR THE UNIFORM BANK
PERFORMANCE REPORT " FORWARDED TO YOUR BANK UNDER SEPARATE COVER.
ADDITIONAL COPIES OF THE USER'S GUIDE CAN BE OBTAINED USING THE
ORDER BLANK' ATTACHED TO THIS REPORT.

AS OF THE DATE OF PREPARATION OF THIS REPORT, YOUR BANK'S FEDERAL
REGULATOR WAS THE OFFICE OF THE COMPTROLLER OF THE CURRENCY.

YOUR CURRENT PEER GROUP # 08
INCLUDES ALL INSURED COMMERCIAL BANKS HAVING ASSETS
BETWEEN $100 MILLION AND $300 MILLION, WITH 3 OR MORE
BANKING OFFICES, AND LOCATED IN A NON-METROPOLITAN AREA.
FOR INFORMATION CONCERNING THE PEER GROUP(S) WHICH YOU WERE
PREVIOUSLY IN, SEE APPENDIX A.

ADDRESSEE

SUMMARY RATIOS

	12/31/86 BANK	PEER 08	PCT	12/31/85 BANK	PEER 12	PCT	12/31/84 BANK	PEER 12	PCT	12/31/83 BANK	PEER 12	12/31/82 BANK	PEER 12
AVERAGE ASSETS ($000)	113210			78816**			73775			70291		64624	
NET INCOME ($000)	748			665			680			307		375	
# BANKS IN PEER GROUP	412			732			711			679		635	

EARNINGS AND PROFITABILITY

PERCENT OF AVERAGE ASSETS:

	12/31/86 BANK	PEER 08	PCT	12/31/85 BANK	PEER 12	PCT	12/31/84 BANK	PEER 12	PCT	12/31/83 BANK	PEER 12	12/31/82 BANK	PEER 12
NET INTEREST INCOME (TE)	4.38	4.71	32	5.06	4.79	65	4.61	4.53	57	4.58	4.60	4.86	4.65
+ NONINTEREST INCOME	.94	.61	88	1.03	.62	89	1.10	.61	92	.85	.56	.85	.55
- OVERHEAD EXPENSE	4.12	2.95	92	4.13	3.03	90	3.99	2.96	89	4.10	2.93	4.06	2.92
- PROVISION: LOAN/LEASE LOSSES	.11	.46	12	.50	.53	60	.24	.35	46	.65	.34	.71	.31
= PRETAX OPERATING INCOME (TE)	1.09	1.89	18	1.46	1.84	32	1.48	1.81	33	.67	1.86	.94	1.93
+ SECURITIES GAINS (LOSSES)	.18	.06	82	.15	.03	83	.05	.00	88	.08	.00	.08	-.01
= PRETAX NET OPER INC (TE)	1.27	2.01	20	1.61	1.91	34	1.53	1.80	35	.76	1.87	1.02	1.89
NET OPERATING INCOME	.66	1.08	18	.84	1.07	30	.92	1.00	42	.44	1.04	.58	1.04
ADJ. NET OPER INCOME	-.30	1.14	03	1.04	1.16	39	1.02	1.06	44	.29	1.09	.74	1.09
ADJ. NET INCOME	.10	1.11	07	.97	1.08	37	.89	.99	39	.07	1.02	.42	1.01
NET INCOME	.66	1.09	17	.84	1.08	30	.92	1.00	42	.44	1.04	.58	1.04

PERCENT OF AVG EARNING ASSETS:

	12/31/86 BANK	PEER 08	PCT	12/31/85 BANK	PEER 12	PCT	12/31/84 BANK	PEER 12	PCT	12/31/83 BANK	PEER 12	12/31/82 BANK	PEER 12
INTEREST INCOME (TE)	10.39	10.97	20	11.87	11.97	46	12.64	12.51	59	12.40	12.23	13.42	13.47
INTEREST EXPENSE	5.64	5.92	26	6.33	6.77	20	7.62	7.55	54	7.36	7.16	8.08	8.37
NET INT INCOME (TE)	4.74	5.07	35	5.54	5.21	67	5.02	4.95	59	5.05	5.06	5.34	5.12

LOAN & LEASE LOSSES, RESERVES AND NON-CURRENT LOANS AND LEASES

	12/31/86 BANK	PEER 08	PCT	12/31/85 BANK	PEER 12	PCT	12/31/84 BANK	PEER 12	PCT	12/31/83 BANK	PEER 12	12/31/82 BANK	PEER 12
NET LOSS TO AVG TOT LOAN & LEASE	1.74	.72	86	.46	.85	42	.23	.61	30	1.42	.60	.97	.53
EARNINGS COVERAGE OF NET LOSS(X)	.93	9.16	08	5.15	8.18	47	9.10	9.97	60	.99	10.14	1.61	9.55
LOSS RESERVE TO NET LOSSES (X)	.84	3.63	15	8.73	2.62	88	4.13	3.18	69	.63	3.15	1.25	3.06
LOSS RESV TO TOT LOANS & LEASE	1.49	1.22	76	3.00	1.19	96	.82	1.02	26	.86	1.03	1.23	1.00
% NON-CURRENT LOANS & LEASES	1.08	1.74		2.07	2.36		.47	2.24		.95	2.19	NA	NA

LIQUIDITY AND RATE SENSITIVITY

	12/31/86 BANK	PEER 08	PCT	12/31/85 BANK	PEER 12	PCT	12/31/84 BANK	PEER 12	PCT	12/31/83 BANK	PEER 12	12/31/82 BANK	PEER 12
VOLATILE LIABILITY DEPENDENCE	-15.16	-8.20	26	-10.69	-11.83	49	3.77	-12.55	85	4.02	-12.42	6.54	-10.32
NET LOANS & LEASES TO ASSETS	58.85	54.47	62	58.93	51.68	72	63.97	52.17	87	58.40	49.92	55.33	50.61
NET ASSETS REPRICABLE IN 1 YR OR LESS TO ASSETS	-2.30	-10.73	76	-2.01	-5.27	60	-9.59	-6.96	40	-11.10	-5.13	NA	NA

CAPITALIZATION

	12/31/86 BANK	PEER 08	PCT	12/31/85 BANK	PEER 12	PCT	12/31/84 BANK	PEER 12	PCT	12/31/83 BANK	PEER 12	12/31/82 BANK	PEER 12
PRIM CAPITAL TO ADJ AVG ASSETS*	8.15	8.66	42	11.83	8.88	93	8.50	8.65	51	8.33	8.53	9.22	8.63
CASH DIVIDENDS TO NET INCOME	48.40	36.62	74	80.15	36.68	87	24.26	37.06	32	71.66	34.86	58.67	33.00
RET EARNS TO AVG TOTAL EQUITY	4.77	8.46	25	1.68	7.57	20	8.65	6.87	57	1.54	8.10	2.78	8.37

GROWTH RATES

	12/31/86 BANK	PEER 08	PCT	12/31/85 BANK	PEER 12	PCT	12/31/84 BANK	PEER 12	PCT	12/31/83 BANK	PEER 12	12/31/82 BANK	PEER 12
ASSETS	-.96	9.83	05	NA	6.69	NA	13.85	7.81	81	7.51	10.04	-4.44	9.28
PRIMARY CAPITAL*	-2.75	9.59	05	NA	9.62	NA	9.78	8.33	55	-.20	9.27	-4.40	9.21
NET LOANS & LEASES	-1.09	9.66	19	NA	6.83	NA	24.71	12.85	84	13.48	8.30	-1.57	6.54
VOLATILE LIABILITIES	-56.28	7.19	01	NA	8.75	NA	19.08	22.27	50	-8.34	-3.63	-22.81	10.03

*REFER TO THE UBPR USERS GUIDE FOR PRIMARY CAPITAL DEFINITION.

**PRE-MERGER DATA HAS BEEN EXCLUDED FROM PERIOD ENDING CALCULATIONS AS A RESULT OF MERGERS/CONSOLIDATIONS.

INCOME STATEMENT - REVENUES AND EXPENSES ($000)

PAGE 02

	12/31/86	12/31/85	12/31/84	12/31/83	12/31/82	PERCENT CHANGE 1 YEAR	PERCENT CHANGE 4 YEARS
INTEREST AND FEES ON LOANS	7896	6373	6035	5170	5338	23.90	NA
INCOME FROM LEASE FINANCING	23	44	53	71	0	-47.73	NA
FULLY TAXABLE	7915	6417	6088	NA	NA		
TAX EXEMPT	4	0	0	NA	NA		
ESTIMATED TAX BENEFIT	2	0	0	NA	NA		
INCOME ON LOANS & LEASES(TE)	7921	6417	6088	5241	5338	21.33	NA
US TREAS & AGENCY SECURITIES	1788	975	NA	NA	NA	83.38	NA
MUNICIPAL SECURITIES	275	359	393	446	572	-23.40	NA
TAX BENEFIT ON MUNICIPALS	234	305	334	379	486		NA
OTHER SECURITIES INCOME	45	11	1309	1596	1363	309.09	NA
INVESTMT INTEREST INCOME(TE)	2342	1650	2036	2421	2421	41.97	NA
INTEREST ON DUE FROM BANKS	242	280	253	145	0	-13.57	NA
INT ON FED FUNDS SOLD/RESALES	352	198	181	107	126	77.78	NA
TRADING ACCOUNT INCOME	0	0	0	NA	NA	NA	NA
TOTAL INTEREST INCOME (TE)	10858	8545	8558	7914	7885	27.07	NA
INTEREST ON CDS OVER $100M	381	579	875	875	1078	-34.20	NA
INTEREST ON OTHER DEPOSITS	5353	3787	4009	3552	3261	41.35	NA
INT ON FED FUNDS PURCH & REPOS	75	103	191	209	317	-27.18	NA
INT BORROWED MONEY (+NOTE OPT)	90	88	82	59	91	2.27	NA
INT ON MORTGAGES & LEASES	0	0	0	NA	NA	NA	NA
INT ON SUBORD NOTES & DEBS	0	0	0	0	0	NA	NA
TOTAL INTEREST EXPENSE	5899	4557	5157	4695	4747	29.45	NA
NET INTEREST INCOME (TE)	4959	3988	3401	3219	3138	24.35	NA
NONINTEREST INCOME	1067	811	815	597	552	31.57	NA
ADJUSTED OPERATING INCOME (TE)	6026	4799	4216	3816	3690	25.57	NA
OVERHEAD EXPENSE	4665	3253	2945	2883	2622	43.41	NA
PROVISION FOR LOAN/LEASE LOSSES	125	398	178	460	461	-68.59	NA
PROV: ALLOCATED TRANSFER RISK	NA	NA	NA	NA	NA		
PRETAX OPERATING INCOME (TE)	1236	1148	1093	473	607	7.66	NA
SECURITIES GAINS(LOSSES)	199	120	35	58	50	65.83	NA
PRETAX NET OPERATING INC (TE)	1435	1268	1128	531	657	13.17	NA
APPLICABLE INCOME TAXES	450	298	114	-155	-204		
CURRENT TAX EQUIV ADJUSTMENT	237	305	334	152	171		
OTHER TAX EQUIV ADJUSTMENTS	0	0		227	315		
APPLICABLE INCOME TAXES (TE)	687	603	448	224	282		
NET OPERATING INCOME	748	665	680	307	375	12.48	NA
NET EXTRAORDINARY ITEMS	0	0	0	0	0		
NET INCOME	748	665	680	307	375	12.48	NA
CASH DIVIDENDS DECLARED	362	533	165	220	220	-32.08	NA
RETAINED EARNINGS	386	132	515	87	155	192.42	NA

RELATIVE INCOME STATEMENT AND MARGIN ANALYSIS

PERCENT OF AVERAGE ASSETS	12/31/86 BANK	12/31/86 PEER 08	12/31/86 PCT	12/31/85 BANK	12/31/85 PEER 12	12/31/85 PCT	12/31/84 BANK	12/31/84 PEER 12	12/31/84 PCT	12/31/83 BANK	12/31/83 PEER 12	12/31/82 BANK	12/31/82 PEER 12
INTEREST INCOME (TE)	9.59	10.19	18	10.84	11.01	39	11.60	11.46	60	11.26	11.14	12.20	12.26
LESS: INTEREST EXPENSE	5.21	5.50	26	5.78	6.22	18	6.99	6.92	52	6.68	6.53	7.35	7.61
EQUALS: NET INT INCOME (TE)	4.38	4.71	32	5.06	4.79	65	4.61	4.53	57	4.58	4.60	4.86	4.65
PLUS: NONINTEREST INCOME	.94	.61	88	1.03	.62	89	1.10	.61	92	.85	.56	.85	.55
EQUALS: ADJ OPER INCOME (TE)	5.32	5.32	51	6.09	5.41	77	5.71	5.15	75	5.43	5.17	5.71	5.20
LESS: OVERHEAD EXPENSE	4.12	2.95	92	4.13	3.03	90	3.99	2.96	89	4.10	2.93	4.06	2.92
LESS: PROVISION FOR LN/LS LOSS	.11	.46	12	.50	.53	60	.24	.35	46	.65	.34	.71	.31
LESS: PROV ALLOCATED TRAN RISK	NA	NA	NA	NA	NA	NA	NA	NA	NA	NA	NA	NA	NA
PLUS: SECURITIES GAINS(LOSSES)	.18	.06	82	.15	.03	83	.05	.00	88	.08	.00	.08	-.01
EQUALS: PRETAX NOI (TE)	1.27	2.01	20	1.61	1.91	34	1.53	1.80	35	.76	1.87	1.02	1.89
LESS: APPLICABLE INC TAX (TE)	.61	.94	22	.77	.87	40	.61	.80	31	.32	.83	.44	.84
EQUALS: NET OPERATING INCOME	.66	1.08	18	.84	1.07	30	.92	1.00	42	.44	1.04	.58	1.04
PLUS EXTRAORD EQUALS: NET INCOME	.66	1.09	17	.84	1.08	30	.92	1.00	42	.44	1.04	.58	1.04
MARGIN ANALYSIS													
AVG EARNING ASSETS TO AVG ASST	92.34	93.00	37	91.37	92.13	34	91.77	91.73	49	90.76	91.18	90.90	91.08
AV INT-BEARING FUNDS TO AV AST	76.92	78.85	30	111.71	77.28	99	77.31	76.79	50	73.25	75.23	71.71	73.47
INT INC (TE) TO AVG EARN ASSTS	10.39	10.97	20	11.87	11.97	46	12.64	12.51	59	12.40	12.23	13.42	13.47
INT EXPENSE TO AVG EARN ASSETS	5.64	5.92	26	6.33	6.77	20	7.62	7.55	54	7.36	7.16	8.08	8.37
NET INT INC-TE TO AV EARN ASST	4.74	5.07	35	5.54	5.21	67	5.02	4.95	59	5.05	5.06	5.34	5.12
YIELD ON OR COST OF:													
TOTAL LOANS & LEASES (TE)	11.39	11.60	43	12.33	12.64	34	13.44	13.19	61	13.17	12.93	14.41	14.20
TOTAL LOANS	11.45	11.42	54	12.46	12.52	47	13.60	13.09	73	13.09	12.92	14.41	14.20
REAL ESTATE**	11.45	11.46	53	12.30	12.03	59	12.64	12.00	66	NA	NA	NA	NA
COMMERCIAL TIME,DEMAND,OTH**	9.29	10.64	12	9.17	12.31	02	13.37	13.50	49	NA	NA	NA	NA
INSTALLMENT**	15.10	12.72	93	17.11	13.60	95	14.96	14.06	71	NA	NA	NA	NA
CREDIT CARD PLANS**	17.27	16.16	60	15.81	15.91	39	15.68	16.32	32	NA	NA	NA	NA
MEMO: AGRICULTURAL. IN ABOVE	10.74	10.92	42	12.30	11.99	50	NA	12.84	NA	NA	NA	NA	NA
TOTAL INVESTMT SECURITIES (TE)	8.74	10.74	08	11.05	11.58	36	11.16	11.70	32	11.38	11.73	11.72	12.36
US TREAS & AGENCY	8.13	9.38	13	9.89	NA	NA	NA	NA	NA	11.21	11.14	11.92	12.23
MUNICIPALS (BOOK)	6.40	7.26	17	7.21	7.27	48	6.42	7.06	31	6.25	6.89	6.36	6.80
MUNICIPALS (TE)	11.86	13.23	21	13.35	13.18	51	11.88	12.75	34	11.55	12.54	11.77	12.38
OTHER SECURITIES	8.57	6.71	72	10.28	##	NA	NA	##	NA	NA	5.84	NA	3.71
INTEREST BEARING BANK BALANCES	7.54	8.03	37	10.16	9.86	63	11.17	11.09	54	10.35	9.36	.00	12.16
FEDERAL FUNDS SOLD & RESALES	7.10	6.72	86	8.70	8.13	81	9.45	10.28	14	8.11	9.41	12.46	12.27
TOTAL INT-BEARING DEPOSITS	6.83	7.00	34	5.19	8.07	00	9.10	9.03	55	9.13	8.69	10.12	10.32
LARGE CERTS OF DEPOSIT	8.29	7.39	84	10.76	8.72	93	10.22	9.92	62	9.51	9.18	12.95	11.99
ALL OTH UNREGULATED DEP	6.56	7.08	18	7.95	8.47	21	8.44	9.97	10	NA	NA	NA	NA
FEDERAL FUNDS PURCH & REPOS	5.06	6.40	15	5.42	7.06	18	9.31	8.68	43	9.78	6.94	11.63	10.55
OTHER BORROWED MONEY	5.65	4.45	71	4.47	4.86	25	6.36	7.05	30	6.96	6.94	12.56	10.82
SUBORDINATED NOTES & DEBENTURES	NA	8.74	NA	NA	9.58	NA	NA	9.42	NA	NA	8.96	NA	8.83
ALL INTEREST BEARING FUNDS	6.77	6.99	31	5.18	8.07	00	9.04	9.04	49	9.12	8.67	10.24	10.35

**BANKS HAVING <$300 MILLION IN TOTAL ASSETS REPORT THIS LOAN DETAIL(BY TYPE) USING THEIR OWN INTERNAL CATEGORIZATION SYSTEMS.

NON-INTEREST INCOME AND EXPENSE RATIOS

	12/31/86			12/31/85			12/31/84			12/31/83		12/31/82	
NONINTEREST INCOME ($000)													
FIDUCIARY ACTIVITIES	436			419			NA			306		266	
DEPOSIT SERVICE CHARGES	338			194			226			178		175	
TRADING COMMISSIONS & FEES	0			0			NA			NA		NA	
FOREIGN EXCHANGE TRADING	0			0			NA			NA		NA	
OTHER FOREIGN TRANSACTIONS	0			0			NA			NA		NA	
OTHER NONINTEREST INCOME	293			198			589			419		377	
NONINTEREST INCOME	1067			811			815			597		552	
OVERHEAD EXPENSES ($000)													
PERSONNEL EXPENSE	2173			1678			1547			1580		1471	
OCCUPANCY EXPENSE	858			485			484			443		424	
OTH OPER EXP(INCL INTANGIBLES)	1634			1090			914			860		727	
TOTAL OVERHEAD EXPENSE	4665			3253			2945			2883		2622	
:INCLUDING INT ON MORTG & LEASE	4665			3253			2945			2883		2622	
NUMBER OF EQUIV EMPLOYEES	101			72			78			80		81	
AVG PERS EXP PER EMPLOYEE ($)	21510			23310			19830			19750		18160	
AVG ASSETS PER DOMESTIC OFFICE	12578			8757			14755			14058		12924	
DOMESTIC BANKING OFFICES (#)	9			9			5			5		5	
FOREIGN BRANCHES (#)	0			0			0			0		0	

PERCENT OF AVERAGE ASSETS	BANK	PEER 08	PCT	BANK	PEER 12	PCT	BANK	PEER 12	PCT	BANK	PEER 12	BANK	PEER 12
PERSONNEL EXPENSE	1.92	1.46	87	2.13	1.51	93	2.10	1.50	93	2.25	1.48	2.28	1.50
OCCUPANCY EXPENSE	.76	.45	93	.62	.46	81	.66	.45	87	.63	.45	.66	.45
OTH OPER EXP(INCL INTANGIBLES)	1.44	1.02	86	1.38	1.05	84	1.24	1.00	80	1.22	.98	1.12	.96
TOTAL OVERHEAD EXPENSE	4.12	2.95	92	4.13	3.03	90	3.99	2.96	89	4.10	2.93	4.06	2.92
:INCLUDING INT ON MORTG & LEASES	4.12	2.96	92	4.13	3.04	90	3.99	2.97	89	4.10	2.93	4.06	2.92
OVERHEAD LESS NON-INT INCOME	3.18	2.34	90	3.10	2.40	87	2.89	2.34	83	3.25	2.36	3.20	2.37
PERCENT OF ADJ OPER INCOME (TE)													
PERSONNEL EXPENSE	36.06	27.56	92	34.96	28.08	89	36.69	29.33	89	41.40	28.99	39.86	29.07
OCCUPANCY EXPENSE	14.24	8.33	94	10.11	8.57	70	11.48	8.65	81	11.61	8.83	11.49	8.73
OTH OPER EXP(INCL INTANGIBLES)	27.12	19.57	87	22.71	19.32	75	21.68	19.46	69	22.54	19.22	19.70	18.80
TOTAL OVERHEAD EXPENSE	77.41	55.57	95	67.78	56.23	84	69.85	57.74	85	75.55	57.27	71.05	56.68
:INCLUDING INT ON MORTG & LEASES	77.41	55.72	95	67.78	56.37	83	69.85	57.83	85	75.55	57.27	71.05	56.68
OVERHEAD LESS NON-INT INCOME	59.71	44.24	91	50.88	44.71	75	50.52	45.88	70	59.90	46.67	56.09	46.33
OTHER INCOME/EXPENSE RATIOS													
AVG PERS EXP PER EMPL(THOUSND$)	21.51	20.96	59	23.31	20.30	83	19.83	19.44	59	19.75	18.51	18.16	17.52
AVG ASSETS PER EMPL (MILLIONS)	1.12	1.50	16	1.09	1.40	20	.95	1.36	10	.88	1.31	.80	1.23
TAX RATIOS													
TAX ON SEC GAIN(LOSS)/ AVG ASST	NA	NA	NA	.04	-.14	83	NA	NA	NA	NA	.00	NA	.00
APPL INC TAX TO PRETAX NOI+TE	31.36	12.17	89	23.50	12.62	78	10.11	11.26	50	-29.18	8.98	-31.04	7.12
APPL TAX+TE TO PRETAX NOI+TE	47.88	47.07	61	47.56	45.19	72	39.72	45.19	16	42.20	44.72	42.94	44.53
TAX+CREDITS+TE TO PRETAX NOI+TE	45.79	47.32	30	47.56	46.20	66	39.72	46.07	13	NA	NA	NA	NA
TAX BENEFIT TO PRETAX NOI+TE	16.52	34.38	14	24.06	30.42	31	29.61	32.15	39	71.38	34.43	73.98	37.35
MARGINAL TAX RATE	47.88	47.02	59	47.56	45.27	72	39.72	45.19	11	42.20	44.78	42.94	44.42

BALANCE SHEET - ASSETS SECTION ($000)

PAGE 05

	12/31/86	12/31/85	12/31/84	12/31/83	12/31/82	PERCENT CHANGE 1 YEAR	4 YEARS
REAL ESTATE LOANS	31315	26635	20812	13124	11145	17.57	NA
FINANCIAL INSTITUTION LOANS	97	124	146	165	0	-21.77	NA
AGRICULTURAL LOANS	3524	3740	968	1257	1528	-5.78	NA
COMMERCIAL & INDUSTRIAL LOANS	13595	17339	10838	8601	8122	-21.59	NA
LOANS TO INDIVIDUALS	19299	23503	19399	19895	18294	-17.89	NA
MUNICIPAL LOANS	50	10	0	NA	NA	400.00	NA
ACCEPTANCES OF OTHER BANKS	494	0	963	NA	NA	NA	NA
ALL OTHER LOANS	512	243	235	47	88	110.70	NA
LEASE FINANCING RECEIVABLES	216	881	974	885	0	-75.48	NA
GROSS LOANS & LEASES	69102	72475	54335	43974	39177	-4.65	NA
LESS: UNEARNED INCOME	836	2387	2777	2621	2594	NA	
LOSS RESERVE	1019	2103	425	350	450	-51.55	NA
TRANSFER RISK RESERVE	NA	NA	NA	NA	NA	NA	
NET LOANS & LEASES	67247	67985	51133	41003	36133	-1.09	NA
SECURITIES OVER 1 YEAR	17434	16799	12141	14402	15649	3.78	NA
SUBTOTAL	84681	84784	63274	55405	51782		NA
INTEREST-BEARING BANK BALANCES	2800	3290	2991	2002	200	-14.89	NA
FEDERAL FUNDS SOLD & RESALES	6100	9125	2050	0	1750	NA	NA
TRADING ACCOUNT ASSETS	0	0	0	NA	NA	NA	NA
DEBT SECURITIES 1 YR & LESS	8243	6501	4553	5828	5637	26.80	NA
TEMPORARY INVESTMENTS	17143	18916	9594	7830	7587	-9.37	NA
TOTAL EARNING ASSETS	101824	103700	72868	63235	59369	-1.81	NA
NON-INT CASH & DUE FR BANKS	7875	6797	4715	4243	3603	15.86	NA
ACCEPTANCES	0	0	0	NA	NA	NA	
PREMISES, FIX ASSTS, CAP LEASES	2433	1915	1279	1257	1215	27.05	NA
OTHER REAL ESTATE OWNED	204	520	0	0	0	-60.77	NA
INV IN UNCONSOLIDATED SUBS	0	0	0	NA	NA	NA	
INTANGIBLE ASSETS	38	496	84	106	NA	NA	
OTHER ASSETS	1885	1943	984	1364	1116	NA	
TOTAL ASSETS	114259	115371	79930	70205	65303	-.96	NA
AVERAGE ASSETS DURING QUARTER	112563	78816	77484	72062	65138	42.82	NA
MEMORANDA							
COMMERCIAL PAPER IN LOANS	1488	3011	NA	NA	NA	-50.58	NA
OFFICER, SHAREHOLDER LOANS	158	236	182	63	NA	-33.05	NA
REAL ESTATE ACQ FOR INVESTMENT	NA	NA	NA	NA	NA	NA	NA
TOTAL CURRENT RESTRUCTURED DEBT	294	NA	NA	NA	NA	NA	NA
US TREAS & AGENCY SECURITIES	22940	17987	10457	12058	12402	27.54	NA
MUNICIPAL SECURITIES	2075	5135	5928	6603	8023	-59.59	NA
FOREIGN SECURITIES	0	0	0	NA	NA	NA	NA
ALL OTHER SECURITIES	662	178	309	1569	861	271.91	NA
TOTAL BOOK VALUE	25677	23300	16694	20230	21286	10.20	NA
TOTAL MARKET VALUE	26195	23149	15933	NA	NA	13.16	NA
APPRECIATION(DEPRECIATION)	518	-151	-761	NA	NA	-443.05	NA
PLEDGED SECURITIES (BOOK)	9849	10329	13753	NA	NA	-4.65	NA

BALANCE SHEET - LIABILITIES AND CAPITAL SECTION ($000)

	12/31/86	12/31/85	12/31/84	12/31/83	12/31/82	PERCENT CHANGE 1 YEAR	PERCENT CHANGE 4 YEARS
DEMAND DEPOSITS	20776	18463	13296	11008	11291	12.53	NA
ALL NOW & ATS ACCOUNTS	19287	14101	9380	7177	5473	36.78	NA
SUPER NOWS INCLUDED IN ABOVE	NA	6382	4092	2759	NA	NA	NA
MMDA SAVINGS	13216	12755	7558	6589	NA	3.61	NA
OTHER SAVINGS DEPOSITS	14466	12607	6157	6647	9886	14.75	NA
TIME DEPOSITS UNDER $100M	32385	37841	24382	21380	20814	-14.42	NA
CORE DEPOSITS	100130	95767	60773	52801	47464	4.56	NA
TIME DEPOSITS OVER $100M	2570	6876	8661	7995	8422	-62.62	NA
DEPOSITS HELD IN FOREIGN OFFICES	NA	NA	NA	NA	NA	NA	NA
FEDERAL FUNDS PURCHASED & RESALE	1738	1010	1349	1762	2028	NA	NA
OTHER BORROWINGS (+NOTE OPT)	0	1968	1969	303	525	-100.00	NA
VOLATILE LIABILITIES	4308	9854	11979	10060	10975	-56.28	NA
ACCEPTANCES	0	0	0	NA	NA	NA	NA
OTHER LIABILITIES	1584	1900	979	1635	1236	-1.39	NA
TOTAL LIABILITIES	106022	107521	73731	64496	59675	NA	NA
MORTGAGES & CAPITALIZED LEASES	0	0	0	25	32	NA	NA
SUBORDINATED NOTES & DEBENTURES	0	0	0	0	0	NA	NA
TOTAL LIABILITIES & DEBT	106022	107521	73731	64521	59707	NA	NA
LIMITED-LIFE PREFERRED STOCK	0	0	0	0	NA		
COMMON EQUITY	8237	7850	6199	5684	5596	4.93	NA
PERPETUAL PREFERRED STOCK	0	0	0	0	0	NA	NA
TOTAL EQUITY CAPITAL	8237	7850	6199	5684	5596	4.93	NA
TOTAL LIABILITIES AND CAPITAL	114259	115371	79930	70205	65303	-.96	NA
ALTERNATE DEPOSIT PRESENTATION							
NONINTEREST-BEARING DEPOSITS	20776	18463	13296	11008	11291	12.53	NA
DOMESTIC OFFICES	20776	18463	13296	11008	11291	12.53	NA
FOREIGN OFFICES	NA	NA	NA	NA	NA	NA	NA
INTEREST-BEARING DEPOSITS	81924	84180	56138	49788	44595	-2.68	NA
DOMESTIC OFFICES	81924	84180	56138	49788	44595	-2.68	NA
FOREIGN OFFICES	NA	NA	NA	NA	NA	NA	NA
TOTAL DEPOSITS	102700	102643	69434	60796	55886	.06	NA
TRANSACTION ACCOUNTS	40063	32564	22676	18185	16764	23.03	NA
MONEY MARKET DEPOSIT ACCTS	13216	12755	7558	6589	NA	3.61	NA
OTHER NON-TRANSACTION DEPS	49421	57324	39200	36022	39122	-13.79	NA
TOTAL BROKERED DEPOSITS	0	0	0	0	NA	NA	NA
RETAIL DEP ACQUIRED FR BROKERS	0	0	0	NA	NA	NA	NA

PAGE 06A

COMMITMENTS AND CONTINGENCIES

	12/31/86	12/31/85	12/31/84	12/31/83	12/31/82	PERCENT CHANGE 1 YEAR	PERCENT CHANGE 4 YEARS
LOAN & LEASE COMMITMENTS	2337	3290	913	0	NA	-28.97	NA
FUTURES BUY CONTRACTS	0	0	0	0	NA	NA	NA
FUTURES SELL CONTRACTS	0	0	0	0	NA	NA	NA
STANDBY OPTION BUY CONTRACTS	0	0	0	0	NA	NA	NA
STANDBY OPTION SELL CONTRACTS	0	0	0	0	NA	NA	NA
COMMIT TO PURCH FOREIGN CURR	0	0	NA	NA	NA	NA	NA
GROSS STANDBY LETTERS OF CREDIT	352	305	305	344	225	15.41	NA
COMMERCIAL LETTERS OF CREDIT	0	0	0	0	0	NA	NA
COMMIT:BUY SECURITY WHEN ISSUED	0	0	NA	NA	NA	NA	NA
COMMIT:SELL SECURITY WHEN ISSUE	0	0	NA	NA	NA	NA	NA
PARTICIPATIONS IN ACCEPTANCES:							
ACQUIRED BY THE BANK	0	0	0	0	NA	NA	NA
CONVEYED TO OTHERS	0	0	NA	NA	NA	NA	NA
SECURITIES BORROWED	0	0	0	0	NA	NA	NA
SECURITIES LENT	0	0	0	0	NA	NA	NA
OTH COMMITMENT & CONTINGENCY	0	0	NA	NA	NA	NA	NA
MEMO: LOANS SOLD DURING QUARTER	0	329	296	0	NA	-100.00	NA
NOTIONAL VALUE OF INT RATE SWAPS	0	0	NA	NA	NA	NA	NA

	12/31/86 BANK	PEER 08	PCT	12/31/85 BANK	PEER 12	PCT	12/31/84 BANK	PEER 12	PCT	12/31/83 BANK	PEER 12	12/31/82 BANK	PEER 12
COMMIT & CONTIN TO TOTAL ASSETS	2.05	2.96	55	2.85	.96	81	1.14	.86	71	.00	.61	NA	NA
LOAN & LEASE COMMITMENTS	.00	.00	98	.00	.00	99	.00	.00	99	.00	.00	NA	NA
FUTURES BUY CONTRACTS	.00	.00	98	.00	.00	99	.00	.00	99	.00	.00	NA	NA
FUTURES SELL CONTRACTS	.00	.00	99	.00	.00	99	.00	.00	99	.00	.00	NA	NA
STANDBY OPTION BUY CONTRACTS	.00	.00	98	.00	.00	99	.00	.00	99	.00	.00	NA	NA
STANDBY OPTION SELL CONTRACTS	.00	.00	99	.00	.00	99	.00	.00	99	.00	.00	NA	NA
COMMIT TO PURCH FOREIGN CURR	.00	.00	98	.00	.00	83	NA	.00	##	NA	NA	NA	NA
GROSS STANDBY LETTERS OF CREDIT	.31	.39	58	.26	.23	68	.38	.21	74	.49	.25	.34	NA
COMMERCIAL LETTERS OF CREDIT	.00	.00	77	.00	.00	81	.00	.00	80	.00	.03	.00	NA
COMMIT:BUY SECURITY WHEN ISSUED	.00	.00	97	.00	.00	83	NA	.00	##	.00	.00	NA	NA
COMMIT:SELL SECURITY WHEN ISSUE	.00	.00	99	.00	.00	83	NA	.00	##	.00	.00	NA	NA
PARTICIPATIONS IN ACCEPTANCES:													
ACQUIRED BY THE BANK	.00	.00	98	.00	.00	97	.00	.00	95	NA	NA	NA	NA
CONVEYED TO OTHERS	.00	.00	99	.00	.00	83	NA	.00	##	.00	.00	NA	NA
SECURITIES BORROWED	.00	.00	99	.00	.00	99	.00	.00	99	NA	NA	NA	NA
SECURITIES LENT	.00	.00	99	.00	.00	99	.00	.00	98	NA	NA	NA	NA
OTH COMMITMENT & CONTINGENCY	.00	.00	98	.00	##	99	NA	.00	##	NA	NA	NA	NA
NOTIONAL VALUE OF INT RATE SWAPS	.00	.00	96	.00	.00	99	NA	.00	##	NA	NA	NA	NA

BALANCE SHEET - PERCENTAGE COMPOSITION OF ASSETS AND LIABILITIES

PAGE 07

ASSETS, PERCENT OF AVG ASSETS	12/31/86			12/31/85			12/31/84			12/31/83		12/31/82	
	BANK	PEER 08	PCT	BANK	PEER 12	PCT	BANK	PEER 12	PCT	BANK	PEER 12	BANK	PEER 12
TOTAL LOANS	59.91	55.02	64	59.99	52.66	72	59.84	52.11	75	56.24	50.62	55.83	52.28
LEASE FINANCING RECEIVABLES	.49	.03	89	.76	.00	94	1.20	.00	98	.45	.00	.00	.00
LESS: LOSS RESERVES	1.41	.66	96	1.82	.58	98	.52	.53	50	.62	.51	.56	.51
TRANSFER RISK RESERVE	NA	NA	NA	NA	NA	NA	NA	NA	NA	NA	NA	NA	NA
NET LOANS & LEASES	58.98	54.67	62	58.93	52.19	71	60.52	51.68	79	56.07	50.18	55.27	51.84
SECURITIES OVER 1 YEAR	14.75	20.51	27	14.56	21.01	27	18.36	21.84	37	22.43	23.37	24.01	22.23
SUBTOTAL	73.73	75.35	37	73.49	73.38	45	78.89	73.58	72	78.49	73.56	79.29	74.07
INTEREST-BEARING BANK BALANCES	2.73	1.56	76	2.85	1.60	76	3.16	1.60	78	2.02	1.85	.06	1.77
FEDERAL FUNDS SOLD & RESALES	5.25	4.36	68	7.91	4.10	88	2.38	3.71	41	1.53	4.42	2.47	4.79
TRADING ACCOUNT ASSETS	.00	.00	97	.00	.00	98	.00	.00	98	NA	.00	NA	.00
DEBT SECURITIES 1 YR & LESS	7.82	8.98	46	5.63	10.59	22	6.03	10.80	22	8.31	9.80	7.24	8.54
TEMPORARY INVESTMENTS	15.80	15.96	55	16.40	17.37	49	11.57	17.10	26	11.86	17.06	9.77	16.33
TOTAL EARNING ASSETS	89.53	91.46	18	89.88	90.78	31	90.46	90.70	41	90.36	90.62	89.06	90.40
NON-INT CASH & DUE FR BANKS	6.38	4.60	84	5.89	4.85	78	6.04	4.86	81	6.09	4.98	7.32	5.21
PREMISES, FIX ASSTS, CAP LEASES	1.79	1.73	61	1.66	1.81	51	1.70	1.85	50	1.71	1.92	1.85	1.96
OTHER REAL ESTATE OWNED	.36	.28	69	.45	.38	68	.06	.30	31	.00	.25	.00	.17
ACCEPTANCES & OTHER ASSETS	1.95	1.79	67	2.11	2.08	58	1.74	2.19	24	1.84	2.11	1.77	2.16
SUBTOTAL	10.47	8.54	81	10.12	9.22	69	9.54	9.30	58	9.64	9.38	10.94	9.60
TOTAL ASSETS	100.00	100.00		100.01	100.00		100.00	100.00		99.99	100.00	100.00	100.00
STANDBY LETTERS OF CREDIT	.26	.38	54	.26	.22	67	.43	.21	79	.50	.23	.34	.19
LIABILITIES, PERCENT OF AVG ASST													
DEMAND DEPOSITS	15.93	12.29	84	16.00	13.08	80	15.21	13.62	69	15.47	14.45	19.60	16.05
ALL NOW & ATS ACCOUNTS	14.62	8.96	92	12.22	8.46	86	11.23	8.12	83	9.50	7.47	6.87	6.32
SUPER NOWS INCLUDED IN ABOVE	NA	NA	NA	5.53	3.28	80	3.80	2.78	72	3.03	1.71	NA	NA
MMDA SAVINGS	11.35	15.38	31	11.06	12.59	46	9.61	11.80	43	7.21	9.48	NA	NA
OTHER SAVINGS DEPOSITS	11.59	7.86	81	10.93	7.55	80	8.54	8.30	58	10.89	10.74	12.98	12.91
TIME DEPOSITS UNDER $100M	31.46	34.95	32	32.80	38.79	25	30.80	38.67	21	29.86	38.09	30.97	42.91
CORE DEPOSITS	84.95	80.41	76	83.01	80.78	57	75.39	80.94	18	72.93	80.59	70.42	78.21
TIME DEPOSITS OVER $100M	4.06	8.46	21	5.96	8.36	41	11.30	7.99	76	12.58	8.06	14.07	9.34
DEPOSITS IN FOREIGN OFFICES	NA	NA	NA	NA	NA	NA	NA	NA	NA	NA	NA	NA	NA
FEDERAL FUNDS PURCH & REPOS	1.11	.91	67	.88	.39	77	2.36	.58	89	3.09	.69	4.13	1.63
OTHER BORROWINGS (+NOTE OPT)	1.39	.34	94	1.71	.24	97	1.72	.28	96	1.22	.26	1.10	.22
VOLATILE LIABILITIES	6.56	10.24	30	8.54	9.45	51	15.38	9.32	83	16.89	9.53	19.30	11.55
ACCEPTANCES & OTHER LIAB	1.44	1.15	78	1.65	1.34	79	1.31	1.42	45	2.01	1.44	1.85	1.77
TOTAL LIABILITIES (INCL MORTG)	92.96	91.95	71	93.20	91.74	83	92.08	91.82	50	91.83	91.75	91.57	91.69
SUBORDINATED NOTES & DEBENTURES	.00	.00	84	.00	.00	86	.00	.00	84	.00	.00	.00	.00
ALL COMMON & PREFERRED CAPITAL	7.04	8.01	30	6.80	8.18	18	7.92	8.08	51	8.17	8.16	8.43	8.18
TOTAL LIABILITIES & CAPITAL	99.99	100.00		100.00	100.00		100.00	100.00		100.00	100.00	100.00	100.00
NONINTEREST BEARING DEPOSITS	15.93	12.33	84	16.00	13.25	78	15.29	13.78	68	15.47	14.45	19.60	16.05
INTEREST BEARING DEPOSITS	73.09	76.32	23	72.96	76.04	22	71.40	75.29	19	70.04	74.21	64.89	71.53
TOTAL BROKERED DEPOSITS	.00	.00	96	.00	.00	97	.00	.00	96	.00	.00	NA	NA

ANALYSIS OF ALLOWANCE FOR LOAN AND LEASE LOSSES AND LOAN MIX

PAGE 08

CHANGE:LOAN&LEASE RESERVE ($000)	12/31/86	12/31/85	12/31/84	12/31/83	12/31/82
BEGINNING BALANCE	2103	425	350	450	350
GROSS LOAN & LEASE LOSSES	1327	290	264	633	432
RECOVERIES	118	49	161	73	71
NET LOAN & LEASE LOSSES	1209	241	103	560	361
PROVISION FOR LOAN, LEASE LOSS	125	398	178	460	461
OTHER ADJUSTMENTS	0	1521	0	0	0
ENDING BALANCE	1019	2103	425	350	450
NET ATRR CHARGE-OFFS	NA	NA	NA	NA	NA
OTHER ATRR CHANGES (NET)	NA	NA	NA	NA	NA
AVERAGE TOTAL LOANS & LEASES	69554	52047	45281	39795	37032

ANALYSIS RATIOS	86 BANK	86 PEER 08	86 PCT	85 BANK	85 PEER 12	85 PCT	84 BANK	84 PEER 12	84 PCT	83 BANK	83 PEER 12	82 BANK	82 PEER 12
LOSS PROVISION TO AVG ASST	.11	.46	12	.50	.53	60	.24	.35	46	.65	.34	.71	.31
LOSS PROV TO AVG TOT LOANS & LS	.18	.84	11	.76	.98	50	.39	.67	39	1.17	.64	1.24	.60
NET LOSSES TO AVG TOT LN & LS	1.74	.72	86	.46	.85	42	.23	.61	30	1.42	.60	.97	.53
GROSS LOSS TO AVG TOT LN & LS	1.91	.87	85	.56	1.02	41	.58	.75	52	1.60	.74	1.17	.67
RECOVERIES TO AVG TOT LN & LS	.17	.15	68	.09	.16	45	.36	.14	87	.18	.14	.19	.12
RECOVERIES TO PRIOR PERIOD LOSS	40.69	27.02	76	18.56	29.63	43	25.43	27.36	57	16.90	29.37	29.71	31.80
LOSS RESERVE TO TOT LOAN & LS	1.49	1.22	76	3.00	1.19	96	.82	1.02	26	.86	1.03	1.23	1.00
LOSS RESV TO NET LOSSES (X)	.84	3.63	15	8.73	2.62	88	4.13	3.18	69	.63	3.15	1.25	3.06
LOSS RESV TO NONACRUAL LN&LS (X)	1.73	2.10		3.73	1.71		5.06	1.59		1.05	1.86	NA	NA
EARN COVERAGE OF NET LOSSES (X)	.93	9.16	08	5.15	8.18	47	9.10	9.97	60	.99	10.14	1.61	9.55

LOAN MIX, % AVG GROSS LOANS&LEASE

	86 BANK	86 PEER 08	86 PCT	85 BANK	85 PEER 12	85 PCT	84 BANK	84 PEER 12	84 PCT	83 BANK	83 PEER 12	82 BANK	82 PEER 12
CONSTRUCTION & DEVELOPMENT	.27	1.95	23	1.02	1.44	54	.20	1.49	27	.13	1.48	.17	1.39
1 - 4 FAMILY RESIDENTIAL	25.89	25.57	51	23.10	24.49	47	22.24	24.13	47	13.89	24.24	13.04	24.07
OTHER REAL ESTATE LOANS	13.05	15.41	42	12.64	14.11	48	13.86	13.94	54	14.93	14.13	14.60	14.02
TOTAL REAL ESTATE	39.21	43.64	37	36.75	40.89	40	36.31	40.22	41	28.96	40.53	27.81	40.14
FINANCIAL INSTITUTION LOANS	.44	.01	84	.17	.00	83	.32	.16	73	.68	.76	.00	1.01
AGRICULTURAL LOANS	5.59	3.52	74	5.16	7.46	56	2.32	8.74	36	3.23	8.11	3.98	7.46
COMMERCIAL & INDUSTRIAL LOANS	22.98	21.02	61	23.92	20.33	67	17.98	20.95	44	20.63	21.83	21.05	22.12
LOANS TO INDIVIDUALS	30.22	24.16	73	32.43	24.71	77	38.22	23.99	87	45.47	24.08	46.87	24.20
MUNICIPAL LOANS	.05	2.45	22	.01	1.39	33	.00	.33	36	NA	NA	NA	NA
ACCEPTANCES OF OTHER BANKS	.42	.11	76	.00	.26	65	2.33	.33	84	NA	NA	NA	NA
LOANS, LEASES IN FOREIGN OFFICES	.00	.99	99	.00	.00	99	.00	.00	99	.00	.00	.00	.00
ALL OTHER LOANS	.31	.99	41	.34	1.19	39	.66	1.29	48	.28	1.39	.28	1.45
LEASE FINANCING RECEIVABLES	.80	.05	88	1.22	.00	94	1.86	.00	97	.74	.00	.00	.00

MEMORANDUM(% OF AVG TOTAL LOANS):

	86 BANK	86 PEER 08	86 PCT	85 BANK	85 PEER 12	85 PCT	84 BANK	84 PEER 12	84 PCT	83 BANK	83 PEER 12	82 BANK	82 PEER 12
COMMERCIAL PAPER IN LOANS	2.16	.00	94	5.88	1.61	83	NA	##	64	NA	.00	NA	.00
OFFICER, SHAREHOLDER LOANS	.23	.32	54	.46	.46	65	.41	.42	64	.16	.46	NA	NA
LOAN & LEASE COMMITMENTS	3.39	5.47	51	6.43	1.90	84	2.06	1.74	69	.00	1.22	NA	NA
LOANS SOLD DURING THE QUARTER	.00	.13	64	.64	.12	79	.67	.12	81	.00	.07	NA	NA

COMPOSITION CHANGES:	86 BANK	86 PEER 08	86 PCT	85 BANK	85 PEER 12	85 PCT	84 BANK	84 PEER 12	84 PCT	83 BANK	83 PEER 12	82 BANK	82 PEER 12
ASSET MIX	6.31	13.71	14	NA	13.69	NA	17.71	14.12	73	12.90	14.96	8.12	14.49
LOAN MIX (INCLUDING LEASES)	18.72	14.20	74	NA	13.22	NA	20.12	15.36	74	7.58	14.31	2.74	14.16
LIABILITY MIX	39.66	23.03	95	NA	11.80	NA	75.59	93.94	18	54.72	79.70	24.63	17.20

ANALYSIS OF PAST DUE, NONACCRUAL & RESTRUCTURED LOANS & LEASES

PAGE 08A

NON-CURRENT LNS & LEASES ($000)	12/31/86 BANK	12/31/86 PEER 08	09/30/86 BANK	09/30/86 PEER 08	06/30/86 BANK	06/30/86 PEER 08	03/31/86 BANK	03/31/86 PEER 08	12/31/85 BANK	12/31/85 PEER 12
90 DAYS AND OVER PAST DUE	156		851		847		481		935	
TOTAL NONACCRUAL LNS & LEASE	590		953		997		1231		564	
TOTAL NON-CURRENT LNS & LEASES	746		1804		1844		1712		1499	
NON-CURR AS % OF AVERAGE LN&LS**										
REAL ESTATE LNS-90+ DAYS P/D	.15	.72	.80	.97	1.02	1.03	.48	1.05	.26	1.10
-NONACCRUAL	.25	.92	.63	.97	.54	1.06	.36	1.02	.96	1.02
-TOTAL	.41	1.86	1.43	2.08	1.56	2.33	.83	2.26	1.22	2.33
COML. OTHER LNS-90+ DAYS P/D	.26	.61	2.00	.69	1.74	.80	1.09	.82	2.38	.93
-NONACCRUAL	1.78	1.34	2.07	1.62	1.28	1.53	1.97	1.58	2.00	1.65
-TOTAL	2.04	2.11	4.08	2.50	3.02	2.51	3.06	2.70	4.38	2.74
INSTALLMENT LNS-90+ DAYS P/D	.29	.69	.32	.68	.55	.68	.30	.70	.42	.79
-NONACCRUAL	.08	.09	.08	.12	.14	.09	.08	.11	.10	.07
-TOTAL	.37	.88	.40	.94	.68	.91	.39	.95	.52	1.00
CREDIT CARD PLANS-90+ DAYS P/D	.26	.32	.34	.39	.74	.42	.51	.42	.58	.38
-NONACCRUAL	.00	.00	.00	.00	.00	.00	.00	.00	.16	.00
-TOTAL	.26	.34	.34	.46	.74	.42	.51	.43	.74	.38
LEASE FINANCING-90+ DAYS P/D	.00	.00	41.39	.00	100.00	.00	.00	.00	42.22	.00
-NONACCRUAL	.00	.00	.00	.00	.00	.00	65.13	.00	.00	.00
-TOTAL	.00	.00	41.39	.00	100.00	.00	65.13	.00	42.22	.00
TOTAL LOANS & LS-90+ DAYS P/D	.23	.74	1.20	.85	1.18	.95	.68	.95	1.29	1.03
-NONACCRUAL	.85	1.02	1.35	1.20	1.38	1.20	1.75	1.22	.78	1.23
-TOTAL	1.08	1.74	2.55	2.10	2.56	2.24	2.43	2.21	2.07	2.36
MEMO-BANKS W/AG LOANS OVER 5%:										
%NON-CURR AGRI LNS-90+ DAYS P/D	.00	.66	.00	.67	1.43	1.65	.00	1.92	.33	1.09
-NONACCRUAL	.00	2.84	.00	4.09	.00	4.04	3.97	3.46	15.02	2.94
-TOTAL	.00	4.51	.00	5.66	1.43	5.91	3.97	5.98	15.34	4.92
OTHER PERTINENT RATIOS:										
NON-CURR LN&LS TO TOTAL ASSETS	.65	.99	1.59	1.17	1.60	1.23	1.47	1.24	1.30	1.27
IENC-LOANS TO TOTAL LOANS	1.01	1.06	1.18	1.23	1.04	1.24	1.01	1.29	1.09	1.60
% CURRENT RESTRUC DEBT BY TYPE:										
REAL ESTATE LOANS	.00	.00	.00	.00	.00	.00	NA	NA	NA	NA
INSTALLMENT LOANS	.00	.00	.00	.00	.00	.00	NA	NA	NA	NA
CREDIT CARD AND RELATED PLANS	.00	.00	.00	.00	.00	.00	NA	NA	NA	NA
COMMERCIAL AND ALL OTHER LOANS	1.01	.00	1.08	.01	1.11	.01	NA	NA	NA	NA
LEASE FINANCING RECEIVABLES	.00	.00	.00	.00	.00	.00	NA	NA	NA	NA
AGRI LOANS INCLUDED ABOVE	.00	.00	.00	.00	.00	.00	NA	NA	NA	NA

**BANKS HAVING <$300 MILLION IN TOTAL ASSETS REPORT THIS LOAN DETAIL(BY TYPE) USING THEIR OWN INTERNAL CATEGORIZATION SYSTEMS

SOURCES AND USES OF FUNDS

| | BALANCE 12/31/87 | YEAR ENDED 12/31/86 | | | | QUARTER ENDED 12/31/86 | | | | QUARTER ENDED 12/31/85 | | | |
| | | SOURCE | | USE | | SOURCE | | USE | | SOURCE | | USE | |
		$	%	$	%	$	%	$	%	$	%	$	%
ASSETS													
INTEREST-BEARING BANK BALANCES	2800	490	2			600	5						
FEDERAL FUNDS SOLD AND RESALES	6100	3025	10					4100	34				
TRADING ACCOUNT ASSETS	0												
DEBT SECURITIES 1 YR & LESS	8243			1742	6	2146	18						
RATE ADJ LOAN&LEASE 1YR & LESS	41454			10018	32	620	5						
ADJUSTABLE RATE ASSETS	58597			8245	26			734	6				
ALL OTHER LOANS & LEASES	25793	10756	34			444	4						
ALL OTHER SECURITIES	17434	10121	32			1524	13						
FIXED RATE ASSETS	43227			635	2	1968	16						
TOTAL EARNING ASSETS	101824												
NON-INT CASH & DUE FROM BANKS	7875	1876	6	1078	3	1234	10	1995	17				
ACCEPTANCES & OTHER ASSETS	4560	314	1			19							
TOTAL ASSETS	114259												
LIABILITIES AND CAPITAL													
CDS OVER $100M 1 YEAR & LESS	2470			3700	12			1060	9				
FOREIGN OFF DEPS 1 YEAR & LESS	NA												
ALL OTHER TIME DEPS 1 YR & LESS	24219	132						166	1				
MMDA SAVINGS & UNREGULATED NOW	32503	13366	42			1162	10						
ALL OTH NONDEP INT-BEAR LIA < 1YR	1738	728	2			595	5						
ADJUSTABLE RATE LIABILITIES	60930	10526	33			531	4						
CDS OVER $100M OVER 1 YEAR	100			606	2			413	3				
ALL OTHER TIME DEPS OVER 1 YR	8166			5588	18			2269	19				
FOREIGN OFF DEPOSITS OVER 1 YR	NA												
OTH SAVINGS, ATS & REGULATED NOW	14466			5860	19	443	4						
ALL OTH NONDEP INT-BEAR LIA > 1YR	0												
FIXED INT-RATE LIABILITIES	22732			12054	38			2239	19				
TOTAL INT-BEARING LIABILITIES	83662			1708	5			1708	14				
DEMAND DEPOSITS	20776	2313	7			4450	37						
ACCEPTANCES & OTHER LIABILITIES	1584			2284	7	1940	16						
EQUITY CAPITAL	8237	387	1					60	1				
NON-INTEREST-BEARING FUNDS	30597	416	1			2450	20						
TOTAL LIABILITIES AND CAPITAL	114259												
TOTAL (SOURCES/USES)		31511		31511		12003		12003		NA		NA	
NET CHANGE IN FOOTINGS				-1112				742				NA	
NET CHANGE IN MARKET POSITION				-2281				203				NA	

ANALYSIS OF REPRICING OPPORTUNITIES

PAGE 10

REPRICING OPPORTUNITIES FOR:	1 DAY	3 MONTHS	3-6 MOS	6-12 MOS	1-5 YRS	5 YEARS	ALL OTHER	TOTAL	----% ASSETS
TOTAL LOANS AND LEASES	13418	14743	2687	10606	15905	11153	-	68512	59.96
DEBT SECURITIES	0	2813	802	4628	16445	827	-	25515	22.33
TRADING ACCOUNT ASSETS	-	0	-	-	-	0	-	0	.00
OTHER INTEREST-BEARING ASSETS	6100	2000	400	100	300	0	-	8900	7.79
TOTAL INTEREST-BEARING ASSETS	19518	19556	3889	15334	32650	11980	-	102927	90.08
LOAN & LEASE LOSS RESERVE	-	-	-	-	-	-	-1019	-1019	-.89
NON-ACCRUAL LOANS	-	-	-	-	-	-	590	590	.52
ALL OTHER ASSETS	-	-	-	-	-	-	11761	11761	10.29
TOTAL ASSETS	19518	19556	3889	15334	32650	11980	11332	114259	
DEPOSITS IN FOREIGN OFFICES	NA	NA	NA	NA	NA	NA	-	NA	NA
CDS OVER $100,000	0	1302	200	968	100	0	-	2570	2.25
OTHER TIME DEPOSITS	0	9774	6186	8259	8166	0	-	32385	28.34
MMDA SAVINGS & UNREGULATED NOW	-	32503	-	-	-	-	-	32503	28.45
OTH SAVINGS, ATS & REGULATED NOW	-	-	-	-	-	-	14466	14466	12.66
TREASURY NOTES	-	0	-	-	-	-	0	0	.00
MORTGAGES & CAPITALIZED LEASES	-	0	0	0	0	0	0	0	.00
OTHER NONDEPOSIT INT-BEAR LIABS	1738	-	-	-	-	-	1738	1738	1.52
TOTAL INT-BEARING LIABILITIES	1738	43579	6386	9227	8266	0	14466	83662	73.22
DEMAND DEPOSITS	-	-	-	-	-	-	20776	20776	18.18
ALL OTHER LIABILITIES	-	-	-	-	-	-	1584	1584	1.39
TOTAL LIABILITIES	1738	43579	6386	9227	8266	0	36826	106022	92.79
TOTAL EQUITY (EXCLUDING LIMITED LIFE PREF STOCK)	-	-	-	-	-	-	8237	8237	7.21
TOTAL LIABILITIES & CAPITAL	1738	43579	6386	9227	8266	0	45063	114259	
NET POSITIONS--TOTAL ASSETS LESS LIABILITIES & CAPITAL	17780	-24023	-2497	6107	24384	11980	-33731	0	
CUMULATIVE POSITIONS									
TOTAL ASSETS	19518	39074	42963	58297	90947	102927		114259	
TOTAL LIABILITIES & CAPITAL	1738	45317	51703	60930	69196	69196		114259	
TOTAL ASSETS LESS LIAB & CAP	17780	-6243	-8740	-2633	21751	33731		0	
ESTIMATED DISTRIBUTION FOR BANKS ELECTING OPTION #2 ON SCHEDULE J									
RESIDENTIAL RE LOANS (EST)**	-	NA	NA	NA	NA	NA	-	NA	NA
CONSUMER INSTALLMENT LNS (EST)**	-	NA	NA	NA	NA	NA	-	NA	NA

*BASED ON ESTIMATED PAYMENTS FOR LATEST QUARTER.

PAGE 10A

ANALYSIS OF REPRICING OPPORTUNITIES (CONTINUED)

CUMULATIVE GAP COMPARISONS FOR INTEREST-BEARING ASSETS AND LIABILITIES
(EXCLUDES THOSE CATEGORIZED UNDER "ALL OTHER" ON PAGE 10 DISTRIBUTION)

12/31/86

PERCENT OF ASSETS REPRICED WITHIN	ASSETS			LIABILITIES			NET POSITION			BANK CUMULATIVE NET HISTORY			
	BANK	PEER 08	PCT	BANK	PEER 08	PCT	BANK	PEER 08	PCT	09/30/86	06/30/86	03/31/86	12/31/85
1 DAY	17.08	15.86	60	1.52	1.07	72	15.56	14.39	60	12.75	12.28	14.31	10.96
3 MONTHS	34.20	30.31	67	39.66	43.19	31	-5.46	-12.75	76	-7.85	-7.78	-2.10	-1.39
6 MONTHS	37.60	37.72	49	45.25	52.96	15	-7.65	-14.93	77	-10.47	-8.02	-2.89	-2.20
12 MONTHS	51.02	48.49	58	53.33	59.67	17	-2.30	-10.73	76	-4.35	-6.28	-.95	-2.01
5 YEARS	79.60	77.57	54	60.56	68.74	12	19.04	8.87	84	17.29	15.61	16.89	21.09

SUPPLEMENTAL INFORMATION:

	PEER 08	09/30/86	06/30/86	03/31/86	12/31/85
PEER GROUP AVG YIELD ON FED FUNDS	6.15	6.26	6.87	7.59	8.08
BANK REPORTED FUTURES CONTRACTS OR INTEREST RATE SWAPS	NO	NO	NO	NO	NO

REPRICING DISTRIBUTION COMPARISONS FOR SCHEDULE J ASSETS AND LIABILITIES

SCHEDULE J ASSETS	ITEM TOTAL AS PERCENT OF ASSETS	PERCENT REPRICED WITHIN 3 MONTHS			PERCENT REPRICED WITHIN 6 MONTHS			PERCENT REPRICED WITHIN 12 MONTHS			PERCENT REPRICED WITHIN 5 YEARS		
		BANK	PEER 08	PCT	BANK	PEER 08	PCT	BANK	PEER 08	PCT	BANK	PEER 08	PCT
RESIDENTIAL RE LOANS (EST)**	NA	NA	3.99	54	NA	7.97	NA	NA	15.95	NA	NA	68.92	NA
CONSUMER INSTALLMENT LNS (EST)**	NA	NA	13.70	NA	NA	27.40	NA	NA	54.11	NA	NA	100.00	NA
TOTAL LOANS AND LEASES	59.96	41.10	39.33	54	45.03	48.41	38	60.51	60.26	46	83.72	87.69	28
DEBT SECURITIES	22.33	11.02	9.76	66	14.17	16.71	46	32.31	30.09	62	96.76	74.83	88
OTHER INTEREST-BEARING ASSETS	7.79	91.01	83.71	40	95.51	91.08	35	96.63	96.84	29	100.00	100.00	99
TOTAL SCHEDULE J ASSETS	90.08	37.96	33.11	68	41.74	41.33	52	56.64	53.02	61	88.36	84.52	61

SCHEDULE J LIABILITIES	ITEM TOTAL AS PERCENT OF ASSETS	BANK	PEER 08	PCT	BANK	PEER 08	PCT	BANK	PEER 08	PCT	BANK	PEER 08	PCT
DEPOSITS IN FOREIGN OFFICES	NA	NA	NA	NA	NA	NA	NA	NA	NA	NA	NA	NA	NA
CDS OVER $100,000	2.25	50.66	55.90	38	58.44	76.55	15	96.11	88.80	70	100.00	100.00	99
OTHER TIME DEPOSITS	28.34	30.18	33.65	37	49.28	57.68	26	74.78	74.99	48	100.00	99.95	99
OTHER NONDEPOSIT INT-BEAR LIABS	1.52	100.00	95.92	99	100.00	99.44	99	100.00	99.74	99	100.00	100.00	99
TOTAL SCHEDULE J LIABILITIES	32.11	34.92	40.10	33	52.33	62.58	20	77.47	78.20	47	100.00	99.91	99

**PRESENTED FOR BANKS ELECTING OPTION #2 ON SCHEDULE J.
FIGURES ARE BASED ON ESTIMATED DISTRIBUTION ON PAGE 10.

LIQUIDITY AND INVESTMENT PORTFOLIO

PAGE 11

	12/31/86 BANK	PEER 08	PCT	12/31/85 BANK	PEER 12	PCT	12/31/84 BANK	PEER 12	PCT	12/31/83 BANK	PEER 12	12/31/82 BANK	PEER 12
TEMPORARY INVESTMENTS ($000)	17143	100130		18916	95767		9594	60773		7830	52801	7587	47464
CORE DEPOSITS ($000)		4308			9854			11979			10060		10975
VOLATILE LIABILITIES ($000)													
PERCENT OF TOTAL ASSETS													
TEMPORARY INVESTMENTS	15.00	15.50	51	16.40	17.67	49	12.00	17.68	25	11.15	17.41	11.62	17.48
CORE DEPOSITS	87.63	80.89	86	83.01	81.00	55	76.03	80.90	19	75.21	81.08	72.68	79.12
VOLATILE LIABILITIES	3.77	9.94	14	8.54	9.47	53	14.99	9.37	81	14.33	9.24	16.81	10.95
LIQUIDITY RATIOS													
VOLATILE LIABILITY DEPENDENCE	-15.16	-8.20	26	-10.69	-11.83	49	3.77	-12.55	85	4.02	-12.42	6.54	-10.32
TEMP INV TO VOLATILE LIAB	397.93	219.14	83	191.96	258.91	47	80.09	265.16	14	77.83	267.40	69.13	220.22
BROKERED DEPOSITS TO DEPOSITS	.00	.00	97	.00	.00	97	.00	.00	97	.00	.00	NA	NA
TEMP INV LESS VOL LIAB TO ASSETS	11.23	5.73	73	7.85	8.15	49	-2.98	8.23	14	-3.18	8.08	-5.19	6.41
NET LOANS & LEASES TO DEPOSITS	65.48	60.86	62	66.23	57.73	73	73.64	58.55	90	67.44	55.94	64.65	57.48
NET LNS & LS TO CORE DEPOSITS	67.16	67.32	46	70.99	64.24	69	84.14	64.91	91	77.66	61.98	76.13	64.22
NET LOANS & LEASES TO ASSETS	58.85	54.47	62	58.93	51.68	72	63.97	52.17	87	58.40	49.92	55.33	50.61
NET LOANS, LEASES & SBLC TO ASST	59.16	54.89	61	59.19	51.99	72	64.35	52.46	86	58.89	50.23	55.68	50.88
PERCENT CHANGE IN:													
TEMPORARY INVESTMENTS	-9.37	14.38	32	NA	12.46	NA	22.53	18.06	62	3.20	18.89	1.59	28.97
SECURITIES OVER 1 YEAR	3.78	12.80	39	NA	12.37	NA	-15.70	-3.61	32	-7.97	12.77	-1.63	10.69
NET LOANS & LEASES	-1.09	9.66	19	NA	6.83	NA	24.71	12.85	84	13.48	8.30	-1.57	6.54
CORE DEPOSITS	4.56	10.70	21	NA	7.05	NA	15.10	7.14	87	11.24	12.45	-.29	9.64
VOLATILE LIABILITIES	-56.28	7.19	01	NA	8.75	NA	19.08	22.27	50	-8.34	-3.63	-22.81	10.03
TOTAL ASSETS	-.96	9.83	05	NA	6.69	NA	13.85	7.81	81	7.51	10.04	-4.44	9.28
SECURITIES MIX													
PERCENT OF TOTAL SECURITIES:													
US TREAS & AGENCY	89.34	57.50	95	77.20	60.44	76	62.64	63.84	41	59.60	62.51	58.26	57.28
MUNICIPALS	8.08	33.95	06	22.04	35.99	26	35.51	33.45	59	32.64	35.54	37.69	41.37
FOREIGN SECURITIES	.00	.00	94	.00	.00	83	NA	##	NA	NA	NA	NA	NA
ALL OTHER SECURITIES	2.58	7.09	51	.76	1.00	65	1.85	.74	76	7.76	.41	4.04	.41
DEBT SECURITIES UNDER 1 YEAR	32.31	30.09	62	28.12	32.68	44	27.79	35.29	35	28.81	32.30	27.60	28.72
DEBT SECURITIES 1 TO 5 YEARS	64.45	44.39	90	61.47	45.84	82	53.70	46.45	64	46.52	48.20	46.39	48.35
DEBT SECURITIES 5 TO 10 YEARS	3.24	16.16	15	10.17	14.51	40	17.27	12.54	74	20.52	13.35	18.40	14.17
DEBT SECURITIES OVER 10 YEARS	.00	7.99	24	.24	4.34	35	1.24	3.86	47	4.15	4.40	7.60	7.63
OTHER SECURITIES RATIOS:													
SECURITY APP (DEP) TO INV SEC	2.02	3.14	31	-.65	1.21	16	-4.56	-1.19	12	NA	NA	NA	NA
SECURITY APP (DEP) TO PRIM CAP*	5.60	11.08	30	-1.59	4.66	17	-11.49	-3.64	17	NA	NA	NA	NA
TAXABLE SEC: MKT TO BOOK	101.91	101.87	54	101.06	102.21	23	100.10	100.97	21	NA	NA	NA	NA
NON-TAXABLE SEC: MKT TO BOOK	103.23	105.07	37	93.30	98.68	15	86.98	94.20	12	NA	NA	NA	NA
PLEDGED SECURITIES TO TOTAL SEC	38.36	29.11	69	44.33	26.83	79	82.38	25.81	96	NA	NA	NA	NA

*REFER TO THE UBPR USERS GUIDE FOR PRIMARY CAPITAL DEFINITION.

PAGE 12

CAPITAL ANALYSIS

END-OF-PERIOD CAPITAL ($000)	12/31/86	12/31/85	12/31/84	12/31/83	12/31/82
COMMON EQUITY	8237	7850	6199	5684	5596
LOAN & LEASE LOSS RESERVE	1019	2103	425	350	450
PERM & CONV PREFERRED	0	0	0	0	0
MINORITY INT IN CONS SUBSID	0	0	0	NA	NA
LESS: INTANGIBLE ASSETS	38	496	84	NA	NA
QUALIFYING INTANGIBLE ASSETS	38	61	84	106	0
QUALIF MANDATORY CONV DEBT	0	0	0	106	NA
TOTAL PRIMARY CAPITAL*	9256	9518	6624	6034	6046
SECONDARY CAPITAL COMPONENTS:					
LIMITED LIFE PREFERRED STK	0	0	0	0	NA
QUALIFYING SUBORD DEBT	0	0	0	0	0
TOT PRIMARY & SECONDARY CAPITAL	9256	9518	6624	6034	6046
MEMO:RESID LIM LIFE PFD&SUB DBT	0	0	0	0	0
MORTGAGE SERVICING RIGHTS	0	0	NA	NA	NA
OTH IDENTIFIABLE INTANGIBLES	38	61	NA	NA	NA
GOODWILL	0	435	NA	NA	NA
INT ASSTS BOOKED BEF 4/15/85	38	61	NA	NA	NA
SPECIAL CATEGORY NET CHG-OFF	163	NA	NA	NA	NA
TOTAL MANDATORY CONV DEBT	0	0	0	0	NA

CHANGES IN TOTAL EQUITY ($000)	12/31/86	12/31/85	12/31/84	12/31/83	12/31/82
BALANCE BEGINNING-OF-PERIOD	7851	6199	5684	5596	5441
NET INCOME	748	665	680	307	375
SALE OR PURCH OF CAPITAL	0	0	0	0	0
MERGER & ABSORPTIONS	0	1519	0	0	0
LESS: CASH DIVIDENDS	362	533	165	220	220
NET OTHER INCREASES(DECREASE)	0	0	0	0	0
BALANCE AT END-OF-PERIOD	8237	7850	6199	5683	5596

CAPITAL RATIOS	BANK	PEER 08	PCT	BANK	PEER 12	PCT	BANK	PEER 12	PCT	BANK	PEER 12	BANK	PEER 12
PERCENT OF ADJ AVERAGE ASSETS:													
PRIMARY CAPITAL*	8.15	8.66	42	11.83	8.88	93	8.50	8.65	51	8.33	8.53	9.22	8.63
PRIMARY & SECONDARY CAPITAL*	8.15	8.70	40	11.83	8.95	93	8.50	8.74	49	8.33	8.63	9.22	8.77
PERCENT OF RISK ASSETS:													
PRIMARY CAPITAL*	12.42	12.53	57	12.18	13.36	42	11.09	13.16	31	11.63	13.26	12.77	12.98
PRIMARY & SECONDARY CAPITAL*	12.42	12.63	56	12.18	13.47	40	11.09	13.29	28	11.63	13.39	12.77	13.19
PERCENT OF TOTAL EQUITY:													
NET LOANS & LEASES (X)	8.16	7.28	63	8.66	6.70	79	8.25	6.82	74	7.21	6.45	6.46	6.49
SUBORD NOTES & DEBENTURES	.00	.00	87	.00	.03	88	.00	.00	87	.00	.00	.00	.00
LONG TERM DEBT	.00	.58	63	.00	.03	72	.00	.20	68	.44	.26	.57	.95
PERCENT OF AVG TOT EQUITY:													
NET INCOME	9.24	13.85	18	8.47	13.03	21	11.42	12.20	39	5.42	12.81	6.73	12.81
DIVIDENDS	4.47	4.72	53	6.79	4.53	76	2.77	4.39	32	3.89	4.24	3.95	4.15
RETAINED EARNINGS	4.77	8.46	25	1.68	7.57	20	8.65	6.87	57	1.54	8.10	2.78	8.37
OTHER CAPITAL RATIOS:													
QUALIFYING INTANG TO PRIM CAP*	.41	.00	91	.64	.00	96	1.27	.00	96	1.76	.00	.00	.00
EQUITY CAPITAL TO ASSETS	7.21	7.86	38	6.80	8.14	21	7.76	7.98	49	8.10	7.99	8.57	8.08
PRIM CAP TO TOT LNS & LEASES*	13.56	16.23	38	13.58	17.58	27	12.85	16.87	23	14.59	17.71	16.53	17.27
GROWTH RATES:													
TOTAL EQUITY CAPITAL	4.93	9.38	22	NA	8.59	NA	9.06	7.92	54	1.57	9.13	2.85	9.20
PRIMARY CAPITAL*	-2.75	9.59	05	NA	9.62	NA	9.78	8.33	55	-.20	9.27	4.40	9.21
EQUITY GROWTH LESS ASSET GROWTH	5.89	-.59	82	NA	1.16	NA	-4.79	-.65	25	-5.94	-1.24	7.29	.03

*REFER TO THE UBPR USERS GUIDE FOR PRIMARY CAPITAL DEFINITION.

SUMMARY INFORMATION FOR BANKS IN STATE

PAGE 13

	AVERAGE OF ALL BANKS IN STATE					BANKS WITH ASSETS - $MILL (12/31/86)		
	12/31/86	12/31/85	12/31/84	12/31/83	12/31/82	0-25	25-100	100+
TOTAL ASSETS ($MILLIONS)	88740	81764	72337	67209	63379	991	6876	80872
NET INCOME ($MILLIONS)	927	783	702	518	461	7	69	851
NUMBER OF BANKS IN TABULATION	308	320	320	343	355	67	134	107
EARNINGS AND PROFITABILITY								
NET INT INC (TE) TO AVG ASSETS	4.60	4.69	4.48	4.50	4.47	4.70	4.58	4.58
+ NON-INT INC TO AVG ASSETS	.53	.53	.59	.52	.50	.51	.40	.71
- OVERHEAD EXP TO AVG ASSETS	3.03	3.04	3.03	3.06	3.01	3.60	2.66	3.13
- PROV FOR LN/LS LOSS TO AV AST	.34	.36	.33	.34	.27	.33	.30	.38
= PRETAX OPERATING INCOME (TE)	1.83	1.84	1.75	1.60	1.62	1.41	1.98	1.88
+ SECURITIES GAINS (LOSSES)	.06	.02	.00	.01	.01	.04	.07	.08
= PRETAX NET OPER INC (TE)	1.93	1.90	1.75	1.59	1.60	1.41	2.10	2.03
NET OPER INC TO AVG ASSETS	1.06	1.08	1.00	.93	.93	.88	1.13	1.09
ADJ NET OPER INC TO AVG ASSETS	1.14	1.17	1.07	.99	.98	.94	1.19	1.18
NET INCOME TO AVG ASSETS	1.07	1.09	1.01	.93	.93	.90	1.13	1.10
INT INC (TE) TO AVG EARN ASSTS	10.82	11.63	12.17	11.94	12.91	10.75	10.91	10.74
INT EXPENSE TO AVG EARN ASSETS	5.91	6.67	7.38	7.04	8.12	5.72	6.01	5.92
NET INT INC-TE TO AV EARN ASST	4.95	5.04	4.89	4.91	4.92	5.11	4.88	4.95
LOAN & LEASE LOSSES AND RESERVES								
NET LOSS TO AVG TOT LOAN & LEASE	.53	.56	.55	.61	.52	.59	.49	.56
EARNINGS COVERAGE OF NET LOSS(X)	7.95	7.65	9.91	8.47	7.36	6.10	9.19	7.48
LOSS RESERVE TO NET LOSSES (X)	3.37	3.19	3.73	3.20	2.76	2.80	3.56	3.45
LOSS RESV TO TOT LOANS & LEASE	1.18	1.15	1.07	1.08	1.05	1.19	1.17	1.19
LIQUIDITY AND RATE SENSITIVITY								
VOLATILE LIABILITY DEPENDENCE	-17.37	-17.55	-18.56	-20.02	-17.33	-37.45	-18.30	-4.10
NET LOANS & LEASES TO ASSETS	52.26	50.88	50.66	48.24	48.30	46.01	50.21	58.61
CAPITALIZATION								
MEMBER PRIM CAP TO AVG ASSETS*	9.03	9.00	9.13	9.18	9.32	9.90	9.34	8.18
NONMEMBER PRIM CAP TO AVG ASST*	9.02	8.97	9.13	9.18	9.32	9.89	9.38	8.08
CASH DIVIDENDS TO NET INCOME	34.33	31.99	37.03	39.50	37.22	30.47	29.60	42.23
RET EARNS TO AVG TOTAL EQUITY	7.84	8.41	7.01	5.96	6.35	5.80	8.71	8.01
GROWTH RATES								
ASSETS	8.14	9.96	8.82	8.83	7.81	7.26	7.93	8.99
TOTAL EQUITY CAPITAL	8.80	9.58	8.41	6.76	7.00	6.64	9.36	9.42
CORE DEPOSITS	9.23	9.65	7.83	10.81	7.84	7.77	8.65	10.96
VOLATILE LIABILITIES	-.11	19.74	26.32	-6.28	11.53	4.16	-.10	-2.38
% NON-CURRENT LOANS & LEASES								
TOTAL LNS & LEASES-90+ DAYS P/D	.98	1.14	1.32	1.64		1.37	1.05	.66
-NONACCRUAL	.87	.81	.87	.77		.67	.87	1.00
-TOTAL	1.92	2.05	2.22	2.51		2.28	1.95	1.70

*REFER TO THE UBPR USERS GUIDE FOR PRIMARY CAPITAL DEFINITIONS.

APPENDIX A

PEER GROUP INFORMATION

THE UBPR PEER GROUP DEFINITION FOR A BANK IS BASED ON THREE CRITERIA: AVERAGE QUARTERLY ASSETS, NUMBER OF DOMESTIC OFFICES, AND WHETHER THE BANK IS IN A METROPOLITAN AREA AS DEFINED BY RAND MCNALLY & COMPANY. IF THE BANK HAS MOVED FROM ONE UBPR PEER GROUP DEFINITION TO ANOTHER DURING ANY PERIOD COVERED IN THIS REPORT, THIS PAGE WILL DESCRIBE PREVIOUS UBPR PEER GROUP DEFINITIONS. THE BANK'S CURRENT UBPR PEER GROUP CLASSIFICATION IS DESCRIBED ON THE TABLE OF CONTENTS PAGE.

   PEER GROUP # 12
   INCLUDES ALL INSURED COMMERCIAL BANKS HAVING ASSETS
   BETWEEN $50 MILLION AND $100 MILLION, WITH 3 OR MORE
   BANKING OFFICES AND LOCATED IN A NON-METROPOLITAN AREA.

UNIFORM BANK PERFORMANCE REPORT

ORDERING INSTRUCTIONS AND ORDER BLANK

INFORMATION

THE UNIFORM BANK PERFORMANCE REPORTS ARE PREPARED QUARTERLY AND INCLUDE ALL INSURED COMMERCIAL BANK IN THE UNITED STATES. THERE ARE THREE TYPES OF REPORTS:

* THE BANK REPORT IS PREPARED FOR EACH INSURED COMMERCIAL BANK IN THE UNITED STATES.
* THE STATE AVERAGES REPORT (ABOUT 55 PAGES) CONTAINS ONE PAGE OF RATIO AVERAGES FOR EACH STATE, AS THE DATA APPEAR ON PAGE 13 OF THE BANK REPORT.
* THE PEER GROUP REPORT (ABOUT 262 PAGES) PRESENTS ALL UBPR PEER GROUP RATIO AVERAGES FOR EACH OF THE 25 PEER GROUPS, AND ALSO PRESENTS NATIONWIDE AVERAGES.

THERE IS ALSO A UBPR USER'S GUIDE WHICH DOCUMENTS THE BANK REPORT. PAST EDITIONS OF THE BANK REPORT, THE PEER GROUP REPORT, AND THE STATE AVERAGES REPORT ARE ALSO AVAILABLE, BEGINNING WITH THE DECEMBER, 1981 EDITION. THE FEE SCHEDULE BELOW APPLIES TO ALL ORDERS FOR ALL EDITIONS.

TYPE OF REPORT	PRICE PER COPY
UBPR FOR AN INDIVIDUAL BANK	$30.00
STATE AVERAGES REPORT (COVERS ALL STATES)	$30.00
PEER GROUP REPORT (COVERS ALL UBPR PEER GROUPS)	$50.00
UBPR USER'S GUIDE	$15.00

ALL REQUESTS MUST BE SENT TO:

UBPR
DEPARTMENT 4320
CHICAGO, ILLINOIS 60673

MAKE CHECK PAYABLE TO:

FEDERAL FINANCIAL INSTITUTIONS EXAMINATION COUNCIL

FOR ORDERING ASSISTANCE PHONE: (800) 843-1669.
QUESTIONS REGARDING CONTENT OF REPORTS: (202) 357-0111.

ORDER BLANK

REQUESTOR'S NAME: _____

STREET ADDRESS: _____

CITY: _____ STATE: _____ ZIP: _____

PHONE NUMBER: _____ CONTACT PERSON: _____

AMOUNT ENCLOSED: $ _____

UBPR(S) REQUESTED:

NAME OF BANK	LOCATION (CITY & STATE)	EDITION*
_____	_____	_____
_____	_____	_____
_____	_____	_____
_____	_____	_____

(ATTACH SEPARATE SHEET FOR ADDITIONAL BANKS)

OTHER REPORTS	NUMBER REQUESTED	EDITION*
UBPR USER'S GUIDE:	_____	_____
STATE AVERAGES REPORT:	_____	_____
PEER GROUP REPORT:	_____	_____

*INDICATE QUARTER-ENDING EDITION DATE OF DESIRED REPORT IF YOU WANT OTHER THAN THE LATEST AVAILABLE EDITION.